A
KAUA'I READER

A
KAUA'I READER

Edited and with contributions
by Chris Cook

Mutual Publishing

Library of Congress Catalog Card Number: 95-82260

ISBN-10: 1-56647-832-4
ISBN-13: 978-1-56647-832-8

Design by Jane Hopkins
Cover Design by Wanni

First Printing (large mass market), June 2007

Mutual Publishing, LLC
1215 Center Street, Suite 210
Honolulu, Hawaii 96816
Ph: (808) 732-1709
Fax: (808) 734-4094
email: info@mutualpublishing.com
www.mutualpublishing.com

Printed in Australia

Dedicated to

◈ ──────────────────────────────

CHRISTIAN & DAVID
AND THE KEIKI OF KAUAʻI

TABLE
OF CONTENTS

Chris Cook

PREFACE

Here are choice chapters in the story of Kaua'i and Ni'ihau, the two leeward islands that make up the ancient "Separate Kingdom" of Hawai'i. Myths, adventures, *mele*, recollections and tours bring to life over 1,000 years of history and lore of islands best known for spectacular beauty and isolation.

The centuries-old story of Kaua'i and Ni'ihau is little known off the islands, and known in-depth by only a handful of its residents. This collection will hopefully open up the full story the "Separate Kingdom" to many more.

Over 30 short articles and selections were carefully culled from a wide variety of books ranging from the mythical days of a past that goes back a thousand years to the devastation of Hurricane Iniki just six years ago.

The idea of collecting stories about Hawai'i in an anthology isn't new. A. Grove Day and Carl Stroven, with insights from James Michener, produced *A Hawaiian Reader* in 1959 to mark Hawai'i's statehood. What is new is focusing such an anthology on a Neighbor Island. Kaua'i and Ni'ihau—like Maui, the Big Island and Moloka'i—are often overlooked in the literary world of Honolulu.

The inspiration for *A Kaua'i Reader* goes back to my studies at the University of Hawai'i in the early 1970s when I read extensively about the lore of the islands but knew little of it beyond O'ahu's shores. A Thanksgiving trip to Kaua'i made in 1970, and initiated by a classmate who had relatives there, opened my eyes to a new world. The attraction of the simple, rural ways combined with the knock-out scenery and waves at Hanalei made an impact on me that still underlies my daily life after almost 20 years of living along its shore.

After moving to Kaua'i I began to seek out books and articles about the island's past. That search has accelerated over the years and I've discovered the depth, and richness, of what might be called the literature of Kaua'i.

I've discovered that the Island's past is multi-faceted, observable from a variety of viewpoints, and captured in the writings of missionaries, explorers, noted American authors, early travelers, Hawaiian royalty, sea captains and newspaper reporters.

From these sources I've gathered a set of readable, short selections that paint a well-rounded picture of the island's past.

For a more complete version, the first book on my suggested Kaua'i and Ni'ihau reading list would be Edward Joesting's *Kauai—The Separate Kingdom*. Joesting, a banking executive and historian, compresses complex historical events culled from dozens of sources into an interesting, and accurate, narrative. His chapter on Kaua'i's sugar plantation immigrants is included here.

Prefacing any modern history though, are the myths and legends of the islands, and a look at the rulers and heroes who lived during the era of pre-western contact. The Kaua'i legends of the volcano goddess Pele and her sister Hi'iaka at Hā'ena, and the adventures of the voyager and ali'i Mo'ikeha come from the pen of King David Kalākaua.

While many believe the false tale that Mark Twain toured Waimea Canyon on Kaua'i's west side and named it "The Grand Canyon of the Pacific," one famous author who did visit Kaua'i and wrote about the exploits of a Native Hawaiian hero is Jack London. London's tale "Koolau the Leper" is his most popular Hawai'i story and first appeared in *House of Pride*. It is included here with a brief note about London's ties to Kaua'i.

A look at Ni'ihau from my own writings on the Sinclair and Gay families who bought the island from Kamehameha V in the mid-1860s is matched by Reri Tava and Moses Keale, Sr.'s account of Ni'ihau's native people.

My own interests in surfing and Kaua'i-made movies are also interwoven. The earliest accounts of surfing on Kaua'i I've found appear in missionary leader Hiram Bingham's tour of the island in 1821, and in A. Carrington Bolton's look at surfing on Ni'ihau in the early 1890s. From another of my books, *The Kaua'i Movie Book* which is also published by Mutual, I've updated the account of two life-changing incidents singer and actor Frank Sinatra experienced on Kaua'i.

All selections were carefully chosen to both entertain and educate the reader, and with visitors as well as local residents in mind.

A Kaua'i Reader began as a concept in 1991. The first draft was almost lost when an open beam ceiling took out my home office during Hurricane Iniki. The disaster delayed completion of the book, but now it's ready thanks to the continued support of Bennett Hymer, the design skills of Jane Hopkins, and the *aloha* of my many sources, teachers and supporters on Kaua'i.

Chris Cook
Kaua'i, 1999

Nathaniel B. Emerson

I. THE WATER OF KĀNE
KAUA'I'S POETIC MASTERPIECE

The Water of Kāne, *a mele, or song, was a favorite of
the ali'i of Kaua'i. The holy, spiritual lines of the mele include
references to Lehua, a large serrated rock just north of Ni'ihau
island, and Nihoa, an isolated, tiny island over the horizon
to the northwest of Kaua'i.*

In The Water of Kāne, *the gods Kāne and Kanaloa
journeyed to Hawai'i over the ocean from Kahiki, the mythical
Polynesian homeland of the Hawaiians. Kāne struck his kauila
staff, creating many streams. Kāne became the patron of fresh
waters, while Kanaloa, of salt, or ocean waters. Also symbolic
of Kāne is sunlight.*

The mele, *or song, offers lyrical insight into the
spiritual life of the ancient Hawaiians, especially those of
Kaua'i heritage. Beautiful both in Hawaiian and English,*

the lyrics are perhaps the most revered in the Hawaiian language.

Translator Dr. Nathaniel B. Emerson was born in 1839 to missionary parents at Waialua on O'ahu's north shore. He left Hawai'i to attend college, served as a soldier in the Civil War and eventually became a medical doctor. In 1878 he returned to Hawai'i to serve as an inspector of lepers. Emerson translated David Malo's Hawaiian Antiquities *and the extended myth* Pele and Hi'iaka.

His Hawaiian language translations are known to be credible and infused with the knowledge of Hawaiian culture that he gained growing up in rural O'ahu during the 1840's and 1850's. This knowledge enabled him to accurately translate Hawaiian expressions into English, capturing subtle nuances. Emerson is noted for gathering accurate information about the hula, *and he is considered a primary source for modern-day researches of the dance. His* Unwritten Literature of Hawaii: The Sacred Songs of the Hula *is still a classic.*

IF ONE WERE asked what, to the English-speaking mind, constitutes the most representative romatico-mystical as inspiration that has been embodied in song and story, doubtless he would be compelled to answer the legend and myth of the Holy Grail. To the Hawaiian mind the aspiration and conception that most nearly approximates to this is embodied in the words placed at the head of this chapter, *The Water of Kāne.* One finds suggestions and hints of this conception in many passages of Hawaiian song and story, sometimes a phosphorescent flash, answering to the dip of the poet's blade, sometimes crystallized into a set form; but nowhere else than in the following *mele* have I found this jewel deliberately wrought into shape, faceted, and fixed in a distinct form of speech.

This *mele* comes from Kauaʻi, the island which more than any other of the Hawaiian group retains a tight hold on the mystical and imaginative features that mark the anthropology of Polynesia; the island also which less than any other of the group was dazzled by the glamour of royalty and enslaved by the theory of the divine birth of kings.

HE MELE NO KANE

He u-i he ninau:
E u-i aku ana au ia oe,
Aia i- hea ka wai a Kane?
Aia i ka hikina a ka La,
Puka i Hae-hae;
Aia i-laila ka Wai a Kane.

E u-i aku ana au ia oe,
Aia i- hea ka Wai a Kane?
Aia i Kau-lana-ka-la,
I ka pae opua i ke kai,
Ea mai ana ma Nihoa,
Ma ka mole mai o Lehua;
Aia i-laila ka Wai a Kane.

E u-i aku ana au ia oe,
Aia i-hea ka Wai a Kane?
Aia i-ke kua-hiwi, i ke kua-lono,
I ke awawa, i ke kaha-wai;
Aia i-laila ka Wai a Kane.
E u-i aku ana au ia oe,
Aia i-hea ka Wai a Kane?
Aia i-kai, i ka moana,
I ke Kua-lau, i ke anuenue,

I ka punohu, i ka ua-koko,
I ka alewa-lewa;
Aia i-laila ka Wai a Kane.

Eu-i aku ana au ia oe,
Aia i-hea ka Wai a Kane?
Aia i-luna ka Wai a Kane,
I ke ouli, i ke ao eleele,
I ke ao pano-pano,
I ke ao poplo-hua mea a Kane la, e!
Aia i-laila ka Wai a Kane.

E u-i aku ana au ia oe,
Aia i-hea ka Wai a Kane?
Aia i-lalo, i ka honua, i ka Wai hu,
I ka wai kau a Kane me Kanaloa—
He wai-puna, he wai e inu,
He wai e mana, he wai e ola.
E ola no, e-a!

THE WATER OF KANE

A query, a question,
I put to you:
Where is the water of Kane?
At the Eastern Gate
Where the Sun comes in at Haehae;
There is the water of Kane.

A question I ask of you:
Where is the water of Kane?
Out there with the floating Sun.

Where cloud-forms rest on Ocean's breast,
Uplifting their forms at Nihoa,
This side the base of Lehua;
There is the water of Kane.

One question I put to you:
Where is the water of Kane?
Yonder on mountain peak,
On the ridges steep,
In the valleys deep,
Where the rivers sweep;
There is the water of Kane.

This question I ask of you:
Where, pray, is the water of Kane?
Yonder, at sea, on the ocean,
In the driving rain,
In the heavenly bow,
In the piled-up mist-wraith,
In the blood-red rainfall,
In the ghost-pale cloud-form;
There is the water of Kane.

One question I put to you:
Where, where is the water of Kane?
Up on high is the water of Kane,
In the heavenly blue,
In the black piled cloud,
In the black-black cloud,
In the black-mottled sacred cloud of the gods;
There is the water of Kane.

One question I ask of you;
Where flows the water of Kane?

Deep in the ground, in the gushing spring,
In the ducts of Kane and Loa,
A well-spring of water, to quaff,
A water of magic power—
The water of life!
Life! O give us this life!

✦ ✦ ✦

Notes On Text

Hae-hae. Heaven's eastern gate; the portal in the solid walls that supported the heavenly dome, through which the sun entered in the morning.

Kau-lana-ka-la. When the setting sun, perhaps by an optical illusion drawn out into a boatlike form, appeared to be floating on the surface of the ocean, the Hawaiians named the phenomenon Kau-lana-ka-la—the floating of the sun. Their fondness for personification showed itself in the final conversions of this phrase into something like a proper name, which they applied to the locality of the phenomenon.

Pae opua i ke kai. Another instance of name-giving, applied to the bright clouds that seem to rest on the horizon, especially to the west.

Nihoa (Bird Island). This small rock to the northwest of Kauai, though far below the horizon, is here spoken of as if it were in sight.

Punohu. A red luminous cloud, or a halo, regarded as an omen portending some sacred and important event.

Ua-koko. Literally bloody rain, a term applied to a rainbow when lying near the ground, or to a freshnet-stream swollen with the red muddy water from the wash of the hillsides. These were important omens, claimed as marking the birth of tabu chiefs.

Wai kau a Kane me Kanaloa. Once when Kane and Kanaloa were journeying together Kanaloa complained of thirst. Kane thrust his staff into the pall near at hand, and out flowed a stream of pure water that has continued to the present day. The place is at Keanae, Maui.

II. LOHI'AU–THE LOVER OF A GODDESS

HI'IAKA AND THE PRINCE OF KAUA'I

Hawai'i's King David Kalākaua, who lived from 1836 to 1891 and reigned from 1874 until his death, carefully recorded in writing the myths and interpretations of historic events like the arrival of Captain Cook in 1778. His interest in this field began in his youth and resulted in the publication in 1888, in Honolulu, of his renowned collection, The Legends and Myths of Hawaii.

Some critics believe that the Hon. R.M. Daggett, a United States Minister to the Hawaiian Kingdom during Kalākaua's monarchy, actually ghost-wrote The Legends and Myths of Hawaii *for Kalākaua.*

The publication of the book helped spark a renaissance of the Hawaiian culture, especially of the hula, *in the 1890s. The Merrie Monarch Festival, where Hawai'i's best* halau *present the best in modern and ancient* hula *each spring in Hilo, is named after Kalākaua, who gained notoriety in his later years for his parties and lavish* luau.

The story of Kaua'i's Lohi'au, the lover of Pele, the volcano goddess, is a Hawaiian Odyssey that takes the reader from the volcanoes of the Big Island to Kaua'i, and back.

Underlying the legend are historic details gleaned by Kalākaua regarding Hawaiian sailing canoes, surfing and Hawaiian place names.

The Kaua'i focus of the tale is the romantic, verdant, north shore coastal village of Hā'ena, named Kaena by Kalākaua.

OF ALL THE legends of the adventures with mortals of Pele, the dreadful goddess of the volcanoes, the most weird and dramatic is the one relating to her love for Lohiau, a prince of the island of Kauai, whose reign was probably contemporaneous with that of Kealiiokaloa, of Hawaii, during the early part of the sixteenth century. The story is not only a characteristic relic of the recklessly imaginative and highly-colored meles of the early poets, but an instructive reflex as well of the superstitions controlling the popular mind of the Hawaiian group at that period, when the forests abounded in mischievous gnomes and fairies, when the streams were guarded by nymphs and monsters, and when the very air was peopled with the spirits of the departed. But a thin veil then divided the living from the dead, the natural from the supernatural, and mortals were made the sport of the elements and the playthings of the gods.

As the mele relates, Pele and her brothers and sisters, to amuse themselves with a taste of mortal enjoyments, one day emerged from their fiery chambers in the crater of Kilauea, and went down to the coast of Puna to bathe, surf-ride, sport in the sands, and gather edible sea-weed, squid, limpets and other delicacies washed by the waves. They assumed human forms for the occasion, and therefore had human appetites.

While the others were amusing themselves in various ways—eating, laughing and sporting in the waves in the manner of mortals—Pele, in the guise of an old woman, sought repose and sleep in the shade of a hala tree. Her favorite sister was Hiiaka, her full name being Hiiaka-ika-pali-opele. She was younger than Pele, and frequently occupied the same grotto with her under the burning lake of Kilauea.

Hiiaka accompanied her sovereign sister to the shade of the hala tree, and, sitting devotedly beside her, kept her cool with a kahili. Her eyelids growing heavy, Pele instructed Hiiaka to allow her under no circumstances to be disturbed, no matter how long she might sleep, whether for hours or days, and then closed her eyes in slumber.

Scarcely had the ears of the sleeper been closed by the fingers of silence before she heard the sound of a drum—distant, but distinct and regular in its beat, as if to the impulse of music. Before leaving the crater she had heard the same sound, but paid little attention to it. Now, however, when hearing it in her dreams, her curiosity was aroused, and, assuming her spiritual form, she resolved to follow it.

Leaving her slumbering earthly body under the eye and care of her sister, Pele mounted the air and proceeded in the direction whence the sound seemed to come. From place to place she followed it over the island of Hawaii; but it was always before her, and she could not overtake it. At Upolu it came to her from over the sea, and she followed it to the island of Maui. It was still beyond, and she sped to Molokai; still beyond, and she flew to Oahu;

still beyond, and she crossed the channel and listened on the shores of Kauai, where it was more distinct than she had heard it before. Now encouraged, she continued the pursuit until she stood upon the mountain peak of Haupu, when she discovered at last that the sound came from the beach at Kaena.

Proceeding thither, and hovering over the place unseen, she observed that the sound she had so long been following was that of a *pahu-hula* or *hula* drum, beaten by Lohiau, the young and comely prince of Kauai, who was noted not only for the splendor of his hula entertainments, participated in by the most beautiful women of the island, but for his personal graces as a dancer and musician. The favorite deity of Lohiau was Lakakane, the god of the hula and similar sports, who in a spirit of mischief had conveyed the sound of the drum to the ears of Pele.

The beach was thronged with dancers, musicians and spectators, all enjoying themselves under the shade of the *hala* and cocoa trees, with the prince as master of ceremonies and the centre of attraction. Assuming the form of a beautiful woman, Pele suddenly appeared before the festive throng. Attaching to her person every imaginable charm of form and feature, her presence was immediately noted; and, a way being opened for her to the prince, he received her most graciously and invited her to a seat near him, where she could best witness the entertainment.

Glancing at the beautiful stranger from time to time in the midst of his performances, Lohiau at length became so fascinated that he failed to follow the music, when he yielded the instrument to another and seated himself beside the enchantress. In answer to his inquiry she informed the prince that she was a stranger in Kauai, and had come from the direction of the rising sun. Gazing into her face with a devouring passion, Lohiau smilingly said:

"You are most welcome, but I cannot rejoice that you came."

"And why, since I do not come as your enemy?" inquired Pele, archly.

"Because, until now," returned the prince, "my thought has been that there were beautiful women in Kauai; but in looking at yours I find their faces are plain indeed."

"I see you know how to speak flattering words to women," said Pele, casting a languishing look upon the prince.

"Not better than I know how to love them," replied Lohiau, with ardor. "Will you be convinced?"

"Lohiau is in his own kingdom, and has but to command," answered Pele, with a play of modesty which completed the enthralment of the prince.

Thus Pele became the wife of Lohiau. He knew nothing of her or her family, and cared not to inquire. He saw only that she was beautiful above all women, and for a few days they lived so happily together that life seemed to be a dream to him. And Pele loved the prince scarcely less than he loved her; but the time had come for her return to Hawaii, and, pledging him to remain true to her, she left him with protestations of affection and the promise of a speedy return, and on the wings of the wind was wafted back to the shores of Puna, where she had left her sister waiting and watching in the shade of the hala.

Lohiau was inconsolable. Every day he thought she would be with him the next, until more than a month passed, when he refused food and died of grief at her absence. The strange death of the prince occasioned much comment, for he was naturally strong and without disease. Some said he had been prayed to death by his enemies, and others that he had been poisoned; but an old *kaula* [prophet, seer, *ed.*], who had seen Pele at Kaena and noted her actions, advised against further inquiry concerning the cause of Lohiau's death, offering as a reason the opinion that the strangely beautiful and unknown woman he had taken as a wife was an immortal, who had become attached to her earthly husband and called his spirit to her.

The prince was greatly beloved by his people, and his body, carefully wrapped in many folds of *kapa*, was kept in state for some time in the royal mansion. It was guarded by the high chiefs of the kingdom, and every night funeral hymns were chanted around it, and *meles* recited of the deeds of the dead sovereign and his ancestors. Thus lying in state we will leave the remains of Lohiau, and follow Pele back to Hawaii.

II.

During all the time the spirit of Pele was absent the family kept watch over the body left by her under the hala tree, not daring to disturb it, and were overjoyed when it was at last reanimated, for the fires of the crater of Kilauea had nearly died out from neglect. Pele rose to her feet in the form of the old woman she had left asleep under the care of Hiiaka, and, without at the time mentioning her adventures in Kauai or the cause of her protracted slumber, returned with all but one of the family to Kilauea, and with a breath renewed the dying fires of the crater. Hiiaka asked and received the permission of Pele to remain for a few days at the beach with her much-loved friend Hopoe, a young woman of Puna, who had been left an orphan by an irruption from Kilauea, in which both of her parents had perished.

On leaving Kauai it is probable that Pele, notwithstanding her fervent words to the contrary, never expected or particularly desired to see Lohiau again; but he had so endeared himself to her during their brief union that she did not find it easy to forget him, and, after struggling with the feeling for some time, she resolved to send for him. But to whom should she entrust the important mission? One after another she applied to her sisters at the crater, but the way was beset with evil spirits, and they refused to go.

In this dilemma Pele sent her favorite brother, Lonoikaonolii, to bring Hiiaka from the beach, well knowing that she would not refuse to undertake the journey, however hazardous. Hiiaka accepted the mission, with the understanding that during her absence her friend Hopoe should be kept under the eye and guardianship of Pele.

Arrangements were made for the immediate departure of Hiiaka. Pele conferred upon her some of her own powers, with an injunction to use them discreetly, and for a companion and servant gave her Pauopalae, a woman of approved sagacity and prudence.

With a farewell from her relatives and many an admonition from Pele, Hiiaka took her departure for Kauai, accompanied by Pauo-palae. They traveled as mortals, and were therefore subject to the fatigues and perils of humanity. Proceeding through the forests toward the coast of Hilo, they encountered an old woman, who accosted them politely and expressed a desire to follow them. Her name was Omeo, and she was leading a hog to the volcano as a sacrifice to Pele. No objection being made, she hurried to the crater with her offering, and returned and followed Hiiaka and her companion.

Not long after, their journey was impeded by a demon of hideous proportions, who threw himself across their path in a narrow defile and attempted to destroy them. Pele knew their danger, however, and ordered her brothers to protect them with a rain of fire and thunder, which drove the monster to his den in the hills and enabled them to escape.

After a little time they were joined by another woman, whose name was Papau. She desired to accompany them, and proceeded a short distance on the way, when they were confronted by a ferocious-looking man who was either insane or under the influence of evil spirits. He lacked either the power or the disposition to molest the party, however, and they passed on unharmed; but Papau screamed with fright and hastily returned to her home, where she was turned into a stone as a punishment for her cowardice.

Coming to a small stream crossed by their path, they found the waters dammed by a huge *moo*, or lizard, lying in the bed. He was more than a hundred paces in length, and his eyes were of the size of great *calabashes*. He glared at the party viciously and opened his mouth as if to devour them; but Hiiaka tossed into it a stone, which became red-hot when it touched his throat, and, with a roar of pain which made the leaves of the trees tremble, he disappeared down the stream.

After many other adventures with monsters and evil spirits, which Hiiaka was able to control and sometimes punish, the party reached the coast at a place called Honoipo, where they found a number of men and women engaged in the sport of surf-riding. As they were about to start for another trial, in a spirit of mischief Hiiaka turned their surf-boards into stone, and they fled in terror from the beach, fearing that some sea-god was preparing to devour them.

Observing a fisherman drawing in his line, Hiiaka caused to be fastened to the submerged hook a human head. Raising it to the surface, the man stared at it for a moment with horror, then dropped the line and paddled swiftly away, to the great amusement of Hiiaka and her companions.

Embarking in a canoe with two men as assistants, the travelers sailed for the island of Maui, which they reached without delay or accident. Landing at Kaupo, they traveled overland toward Honuaula, near which place, in approaching the palace of the king, whose name was Olepau, and who was lying within at the point of death, Hiiaka observed a human spirit hovering around the outer enclosure. Knowing that it was the half-freed soul or spirit of the *moi* (king), she seized and tied it up in a corner of her *pau* [wrap-around tapa cloth garment, *ed.*].

Passing on with the soul of the king in her keeping, she met the queen, Waihimano, and told her that her husband had just died. But the queen denied that Olepau was dead, for she was a worshipper of two powerful lizard divinities, and the gods had assured her that morning that her husband would recover.

Saying no more, Hiiaka and her companions went on their way, and the queen, returning to the palace, found her husband insensible and apparently dead. Trying in vain to restore him, she hastily consulted a kaula, telling him what the strange woman had said to her. The seer by the description recognized at once the sister of Pele, who had come to heal the king, but had been deterred in her errand of mercy by the queen's obstinate assurances of his recovery. He therefore advised that she be followed by a messenger with a spotless pig to be placed as an offering in the path before her, when she perchance might return and restore the king to life. But Hiiaka dropped behind her companions and assumed the form of an old woman, and, as the messenger did not recognize her, he returned with the report that the object of his search could not be found.

"Did you meet no one?" inquired the seer.

"No one answering the description," replied the messenger. "I saw only an old woman, so infirm as to be scarcely able to walk."

"Fool!" exclaimed the kaula. "That old woman was Hiiaka in disguise. Hasten back to her, if you would save the life of your king!"

The messenger again started in pursuit of Hiiaka, but the pig was obstinate and troublesome and his progress was slow. Seizing the struggling animal in his arms, the messenger ran until he came within sight of the women, who were again traveling together, when Hiiaka struck the fold of her pau against a rock, and that instant the king expired.

Reaching the coast and embarking with a fisherman, Hiiaka and her companions sailed for Oahu. Landing at Makapuu, they journeyed overland to Kou—now Honolulu—and from Haena made sail for Kauai. Arriving at Kaena, Hiiaka saw the spirit hand of Lohiau beckoning to her from the mouth of a cave among the cliffs. Turning to her companions, she said:

"We have failed; the lover of Pele is dead! I see his spirit beckoning from the *pali*! There it is being held and hidden by the lizard-women, Kilioa and Kalamainu."

Instructing her companions to proceed to Puoa, where the body of Lohiau was lying in state, Hiiaka started at once for the pali, for the purpose of giving battle to the female demons and rescuing the spirit of the dead prince.

Ascending the cliff and entering the cave, Hiiaka waved her pau, and with angry hisses the demons disappeared. Search was made, and the spirit of Lohiau was found at last in a niche in the rocks, where it had been placed by a moonbeam. Taking it tenderly in her hand, she enclosed it in a fold of her pau, and in an invisible form floated down with it to Puoa.

Waiting until after nightfall, Hiiaka entered the chamber of death unseen, and restored the spirit to the body of Lohiau. Recovering his life and consciousness, the prince looked around with amazement. The guards were frightened when he raised his head, and would have fled in alarm had they not been prevented by Hiiaka, who at that instant appeared before them in mortal form. Holding up her hand, as if to command obedience, she said:

"Fear nothing, say nothing of this to any one living, and do nothing except as you may be ordered. The prince has returned to life, and may recover if properly cared for. His body is weak and wasted. Let him be secretly and at once removed to the sea-shore. The night is dark, and it may be done without observation."

Not doubting that these instructions were from the gods, the guards obeyed them with so much prudence and alacrity that Lohiau was soon comfortably resting in a hut by the sea-shore, with Hiiaka and her companions ministering to his wants.

The return of the prince to health and strength was rapid, and in a few days he reappeared among his friends, to their amazement and great joy. In answer to their inquiries he informed them that he owed to the gods his restoration to life. This did not entirely satisfy them, but no further explanation was offered.

After celebrating his recovery with feasts and sacrifices to the gods, Lohiau announced to the chiefs of his kingdom that he was about to visit his wife, whose home was on Hawaii, and that he should leave the government of the island in the hands of his friend, the high-chief

Paoa, to whom he enjoined the fealty and respect of all during his absence.

In a magnificent double canoe, bearing the royal standard and equipped as became the *kaulua* of an *alii-nui*, Lohiau set sail for Hawaii, accompanied by Hiiaka and her companions, and taking with him his high-priest, chief navigator, and the customary staff of personal attendants.

Touching at Oahu, Hiiaka ascended the Kaala mountains, and saw that her beautiful lehua and hala groves near the beach of Puna, on the distant island of Hawaii, had been destroyed by a lava flow. Impatient at the long absence of Hiiaka, and jealous as well, Pele had in a fit of rage destroyed the beautiful seashore retreats of her faithful sister. She scarcely doubted that Hiiaka had dared to love Lohiau, and in her chambers of fire chafed for her return.

After bewailing her loss Hiiaka rejoined her companions, and Lohiau embarked for Hawaii. Landing at Kohala, the prince ordered his attendants to remain there until his return, and started overland for Kilauea with Hiiaka and her two female companions. Before reaching the volcano Hiiaka learned something of the jealous rage of Pele, and finally saw from a distant eminence her dear friend Hopoe undergoing the cruel tortures of volcanic fire, near the beach of Puna, which ended in her being turned into stone.

Approaching the crater with apprehensions of further displays of Pele's fury, Hiiaka sent Omeo and Pauo-palae in advance to announce to the goddess her return with Lohiau. In her wrath she ordered both of the women to be slain at once, and resolved to treat her lover in the same manner.

Aware of this heartless resolution, and unable to avert the execution of it, on their arrival at the verge of the crater Hiiaka threw her arms around the neck of the prince, whom she had learned to love without wrong to her sister, and, telling him of his impending fate, bade him a tender farewell.

This scene was witnessed by Pele. Enraged beyond measure, she caused a gulf of molten lava to be opened between Hiiaka and the prince, and then ordered the instant destruction of Lohiau by fire.

While the sisters of Pele were ascending the walls of the crater to execute her orders, Lohiau chanted a song to the goddess, avowing his innocence and pleading for mercy; but her rage was rekindled at the sound of his voice, and she turned a deaf ear to his entreaties.

Approaching Lohiau, and pitying him, the sisters merely touched the palms of his hands, which turned them into lava, and then retired. Observing this, Pele ordered them to return at once, under the penalty of her displeasure, and consume the body of her lover.

Lohiau again appealed to Pele, so piteously that the trees around him wept with grief; but her only answer was an impatient signal to her sisters to resume their work of destruction. In his despair he turned to Hiiaka and implored her intercession, but she answered in agony that she could do nothing.

The sisters returned to Lohiau, and reluctantly touched his feet, which became stone; then his knees; then his thighs; then his breast. By the power conferred upon her by Pele, and of which she had not yet been deprived, Hiiaka rendered the body of the prince insensible to pain, and it was therefore without suffering that he felt his joints hardening into stone under the touch of his sympathizing executioners.

As the remainder of his body was about to be turned into lava, Hiiaka said to the prince:

"Listen! When you die go to the leeward, and I will find you!"

The next moment Lohiau was a lifeless pillar of stone.

Observing that the cruel work of her sister had been accomplished, and that all that remained of the shapely form of Lohiau was a black mass of lava, Hiiaka caused the earth to be opened at her feet, and started downward at once for the misty realm of Milu to overtake the soul of Lohiau, and, with the consent of the god of death, restore it to its body.

Passing downward through each of the five spheres dividing the surface of the earth from the regions of Po, where Milu sits in state in the gloomy groves of death, Hiiaka finally stood in the presence of the august sovereign of the world of spirits.

The king of death welcomed her to his dominions, and, in response to her inquiry, informed her that the soul of Lohiau had not yet reached the abode of spirits. Having no desire to return to earth, Hiiaka accepted the invitation of Milu, and, watching and waiting for the soul of Lohiau, remained for a time in the land of spirits.

III.

The attendants of Lohiau remained in Kohala until they learned of his fate at the hands of Pele, when they returned to Kauai in the royal kaulua, and horrified the friends of the prince by relating to them the story of his death.

Enraged and desperate, Paoa, the faithful and sturdy chief to whom Lohiau had confided the government of his kingdom, started at once for Hawaii with a small party of retainers, determined, even at the sacrifice of his life, to denounce the powers that had slain his royal friend.

Landing on the coast of Puna, he ascended to the crater of Kilauea, and, standing upon the brink of the seething lake of fire, denounced the cruelty of Pele and defied her power. He contemptuously threw to her offerings unfit for sacrifice, and stigmatized all the volcanic deities as evil spirits who had been driven with Kanaloa from the presence of Kane and the society of the gods.

Paoa expected to be destroyed at once, and recklessly courted and awaited death. The brothers and sisters of Pele, with their several agencies of destruction, were momentarily expecting an order from the goddess to consume the audacious mortal in his tracks. Never before had such words of reproach and defiance been uttered by human tongue, and they could not doubt that swift vengeance would be hurled upon the offender.

But Pele refused to harm the desperate champion of Lohiau, for circumstances had convinced her of the innocence of Hiiaka and the fidelity of the prince. Therefore, instead of punishing the brave Paoa, Pele and her relatives received him with friendship, gently chided him for his words of insult and defiance, and disarmed his anger by forgiving the offence.

Satisfied of the great wrong she had done her faithful sister, and longing for her presence again in the chambers of the crater, Pele restored Pauo-palae and Omeo to life, and, endowing the latter with supernatural powers, sent her down to the regions of the dead to induce Hiiaka to return to earth.

Descending through the opening made by Hiiaka, Omeo was stopped at the intervening spheres, owing to the aspects of mortality which she unconsciously retained, and encountered many difficulties in reaching the kingdom of Milu. Arriving there and making known the object of her visit, Omeo was neither assisted nor encouraged in her search for Hiiaka. Milu was not anxious to part with his distinguished guest, and attempted to deceive Omeo by intimating that Hiiaka had returned to earth and was then on a visit to some of the relatives of her family in Kahiki.

Omeo was about to return, disappointed, to earth, when she discovered Hiiaka as she was listlessly emerging from a thick grove of trees where she had spent the most of her time since her arrival there in quest of the soul of Lohiau. Their greeting was most friendly, and when Omeo informed her of what had occurred at the volcano since her departure, she consented to leave the land of death and rejoin her relatives at the crater.

The brothers and sisters of Hiiaka were overjoyed at her return, and Pele welcomed her with assurances of restored affection. Paoa was still there. He was at once recognized by Hiiaka, and the next day she descended from Kilauea and embarked with him for Kauai in search of the soul of Lohiau.

The canoe of Paoa had scarcely left the shores of Puna before a strange craft swept in from the ocean, and was beached at the spot from which Hiiaka and her companion had embarked less than half a day before. It was a huge cowrie shell, dazzling in the brilliancy of its colors, and capable of indefinite expansion. Its masts were of ivory, and its sails were mats of the whiteness of milk. Both seemed to be mere ornaments, however, since the shell moved quite as swiftly through the water without wind as with it.

The sole occupant of the little vessel was the god Kanemilohai. He was a relative of the Pele family, and came from Kahiki on a visit to the volcanic deities of Hawaii. Remaining two or three days with Pele, and learning all that had happened to the family since they left Kahiki, the god started for Kauai to extend a greeting to Hiiaka.

Proceeding in a direct route, when about midway between the two islands the god caught the soul of Lohiau, which had misunderstood the final directions of Hiiaka and was on its way to Kauai. Not having gone to the land of spirits, it had been searching everywhere for Hiiaka, and had at last taken flight for Kauai, when it was intercepted by Kanemilohai.

The god returned to the crater with the captured spirit, and, finding the pillar of stone into which Lohiau had been turned, restored the prince to life. As he recovered his consciousness and opened his eyes he recognized Pele standing before him. Apprehensive of further persecution, he was about to appeal to her again for mercy when she said, in a tone as tender as that in which she had first replied to his welcome on the beach at Kaena:

"Fear me no longer. I have been unjust to you as well as to Hiiaka. After what I have done I cannot expect your love. Find Hiiaka and give it to her. She loves you, and knows how to be kind to a mortal."

Lohiau would have thanked the goddess, but when he looked again she was gone, and in her place stood Kanemilohai, who told him to take the shell vessel he would find at the beach below, and proceed to Kauai, where he would probably meet Hiiaka and his friend Paoa.

Lohiau hesitated, for there was something in the appearance of Kanemilohai that inspired a feeling of awe.

"Go, and fear nothing," said the god, who knew the thoughts of the prince. "The shell was not made in the sea or by human hands, but it will bear you safely on your journey, no matter how rough the waves or great its burden."

"The coast of Puna is a day's journey in length," said Lohiau. "Where and how will I be able to find the shell?"

"Hasten to the shore at Keauhou," returned the god, "and you will see me there."

Arriving at the beach designated, the prince was surprised to find Kanemilohai already there; but he found something more to excite his wonder when the god took from a crevice in the rocks, where it had been secreted, a shell no larger than the palm of his hand, and passed it to him with the announcement that it was the barge in which he was to sail for Kauai.

Lohiau examined the little toy with something of a feeling of amusement, but more of perplexity, and was about to return it to his strange companion, when the latter instructed him to place the shell in the edge of the waters. The prince obeyed, and instantly found before him the beautiful craft in which the god had made his journey from Kahiki.

The power being conferred upon him by the god to contract or extend the proportions of the shell at his will, Lohiau entered the enchanted vessel of pink and pearl, and, directing its course by simply pointing his finger, was swiftly borne out into the ocean.

Rounding the southern cape of Hawaii, Lohiau thought of proceeding directly to Kauai; but he pointed too far to the northward, and the next morning sighted Oahu. Passing the headland of Leahi, he turned and entered the harbor of Hou. Landing, he contracted to the dimensions of a limpet, and secreted in a niche in the rocks, his obedient barge, and then proceeded to the village, where, he learned to his great joy, Hiiaka and Paoa were tarrying on a visit. Hou was at that time the scene of great merriment and feasting. It had become the temporary residence of the alii-nui, and high-chiefs, kahunas, adventurers, and noted surf-riders and hula performers had congregated there from all parts of the island.

Ascertaining that an entertainment of great magnificence was to be given that evening by a distinguished chiefess in honor of Hiiaka and her companion, Lohiau resolved to be present. Had he made himself known he would have been entitled to the consideration of the highest—would have been, indeed, the guest of the alii nui, with the right of entrance anywhere; but fancy prompted him to hide his rank and appear in disguise among the revelers.

Early in the evening the grounds of the chiefess were lighted with hundreds of torches, and under a broad pavilion, festooned and scented with fragrant vines and flowers, the favored guests, enwreathed and crowned with leaf and blossom, partook without stint of such delicacies as the land and sea produced. After the feast, song and music filled the air, and bands of gaily-decked dancers kept step among the flaring torches, while around the doors of the mansion white-bearded bards chanted wild legends of the past and sang the *mele-inoas* of the hostess and her distinguished guests.

In the midst of this inspiring revelry the guests divided into groups as their several tastes suggested. Some strolled out among the dancers, others listened to the stories of the bards, and one party, including Hiiaka, Paoa and the hostess, entered the mansion to engage in the game of *kilu*. It was a pastime of which singing or chanting was a part, and the chiefess was noted for her proficiency in the popular amusement.

Lohiau entered the grounds at the close of the feast, and stood watching the festivities when the party of kilu players retired to the mansion. He had turned inward the feathers of his mantle of royal yellow, and, with his long hair falling over his face and shoulders, was readily mistaken for a kahuna.

Quite a number of persons thronged around the kilu players to witness the game, and Lohiau entered the room without hindrance. Approaching the players, he screened himself behind the kapas of two old chiefs who were so intently regarding the performance that they did not observe him.

The game progressed until the kilu fell to Hiiaka, and as she threw it she chanted a song of her own composing, in which the name of Lohiau was mentioned with tenderness. The song ceased, and from behind the spectators came the answering voice of the prince. As he sang he brushed back the hair from his handsome face and turned outward the yellow feathers of his mantle. The throng divided, the singer advanced, and before the players stood Lohiau, the prince of Kauai.

He was recognized at once. Hiiaka threw herself into his arms, and the faithful Paoa wept with joy. Informed of the rank of the distinguished visitor, the guests vied with each other in showing him honor, and the festivities were renewed and carried far into the night.

Learning the next day of the presence near his court of the sovereign of Kauai, the alii-nui would have entertained him in a manner befitting the high rank of both; but Lohiau was anxious to return to his people, and set sail for Kauai at once in the shell barge of Kanemilohai, expanded to adequate dimensions, taking with him Hiiaka and Paoa.

Although Hiiaka soon after returned to Hawaii and effected a complete reconciliation with her sister, while Lohiau lived she spent much of her time in Kauai. Hopoe was restored to life, and Omeo, or Wahineomeo, was given an immortal form for what she had done, and became thereafter the mediator between the volcanic deities.

Chris Cook

III. THE MENEHUNE OF KAUA'I
THE LEGENDARY EARLY SETTLERS

The menehune of Kaua'i have been reduced in status to a small leprechaun-like people. However, as revealed in Kaua'i's menehune legends, especially those collected by William Hyde Rice describing the menehune ties to the Polynesian islands of the South Pacific that sent settlers to Hawai'i over 1,400 years ago, as well as their local legends and physical appearance, the menehune are at the root of Kaua'i's Hawaiian culture and were once a very powerful people on the island.

William Hyde Rice was a missionary son born in 1846 at Punahou, the private missionary school in Honolulu, to school-teacher parents. In 1854 the family was transferred to Līhue, Kaua'i, where Rice remained for most of his life. Growing up, his playmates were mostly Hawaiian boys who *spoke their native tongue as their first language. Rice quickly picked up the Hawaiian language and heard many legends from Hawaiian sources.*

Other Hawaiian myth collectors, such at Pedric Column and William Westervelt, present stories complementary to Rice's.

Were the menehune *a real people? Do their descendants live on today on Kaua'i? The historical record says yes. A look at the fact and fancy of the* menehune *legends follows.*

WANDERING DEEP IN the inner highlands of Wainiha Valley on a moonless night you can almost hear the ring of stone upon stone that once echoed through the valley in long ago days when *menehune* stacked the rock walls that held water and rich stream soil in micro-sized *taro* patches.

According to a census taken by the *konohiki*, or ruler, of the valley in the 1820's, during the reign of Kaumuali'i, Kaua'i's last king, the "65 men" of the village of La'au ("forest" in Hawaiian) in the uppermost reaches of Wainiha Valley were *menehune*.

This off-chance that the *menehune* were real, let alone active and counted in a 19th-century census, is virtually unknown among many residents of Hawai'i.

What is generally known of the *menehune* is the stuff of popular legend rivaled today in Hawai'i only by the tales of the volcano goddess Pele. Many of the tales include a charming twist, and perhaps the most considered came from the pen of master Hawaiian myth collector William Hyde Rice several generations ago. Many of Rice's tales contain references to *menehune* and possibly veiled references to actual historic events which occurred on Kaua'i in the 1700's and 1800's.

In his highly regarded book *Hawaiian Legends*, Rice, who grew up on Kaua'i as a Hawaiian-speaking missionary descendant with close contact with aged Hawaiian informants, described the *menehune* as "A race of mythical dwarfs from two to three feet in height, who were possessed of great strength; a race of pygmies who were squat, tremendously strong, powerfully built, and very ugly of face. They were credited with the building of many temples, roads, and other structures. Trades among them were well-systematized, every Menehune being restricted to his own particular craft in which he was a master. It was believed that they would work only one night on a construction and if unable to complete the work, it was left undone."

Rice's tales and other references to *menehune* in Hawaiian myths credit them with performing prodigious construction feats overnight. In fact, these stories claim the *menehune* work only at night, and in great numbers.

In a book of Hawaiian legends culled from the work of T. G. Thrum, who produced a popular Hawaiian almanac for decades and avidly filled its pages with his own research into Hawai'i's *heiau*, legends, history and other aspects of Hawaiian culture, is a chance meeting with a *menehune* in the highland forests of Kaua'i at Kōke'e. A Hawaiian couple, the story goes, was gathering sandalwood at Kōke'e when they met up with *menehune*. The Hawaiians described the *menehune* as "...having short, hairy bodies...muscular and very strong. Set in a red-skinned face are big eyes hidden by long eyebrows. A low, protruding forehead is covered with hair of undescribed color and texture. The nose is short and thick...the Menehune have a set expression that makes them unpleasant to look at and inspires fear, though they are neither angry nor quarrelsome, but are good people who molest no one without cause."

The *menehune* may not have been as dour as Thrum's writing made them out, for Rice records that once the great laughter of the *menehune* frightened the birds on distant O'ahu.

They may have been great revelers, too, for Rice tells of a party before the *menehune* left Kaua'i in great numbers held around a monument to their king. The celebration grew so noisy that it caused the fish in a pond located across the island to jump and caused the tiny *moi* to leave the beach for deep waters.

The legendary *menehune* played games like children. They would throw rocks off diving spots, especially around Kalapak'i Bay at Nāwiliwili, and dive underwater to retrieve them. They also had lively musical bands who played nose flutes, *ti*-leaf trumpets, mouth harps and hollow log drums. Their games included dart tossing, tops, boxing, wrestling, tug of war, foot races, sledding down grassy hills, and a version of bowling with basalt disks known as *'ulu maika*. The fastest *menehune* were said to be able to run the perimeter of Kaua'i six times in one day.

The *menehune* legends were not limited to Kaua'i. The 19th-century Hawaiian historian Kamakau wrote, "On the edge of the cliff at Kalaupapa (Molokai), that is at Kukui-o-Hapuu, they made a heiau with long ala stones. It is beautiful to behold."

The least-considered of the popular images of the *menehune* is that of small, brown, smiling, elf-sized creatures which have been used to sell a variety of products and, molded in rubber and plastic, purchased as cheap souvenirs by Kaua'i's tourists since World War II pumped Hawai'i's mass market tourist industry to life.

Among the locals on Kaua'i, modern tales of contemporary visits by *menehune* sometimes spread across the island by word of mouth. The tales are cute and usually involve a Kaua'i school child and are frequently taken as truth by many tellers and listeners. These stories usually describe a chance encounter behind a school while a child is performing a chore; generally the *menehune* quickly disappears under the raised plantation school floor, but some encounters result in the little *menehune* actually entering the classroom to the glee of students and frightening dismay of the teacher.

The *menehune* also became a bogeyman to children of Japanese immigrant sugar plantation workers, who were warned not to wander away, or to behave good or else.

Unlike these modern images, the industrious and skillful *menehune* of Wainiha were probably of normal stature, not the stereotyped leprechaun elves many think of when talk turns to the legendary adventures and stone works of Kaua'i's *menehune*.

Unlike this image of little Hawaiian-like people, historical *menehune* of Wainiha were not small in stature, as modern-day lore has it, but rather small in social status. They were probably the descendants of Kaua'i's first settlers, who it is believed journeyed from the Marquesas in the South Pacific to Kaua'i. This first wave of settlers may have grown to a population of 500,000 before they were subjugated to the rule of warriors from the islands of Tahiti led by the high priest Pa'ao, who arrived generations after the supposed date of the arrival of the *menehune*.

In the ancient Polynesian culture of Tahiti the word *menehune* becomes *manahune* and is the name for a caste of commoners, who like the historical *menehune* of Kaua'i, were conquered by Tahitians who probably set out from the sacred Tahitian island of Raiatea.

An ancient Tahitian chant tells of the plight of the *manahune* of Tahiti:

> Go to the mountains where you belong,
> Far, far away up there;
> Far away where the red skies lie,
> Away to the road of separation.

The name became *menehune* during the evolution of the Tahitian princedoms which culminated in the reign of Kamehameha the Great, who united by force all the Hawaiian Islands, save Kaua'i. The original settlers were virtually wiped out during this millennium of Tahitian rule and assimilated into the new settler's culture, or treated like outcasts and isolated in small villages like that in Wainiha.

The unique ring and stirrup basalt stone *poi* pounders that in all of Hawai'i are found only on Kaua'i are the key links between Kaua'i and the Marquesas. In recent times a stirrup *poi* pounder was unearthed on the northern Marquesas island of Uahuka. Archaeologists now point to the find as proof of the connection between the two distant islands.

Some say the legendary *menehune* was birthed when early western visitors asked the Hawaiian who built various ruined Hawaiian sites. In simple reply, the Hawaiian may have answered, "Why, *menehune*," referring to the common people of Hawai'i, rather than mythical little people.

Besides the distinctive stirrup and ring pounders, the *menehune* have left behind perhaps the most striking monuments to the Hawaiian culture still extant on Kaua'i. The Menehune (or more properly, the Alekoko) Fishpond along the Hulē'ia River just inland from Nāwiliwili is credited to the work of a *menehune* who wished to catch a fish for his sister and, in doing so, left behind a tribute to his people.

One Hawaiian language version of the construction of the 'Alekoko Fishpond tells of Pi, a god in other myths told of the *menehune*, and appeared in *Hawaii Holomua*, a Hawaiian language publication.

Pi lived at Hulē'ia on Kaua'i when the chief of that place began a large bank for a *taro* patch to keep the river water out. This chief and his people had worked hard for some time but the task was far from being finished. The chief had paid the workers well in food, fish, *tapa*, and loin cloths, but still the job was not done. Instead Pi, who was quite lazy and scorned by his wife for not working on the bank and for not providing fish to his family, enlisted the *menehune*, whom he regarded as fellow gods, luring them to the site with cakes of *taro*, which he placed in the branches of a *kukui* tree he had uprooted. The *menehune* took the bait and that night, standing in a long line to rapidly move rocks to the construction site, completed the project.

North of Līhu'e, on the south side of the Wailua River tucked away in a dense cane field, is the Malae *heiau*. The thousands of smooth river or ocean basalt rocks used in the foundation, according to legend, were passed hand-to-hand by a wavering double row of thousands of *menehune* from Makaweli on Kaua'i's west side all the way across the island, 25 miles to Wailua.

The most intriguing archaeological site attributed to *menehune* craftsmen is the walls of dressed stones which for hundreds of years have irrigated arid land behind Waimea. Only the topmost blocks of the massive stonework are visible today. If cleared to its original height, which would mean the destruction of the main road into the agricultural lands behind Waimea, the Menehune

Ditch would perhaps tower 20 feet above the banks of the Waimea River. A bronze plaque near the swinging bridge along the river that was placed during the days of the Territory of Hawai'i marks the best spot to view the *menehune*'s carefully laid blockwork.

Real or not, the *menehune* have made their mark on Kaua'i, both in legend and rock. Were they real? We may never know. Will Kaua'i's children still hear them in the night, or just outside the classroom? Probably, as long as the rocks of the Menehune Fishpond and the Menehune Ditch stand.

■ ◆ ◆

IV. MOʻIKEHA FINDS A HOME, AND WIFE, ON KAUAʻI

from The Legends and Myths of Hawaii
by His Hawaiian Majesty Kalākaua

Moʻikeha is a legendary king, voyager and surfer who ended up on Kauaʻi following many adventures. Born in Waipiʻo Valley on the remote Hāmākua Coast of the Big Island, this Homeric figure traveled to his people's ancient homeland of Kahiki in the South Pacific before finding a home near Wailua on Kauaʻi.

Related to the island's earliest settlers, Moʻikeha was a worthy adventurer and hero.

This legend of Moʻikeha, who by all accounts was a real man, tells of how he won his wife Hoʻoipo by sailing in a canoe race to Kaʻula Rock south of Niʻihau and back to Kapaʻa.

Moʻikeha and his adopted family brought an era of peace to the island.

LEAVING KOHALA, MOIKEHA next touched at Hanuaula, on the island of Maui; but, without stopping to exchange courtesies with Haho, the noted moi of that division of the island, he sailed immediately for Oahu. His purpose was to visit his royal father, Mulielealii, whose residence was at Ewa; but his priest and seer so strongly protested against the visit, declaring it to be contrary to the will of the gods, that he directed his course around the northern side of the island, touching at Makapuu and Makaaoa, and then sailing directly for the island of Kauai.

On the evening of the second day after leaving Oahu, Moikeha anchored his canoes in a roadstead not far from Kapaa, Kauai, where Puna, the governing where Puna, the governing alii of the island, held his court, surrounded by the chiefs of his family and a large number of retainers. Puna was one of the most popular rulers in the group, and, strict as he may have been in the exercise of his prerogatives, was always merciful in dealing with offences thoughtlessly or ignorantly committed. He would pardon the humble laborer who might inadvertently cross his shadow or violate a tabu, but never the chief who deliberately trespassed upon his privileges or withheld a courtesy due to his rank. His disposition was naturally warlike, but as the condition of the island was peaceful, and military force was seldom required except in repelling occasiona plundering raids from the other islands, he kept alive the martial spirit of his chiefs and subjects by frequent sham fights, marine drills, and the encouragement of athletic games and friendly contests at arms, in which he himself sometimes took part. Feasting and dancing usually followed these warlike pastimes, and the result was that the court of Puna became somewhat noted for the chivalry of its chiefs and the splendor of its entertainments.

Puna had but one child, a daughter named Hooipo. Tradition describes her as having been, like the most of royal daughters painted by the poets, a very comely maiden. She was therefore the pride and glory of the court, and as she grew to a marriageable age her favor was sought by a number of aspiring chiefs whose rank entitled them to consideration; but, flattered by the contest for her smiles, and naturally vain of a face which the unruffled waters told her was attractive, she evinced no haste in making choice of a husband.

This tardiness or indecision was but very gently rebuked by Puna. Although one tradition gives him two daughters, Hooipo was doubtless his only child, and he was therefore indisposed to hasten an event which would probably lead to their separation. But, as time passed, the suitors of the young chiefess became so persistent, and the rivalry for her assumed so bitter and warlike an aspect, that Puna deenied it prudent for her to restore harmony among the rivals by making a choice at once. But for no one of them did she seem to entertain a decided preference, and therefore suggested that, since a choice must be made, she was willing to leave it to the arbitrament of such manly contest between the rivals as might comport with their dignity and the character of the prize at stake. Puna eagerly accepted the suggestion, as it opened the way to a selection without incurring the enmity of all but the one chosen.

But what should be the nature of the contest? Each of the rival chiefs was probably noted for his skill in some especial accomplishment, and the difficulty was in naming a trial that would seem to be just to all. Unable to decide the matter himself, Puna appealed to the high-priest, and the next day announced that his palaoa—a talisman consisting of a whale's tooth, carved and sanctified—would be sent by a trusty messenger to the little island of Kaula;

that four days thereafter the rival chiefs should, each in his own canoe, start at the same time and place from Kauai, and the one who returned with the palaoa, which the messenger would be instructed to give to the first of the contesting chiefs to land and claim it on the rocks of Kaula, should be the husband of Hooipo, and the others must remain his friends.

The size of the canoes was left to the discretion of the several contestants, but as no more than four assistants would be allowed to each, very large canoes, of course, would not be used. Any means of speed might be employed, including oars, paddles and sails.

The contest was admitted to be as fair as any that could be devised, and the rival chiefs declared themselves satisfied with it, and began to prepare for the race by securing suitable canoes and skilful and stalwart assistants. It promised to be an exciting contest, and the whole of Kapaa was on tiptoe to witness the start.

After a few days of preparation the messenger of Puna was despatchrd with the palaoa to Kaula, with instructions to place it in the hands of the first of the contesting chiefs to claim it on that island. The messenger had been gone two days, and had probably reached his destination, as the distance to be travelled was but little more than a hundred miles, and the rival chiefs had everything in readiness to bend their sails for Kaula, when Moikeha, as already stated, anchored his fleet in the evening off Kapaa.

Early next morning, with his double canoe flying the standard of his rank and otherwise becomingly dressed, Moikeha went ashore, where he was cordially received by the chiefs of the district, and in due time escorted to the sovereign mansion and presented to Puna, without referring to his family connections, he simply announced that he was a chief from the distant land of Kahiki, and was traveling through the Hawallan group on a tour of observation and pleasure. He wore a maro fringed with shells, a kihei or mantle of finely-woven and decorated cloth, and on his head a lei-alii of brilliant feathers, while from his neck was suspended by a cord of plaited hair a curious ornament of mother-of-pearl set in ivory. He was a handsome representative of savage manhood, and his bearing was dignified, correct and courtly.

During his audience with Puna, Moikeha met Hooipo-most likely by accident, but he was so charmed by her bright eyes that he did not leave the mansion until he found occasion to exchange a few pleasant words with her. They seemed to be mutually pleased with each other, and Moikeha accepted the invitation of the chief to consider himself his guest until the next day, at the same time allowing him to send fresh provisions to his people, whose canoes had been drawn up on the beach.

A brilliant entertainment of feasting, music and dancing in honor of the distinguished stranger followed in the evening, during which Moikeha was favored with the companionship of Hooipo, and learned of the contest about to take place between the rival chiefs of Kauai to determine to whom she should be given in marriage.

Hilarity and feasting were the order of the next day and evening, for on the morning following the contesting chiefs were to start for Kaula under the eye of Puna. Their well-equipped canoes were on the beach, and their crews, drilled to work sail and oar together, were in readiness.

Morning came, and with it a large concourse of people to witness the departure of the chiefs. The canoes and their attending crews were examined, and many wagers laid on the result of the race. Finally the contesting chiefs made their appearance, followed shortly after by Puna and the most of his household, including Hooipo, who was conveyed to the beach in a manede borne on the shoulders of four stout attendants, She was attired in an embroidered pau—a short skirt of five thicknesses of thin kapa cloth reaching to the knees—and a cape or short mantle trimmed with feathers. Her hair was braided in a single strand at the back; her head and neck were adorned with leis of flowers and feathers, and her limbs were ornamented with circlets of shells and tinted seeds.

Everything being in readiness, the contending chiefs, eight in number, appeared before the alii-nui, and, bowing low, proceeded in turn to recite their kuauhaus, or genealogies, as they had been called upon to do, to show in a formal manner that all their strains were noble. As each concluded he again bowed, giving Hooipo a smile and look of confidence, and stepped back to await the signal of departure.

The last of them had given his pedigree, the terms of the contest had again been announced in form by a herald, and Puna was about to order the simultaneous launching of the canoes, when Moikeha, whose presence had not before been observed by the chiefs, suddenly presented himself before the alii-nui, and, bowing first to him and then courteously to the chiefs, said : "Great chief, as this trial seems to be free to all of noble blood, I accept the terms, and ask permission to present myself as a contestant for the prize."

The chiefs exchanged glances of surprise, and a pleased expression lighted up the face of Hooipo, who until that moment had manifested but little interest in what was transpiring around her.

Puna hesitated a moment, and then graciously replied: "Noble stranger, if your rank is level with the conditions, and the chiefs now ready for departure urge no objection, my consent will not be withheld."

A hurried consultation among the chiefs showed that some of them objected; but as the stranger, with no knowledge of the coast and apparently no canoe or crew in readiness, did not seem to be a competitor to be feared, it was finally agreed that, should he be able to establish his rank, which a few of them doubted, he might be admitted to the contest.

This resolution having been communicated, Moikeha gracefully bowed his thanks, and then began to recite his genealogy. Curious to learn the strain of the courtly stranger, the chiefs pressed around him, eagerly listening to every word. He began with Wakea, away back in the past, when his ancestors were residents of other lands referred to in Hawaiian story. Giving the record of thirteen generations, he brought the connection down to Nanamaoa, the pioneer of the first migratory influx to the Hawaiian group seven hundred years before. Thence, generation by generation, naming father, mother and heir, he traced down a line of sixteen successors to Maweke. Pausing a moment, while a look of surprise and wonder was exchanged by the listening chiefs, Moikeha continued:

"Maweke the husband,
"Naiolaukea the wife;
"Mulielealii the husband,
"Wehelani the wife;
"Moikeha the husband,
"Hooipo the wife.

Applause followed this announcement by the stranger that he was the son of Mulielealii, the aliinui of Oahu, and the jesting and good-natured manner in which he concluded the kuauhau by predicting his success in the coming contest, and marriage sail sat the friendly deity, from whose exhaustless ipu of imprisoned winds a gale was sent forth which carried the canoe to Kaula before daylight the next morning.

Effecting a landing soon after sunrise, Puna's messenger was found, and at once delivered to Moikeha the palaoa, which he had been instructed to surrender to the chief first demanding it. Content in the possession of the talisman, Moikeha and his companion remained on the island for refreshment until past midday, and then started on their return to Kauai, favored by the same winds that had borne them to Kaula, but proceeding with less haste. Toward night the eight other chiefs landed within a few hours of each other, and great was their astonishment on learning that the palaoa had been delivered to a chief claiming it early that morning.

"He must have had wings," said one of them.

"He was surely helped by the gods," suggested another, who had been the first to land after Moikeha. "But for that the palaoa would have been mine, as you all know. But who can struggle with the gods! Let us not incur their anger by complaint."

As it was easy for the others to reconcile themselves to Moikeha's success, good-humor was soon restored, and the next morning, in company with the messenger, they all re-embarked for Kauai. On the evening of the same day Moikeha landed at Kapaa, and hastened to place in the hands of Puna the talisman which made him the husband of Hooipo. Now assured of the rank of the victor, Puna was gratified at his success, and Hooipo made no disguise of her joy. Tradition says she fell in love with the handsome stranger on first beholding him; but be that as it may, when he returned from Kaula with the palaoa she was frank enough to confess that his success had made her happy.

In the course of a few days all of the defeated chiefs returned to Kapaa, and Moikeha invited them to a feast, over which they forgot their rivalry and renewed the pledges of friendship embraced in the terms and made a condition of the contest. They sought by many ingenious ways to draw from Moikeha the secret of his success; but he failed to enlighten them, and they were compelled to content themselves with the belief that he had been assisted by some supernatural power, possibly by Apukohai, the great fish-god of Kauai, who sometimes seized canoes and bore them onward with almost incredible velocity.

In due time Hooipo became the wife of Moikeha, who, on the death of Puna, succeeded him as the aliinui of Kauai, where he remained to the end of his life. He was blessed with a number of sons, through one of whom, it may be mentioned, the sovereignty of the island was continued in the family after Moikeha was laid under the black kapa.

▨ ▨ ▨

V. MOʻIKEHA—ALIʻI OF KAUAʻI

from The Legends and Myths of Hawaii
by His Hawaiian Majesty Kalākaua

This legend of Moʻikeha takes place late in his life, a time when the adventurer had served as king of Kauaʻi for over two decades. It is a tale of royal life at Wailua, and of the passing of the voyaging mantle to his son Kila of Kauaʻi.

Underlying the story of father and foster-son reunion is the story of the last contact between Kauaʻi and its Polynesian homeland to the South. King Kalākaua wraps up Moʻikehaʻs story by connecting him to the Kamehameha dynasty, and presents his version of why contact was cut off for over 300 years until Captain James Cook arrived off Waimea in 1778.

TRADITION NEXT REFERS to Moikeha about twenty-five years after his marriage with Hooipo. The death of

Puna had left him the sovereignty of Kauai, and his principal residence was at Wailua. He had seven sons, and his court, like that of his predeccesor, was noted for the distinguished chiefs, priests, prophets and poets connected with it.

As the life of Moikeha was drawing to a close as strong desire possessed him to see once more his foster-son Laa, whom, on his departure from Raiatea, he had left with his brother Olopana, whose presumptive heir and successor the young chief had become. In preparation for a journey thither he ordered a number of large double canoes to be repaired and put in order for the open sea, and had some time before dispatched a large party of hunters to the cliffs along the coast for the feathers of the mamo, from which to fabricate a royal mantle for the ward of his youth.

As but a single small yellow feather of the kind used in a royal mantle is found under each wing of the mamo, the task of securing the many thousands required was by no mean a brief or easy service; but in time the feathers were gathered and the cloak was completed. As the choicest feathers along were used, the garment was one of the most brilliant and elaborate ever made on Kauai, and represented the labor of a hundred persons for a year.

But when everything was in readiness for his departure for the south, Moikeha concluded that he was too old and feeble to undertake the voyage. In this conclusion he was sustained by the auguries of the prophets and the persuasion of his sons.

His third son was Kila. He was distinguished for his capacity and courage, and especially for his skill as a navigator, and it was finally decided that he should make the journey to Raiatea as the messenger of Moikeha, and invite Laa to revisit the Hawaiian group, assuring him of the feeble health of his foster-father and of his anxiety to embrace him before death separated them for ever.

Kila was delighted with the mission. For several years intercourse between the Hawaiian and southern groups had been almost completely suspended, but from boyhood his dreams had been of visits to the far-off and misty shores of Kahiki, of which he had heard Moikeha speak; and now that an opportunity was presented for gratifying his appetite for adventure in unknown seas, his joy was boundless, and so vigorously did he push the work of preparation that in a few days the canoes were equipped and provisioned for the voyage. The provisions consisted, in long voyages of that period, of dried fish, dried bananas and plantains, cocoanuts, yams and potatoes, with poi and paiai, fresh fruits and cooked fowls and pigs, for early consumption. Large calabashes of fresh water were also provided, but frequent baths largely diminished the craving for that necessity.

Sacrifices were offered, the auguries were pronounced favorable, and the fleet of double canoes set sail for the south. Kila was accompanied by three of his brothers, and, more important still, by the venerable Kamahualele, the friend and astrologer of Moikeha, who had borne him company from Raiatea more than a quarter of a century before, and chanted his inspired visions of the future off the coast of Kau. He went as Kila's chief navigator and especial counsellor.

The fleet passed through the group and took its final departure from the most southern point of the island of Hawaii. Wind and weather were both favorable, and without a mishap of consequence the expedition arrived in due time at Raiatea, first touching for guidance at some of the other islands of the southern group.

Kila landed at Opoa through the sacred entrance of Avamoa. His flag and state were recognized by Olopana, who was still living, and the sons of Moikeha and their personal attendants were ceremoniously conducted to the royal mansion, where Kila made known the purpose of his visit. Olopana was greatly interested in the story of Moikeha's successful establishment on

Kauai, but refrained from referring to the circumstances which led to their separation many years before. He was also in- formed of the death of his father, Mulielealii, and the succession of his brother Kumuhonua to the rank and authority of alii-nui of Oahu.

With the affectionate greetings of Moikeha, Kila presented to Laa the brilliant mamo, or royal mantle, of which he was made the bearer, and expressed the hope that he would comfort the few remaining days of his foster-father by returning with him on a visit to Kauai. Olopana strongly objected to the proposed journey, urging his advanced years and the probability of his early death; but when assured by Laa of his speedy return he reluctantly consented, and after a round of hospitable feasts and entertainments, in his own double canoes, and attended by his priest, astrologer, master of ceremonies, musicians, and a number of knightly and noble friends, Laa accompanied Kila and his party back to Hawaii.

The voyage was made in good time, and as the combined fleet, with canoes of royal yellow and pennons flying, coursed through the group to Kauai, stopping at several points to exchange courtesies with the ruling chiefs, it attracted unusual attention; and when Laa landed at Wailua, on the island of Oahu, to greet his relatives, and the people learned that the son of Ahukai had returned from the distant land of Kahiki rich in honors and possessions, they strewed his path with flowers and welcomed him as if he were a god.

Proceeding to Kauai, after a brief stay at Wailua, Laa was affectionately received by Moikeha, his foster-father, who had left him a child in Kahiki, and for a month or more the Kauaian court blazed nightly with feasts and festivals given in his honor.

Returning to Oahu, Laa took up his residence for a time at Kualoa. A large mansion was constructed for him, with ample accommodations for his friends and retainers, and the chiefs of the island esteemed it an honor to share his friendship and accept his hospitality.

There was no jealousy of Laa, for it was known that he would soon return to Raiatea, there to permanently remain as the heir and successor of Olopana. In his veins ran the noblest blood of Oahu. He was the son of the great-grandson of the great Paumakua in direct and unchallenged descent, and the adopted heir of the grandson of Maweke, the proud descendant of the Nanaula dynasty of kings.

It was not deemed well that the line of Paumakua, through so distinguished a representative as Laa, should be perpetuated solely on a foreign soil. From a suggestion the matter came to be seriously discussed by the leading chiefs, and finally Laa was approached on the subject. Being a young man, the patriotic proposal of the chiefs very naturally accorded with his tastes, and, without great persuasion, he expressed a willingness to comply with what seemed to be a general request.

But the approval of Laa did not quite settle the delicate question, as the chiefs at once observed on casting around for a suitable wife for so desirable a husband. The most of them had daughters or sisters of eligible rank and age. But which one of them should they select? Whose family should be so honored? They were willing to leave the choice to Laa, but, sagaciously anticipating the result, he declined to make the selection. As usual in momentous cases of doubt, the high-priest was consulted, and the matter was settled in a manner quite satisfactory to Laa. It was agreed that he should marry three wives, all on the same day, and the maidens selected were Hoakanui, daughter of Lonokaehu, of Kualoa; Waolena, daughter of a chief of Kaalaea; and Mane, daughter of a chief of Kaneohe. All were noted for their beauty and distinguished blood.

The three brides were brought to the mansion of Laa, at Kualoa, on the day fixed for the triple marriage, and the event was celebrated with splendor and enthusiasm. The hoao, or marriage agreement, was made public by a herald, as was then the custom among the nobility; the brides, attired becomingly and decked with garlands, were delivered in form to the bridegroom, and in the evening a feast was served on the grounds to more than a thousand guests, with hula, mele, and other festive accompaniments, including mele-inoas, or songs of personal application to the new wives and their husband.

This triple marriage is one of the most thoroughly-established incidents of remote Hawaiian tradition. After his marriage Laa remained a year at Kualoa, and then began to prepare for his return to Raiatea. He looked forward to his departure with mingled feelings of regret and satisfaction, for his brief married life had been singularly as well as most bountifully blessed. On heir of the grandson of Maweke, the proud descendant of the Nanaula dynasty of kings.

It was not deemed well that the line of Paumakua, through so distinguished a representative as Laa, should be perpetuated solely on a foreign soil. From a suggestion the matter came to be seriously discussed by the leading chiefs, and finally Laa was approached on the subject. Being a young man, the patriotic proposal of the chiefs very naturally accorded with his tastes, and, without great persuasion, he expressed a willingness to comply with what seemed to be a general request.

But the approval of Laa did not quite settle the delicate question, as the chiefs at once observed on casting around for a suitable wife for so desirable a husband. The most of them had daughters or sisters of eligible rank and age. But which one of them should they select? Whose family should be so honored? They were willing to leave the choice to Laa, but, sagaciously anticipating the result, he declined to make the selection. As usual in momentous cases of doubt, the high-priest was consulted, and the matter was settled in a manner quite satisfactory to Laa. It was agreed that he should marry three wives, all on the same day, and the maidens selected were Hoakanui, daughter of Lonokaehu, of Kualoa; Waolena, daughter of a chief of Kaalaea; and Mane, daughter of a chief of Kaneohe. All were noted for their beauty and distinguished blood.

The three brides were brought to the mansion of Laa, at Kualoa, on the day fixed for the triple marriage, and the event was celebrated with splendor and enthusiasm. The hoao, or marriage agreement, was made public by a herald, as was then the custom among the nobility; the brides, attired becomingly and decked with garlands, were delivered in form to the bridegroom, and in the evening a feast was served on the grounds to more than a thousand guests, with hula, mele, and other festive accompaniments, including mele-inoas, or songs of personal application to the new wives and their husband.

This triple marriage is one of the most thoroughly-established incidents of remote Hawaiian tradition. After his marriage Laa remained a year at Kualoa, and then began

to prepare for his return to Raiatea. He looked forward
to his departure with mingled feelings of regret and
satisfaction, for his brief married life had been singularly
as well as most bountifully blessed. On the same day he
had been presented with a son by each of his three wives,
and an ancient chant thus refers to the event:

"O Ahukai, O Laa-a, O Laa,
O Laa from Kahiki, the chief;
O Ahukini-a-Laa, O Kukona-a-Laa,
O Lauli-a-Laa, the father
The triple canoe of Laa-mai-kahiki,
The sacred first-born children of Laa,
Who were born on the same one day."

Moikeha died soon after, and Laa bade farewell to
the Hawaiian Islands and returned to Raiatea just in time
to receive the dying blessing of Olopana. As he had
promised, he left his three wives and their sons in Oahu,
where they were well cared for. The names of the children,
as mentioned in the chant quoted, were Ahukini-a-Laa,
Kukona-a-Laa, and Lauli-a-Laa, from whom it was in after-
generations the pride and glory of the governing families
of Oahu and Kauai to trace their lineage. From Ahukini-
a-Laa Queen Kapiolani, wife of Kalakaua, the present
sovereign of the islands, is recorded in descent through a
line of Kauaian chiefs and kings.

Kila, after his return from Raiatea, established
himself in the valley of Waipio, on the island of Hawaii,
and became prosperous in the possessions abandoned
by his uncle Olopana a generation before. He was the
ancestor of several prominent Hawaiian families, who
traced their descent to him as late as during the reign of
Kamehameha I.

With the return of Laa to Raiatea all communication between the Hawaiian and southern groups seems to have abruptly terminated, and for a period of about six hundred years, or until the arrival of Captain Cook in 1778, the Hawaiians learned nothing of the great world beyond their little archipelago, and knew that lands existed elsewhere only through the mysterious mooolelos of their priests, and a folk-lore consisting of broken chains of fables and tales of the past in which the supernatural had finally become the dominant feature.

▣ ⊕ ⊕

Eric Knudsen

VI. THREE MOʻS OF TAHITI
KAUAʻI LEGENDS FROM THE TELLER OF TALES

    *Eric Knudsen, the son of Kauaʻi west-side pioneer
Valdemar Knudsen, grandson of a premier of Norway, was
renowned for his Hawaiian storytelling abilities. During
World War II he hosted a popular radio program featuring
his tales on Kauaʻi's old KTOH station. Sponsored by Coca-
Cola, the Teller of Tales series was recorded on 78 rpm records.
The stories reprinted weekly as giveaway sheets to advertise
their soft drinks on Kauaʻi. The set is now a collector's item.
The younger Knudsen was raised on Kauai's west side and
intimately knew the island, its people and its legends.*

    The location of the moʻo *legend is the Spouting Horn, a
Kauaʻi landmark located along the coast near Kōloa town, to
the west of Poʻipū Beach. Some say the plume of sea spray
that shoots up with each set of waves was once higher and*

more powerful. Reportedly, the hole or puka *was blasted to keep the spray off nearby fields.*

Polihale, the site of the second tale included here, is an otherworldly beach on the west side past Mānā, just before the steep cliffs of Nā Pali begin. This anecdotal piece captures the sometimes amusing crossover of Hawaiian ways with western politics that still highlights local politics on Kaua'i.

Eric Knudsen wrote Kanuka of Kauai *with Gurre Noble in 1944. Kanuka is his father, Valdemar, and the book tells of his loss of gold in the fields of Gold Rush California and his success in making a fortune in sugar on Kaua'i's west side.*

ONCE UPON A time, long years ago, there lived a family of huge lizards, or *mo-os*, on the island of Tahiti. Besides papa and mama Mo-o, there were a lot of young ones.

The young lizards played so many pranks on their older brother and two beautiful sisters that the latter decided to pack up and seek an island where there was more living space and peace. One bright day they said farewell to their weeping parents and swam away, out into the broad Pacific ocean.

Being used to an ocean full of islands, they had no idea how far they would have to swim, but they headed north. Day and night they swam along. For a while the water was warm, and then it began to get colder and colder. No rocks were to be seen, and they finally got so tired that they wished they had never left home.

Their strength was almost spent when one morning they saw land ahead. A long island lay sleeping in the ocean, and they could see a beach of white sand with the waves breaking on it. The two sisters wanted to go to this island, but their brother begged them not to.

"It looks bare and hot," he said. "I see another island

lying only a few miles beyond, and it has tall mountains with clouds hanging on them. That means there are forests and rivers where we can rest and enjoy life. But the two sisters would not listen to him. How human they were! They insisted on crawling up on the wide sandy beach to rest; and so they parted. The sisters landed on the island of Niihau, but the brother kept on toward Kauai.

When the hot sun beat down upon the two sleeping sisters they were too exhausted to crawl back to the ocean. They slept on and on, until they were finally turned to stone.

Many years later, when I was a small boy visiting my Uncle Frank on the island of Niihau, I rode with him along the shore and he pointed out the two sisters. They looked like two great coconut logs lying side by side and over one hundred feet long.

"They must be part of a lava flow," I said.

"No," he told me, "lava doesn't flow like that. The old Hawaiians say they are mo-os, and they swam here from Tahiti."

"Were there any more?" I asked Uncle Frank.

"I have heard that one went to Kauai," he said; "but where he ended up is a mystery to me."

The years rolled on and I grew up. Often I thought of the two black petrified sisters on Niihau, but I never got back to see them. The island of Kauai was a big one to get around on horseback. But when a Ford runabout fell into my hands, I began to explore my home island more thoroughly.

One day I drove down the old Koloa Landing road, and following a dirt road came upon the famed Spouting Horn. It was fascinating to watch this great geyser—to see an ocean swell come racing in from the open sea and splash up against the big lava at my feet, then a great column of white water roar up through an opening in the lava thirty, forty or fifty feet in the air. It had Old Faithful of the Yellowstone Park easily beaten. Old Faithful blew every fifty-eight minutes or so: but this one blew every minute!

As I watched the fountain play, I heard a queer sound coming from the ledge below me. It sounded like the hissing noise a snake makes when angry. I walked down onto the ledge and waited. A long swell came in and, as the column of water rose in a great fountain, the hissing noise sounded at my feet.

As I stood there an old Hawaiian fisherman came along, and when I spoke to him and asked him about the queer noise, he smiled and said, "Listen, and I will tell you all about it." We sat on the bank and he began to talk.

"Once upon a time a giant mo-o, or lizard, landed on Kauai. It had swum all the way from Tahiti. It was a huge monster but quite friendly, and the people called him Lehu. He landed at Lawai Beach and crawled up into the stream and lay exhausted for awhile. Then he recovered his strength and wandered about the countryside. He went over to Koloa, and his favorite spot was the junction of the Poeleele and Omao rivers. He lived on Kauai for many years, and stories came from Niihau of the arrival there of two other mo-os who had become petrified as they lay sleeping on the sand.

"One day Lehu, feeling lonely, swam over to the island of Niihau to visit his two sisters. But when he found that they were dead, he swam back to his beloved Kauai.

"As he swam along the shore he was so fascinated by the fountains of the Spouting Horn that he came in close to land to get a better view. A long narrow lava tube lay under the lava where we now are, and the opening was under the water. He thought he would explore this strange tube. He crawled up into it. Unfortunately, some sharp rocks on the sides that let him slip in caught his legs as he tried to back out, and he was stuck fast in the lava tube.

"He wriggled and fought, but in vain. There he was doomed to lie, and now, every time a wave rushes in and wets him all over, he growls and hisses; and that is what you hear.

"The lava was too hard for Hawaiians of the long ago. They couldn't free him. And now, if we used dynamite to blow up the lava, we would only kill him. There poor Lehu is doomed to stay forever," concluded the Hawaiian.

I thanked the old fisherman. The mystery of the third and last of the three mo-os had finally been cleared up.

THE HEIAU AT POLIHALE

The priests of the old Hawaiians were a clever lot. They chose a perfect place for a temple dedicated to the dead.

The land of the dead, or Po as the Hawaiians called it, lay a mile or two out in the ocean, beneath the waves in the long sweeping bight that lies between Nohili, the Barking Sands, and the point of Nualolo on Kauai.

As you approach the temple, you find the ocean waves crowding you on one side and, on the other, rugged cliffs that rise higher and higher. The last valley–Haeleele–is passed and a straight cliff more than one thousand feet high towers over your head. When the great typhoon swells come roaring in, they wash up the slope of the cliff and cut off all travel toward Napali. And just where the sand beach ends and the rocky shore begins is a well of bubbling water, a sacred spring. Only the priests could drink its waters. At night the sea birds scream and cry as they roost high up in the cliffs, and when the surf is high, the *ehu kai*, or sea spray, rises like smoke along the shore, giving the place a weird look.

Here on the talus slopes of the thousand-foot cliff, almost one hundred yards east of the sacred spring, the priests built their heiau of Polihale. The first terrace is faced with large rocks and is quite large. And so the temple climbs up the hill, terrace upon terrace, five in all. When it was built no one remembers, but the stonework today is as good as when it was first constructed, maybe a thousand years ago.

The priests were tabu, or sacred, and were held in great fear by the common people, for this was the temple of the dead and the soul of everyone who died had to go to Polihale Temple to be purified before it could enter the land of Po. Those who were accepted climbed to a big black rock some eight hundred feet above the temple, and from there they dived into Po. Here human sacrifices were offered. Here came Hawaii's last king—King Kalakaua—about 1886 to pray to the ancient Hawaiian gods to cure him of a sickness the white doctors had pronounced fatal. He sacrificed a black pig and a white rooster, but the god Miru of the land of Po refused to help, and Kalakaua did not get the few extra years to enjoy the life he loved so dearly.

The terraces still stand, though gone are the priests and all their glory. But though the temple is abandoned and neglected, it is still venerated and people go and place little altars upon the terraces.

Near the temple lived a family who later moved to Mana. The son became my father's head *luna*, or overseer, and he told me about the temple and showed me how to build an altar of my own and how to pray. The old religion was gone soon after Captain Cook landed on Kauai, but the old superstitions still lived on, for who isn't a bit superstitious, really?

As time went on, I became manager of the ranch in which this famous *heiau* lies. Still later I was elected to the Hawaiian Legislature. It was the session of 1905, and a long one. I was Speaker of the House. My friend, Billy Harris, was floor leader.

The regular session ran its course. So did an extra session called to pass financial bills. But the last one was hopeless. It seemed that everyone had to put something into the appropriation bills, until almost three times the amount of revenue in sight was given away. And then we adjourned.

I had been away from home almost five months. It was grand to be back on the ranch—away from the noise and bustle of Honolulu and out on the range again. But barely a month had passed when early one morning, as I was walking down to the stables, a carriage drove into the yard and out stepped my friend of the legislature, Billy Harris. He looked sick.

"What's the trouble?" I asked, "What's happened?"

He moaned and sighed. "Haven't you heard the news? The governor called a special session of the legislature to straighten out the appropriation bills, and we meet next week. I jumped the first boat to Kauai. I wanted to talk it over with you."

I saddled another horse and Billy and I rode away toward Mana as we discussed the situation. The more we talked the worse it seemed. In the legislature there were the old *awa*-drinking, watery-eyed hack driver who sat next to Harris; the so-called Cannon Ball of Kohala; and a bunch of other legislators who didn't care a rap if the bills were overloaded, just so long as their own favorite items were there. We laughed as we remembered the emergency bill the governor sent down during the session. It had called for $25,000, but when it finally got out of the House it called for almost half a million!

By the time my work was done we had ridden far away along the land and were quite near the temple of Polihale, so I suggested to my companion that we go take a look at it. We tied our horses to some nearby bushes and climbed up onto the old terraces. And it was then that I had an inspiration! "Billy," I said, "let's try some kahuna business. Let's pray to the god Miru for help."

He laughed at me and said I was crazy, but I started to build an altar. He watched me a few moments, then he began to build one also. Up on the cliff I saw a white flower, the *pua ahiahi* or night flower, that the sun had not yet touched. I clambered up and picked it and placed it upon my altar. Billy, finding nothing better, placed a lantana flower on his. Then, standing beside our altars and facing the land of Po, I prayed to Miru in the best Hawaiian I knew. I told him the session could be over in fifteen days if no one tried any monkey business. "*Pepehe*-strike dead," I cried, "anyone who starts to filibuster. They only bring shame to Hawaii." I finished my prayer and bowed low over our altars. At that very moment a small cloud shut out the sun. "The god Miru has answered our prayer," I cried out. "Mahalo, thank you!"

Of course Billy Harris and I went to Honolulu to attend the special session. All the old gang was there. The old officers were re-elected. In a few minutes the governor's message was in our hands. We took a recess. I stepped down from the Speaker's platform and met the old hack driver face to face.

"Hello, Mr. Speaker," he said. "How long you think this session will last?"

"Oh," I replied, "it won't take long to straighten out those bills. It can be done in fifteen days."

"What!" he exclaimed. "Impossible! It will take all of sixty days and then nothing will be accomplished, only *hopapa, hopapa, hopapa*—wrangling all the time."

"Well," I said, "it's up to you and your gang, but I will tell you a little story. Do you know about the heiau of Polihale?" I asked him.

"Of course," he said. So then I told him all that Billy Harris and I had done at the temple the week before. He looked at me in amazement, his eyes watering, and finally gasped out, "But, Mr. Speaker, you surely don't believe in those things?"

"Well," I said, "I don't know. I was born on Kauai not far from the temple of Polihale and I knew some of the old *kahuna*s who lived and sacrificed there. The Greeks and Romans had Jupiter and Mars. The Japanese worship Buddha-the Chinese, Confucius. I recognize Jehovah, but I am not so sure that the old Hawaiian gods have no power. Anyway, I am not going to take any chances. I will get through in fifteen days if I can."

I left him and went out to lunch. Returning later, I was entering the hall by a back door when I saw the old hack driver sitting near it surrounded by his cronies, and he was talking in Hawaiian. I caught the word "Polihale." I slipped away and entered through the front door.

The session went on. A hundred thousand dollars was cut out of the Cannon Ball's favorite items. I glanced at him but he sat with glassy eyes gazing into space. One of the other leader's pet bills was smothered. He sat and squirmed and kept wiping his eyes. He looked at me but never uttered a word. The top heavy bills were slashed and cut to pieces, but never a peep did we hear from the old gang. The days were full of work, the bills were ready and finished, the last vote recorded, and the new bills went to the governor. Our work was *pau*–finished. And it was the night of the fifteenth day.

Billy Harris rose from his desk. "Mr. Speaker," he said. "I move we adjourn, sine die." The session was over.

I stepped down to the floor and he and I shook hands.

"It worked," he said, in a triumphant voice. "Sure," I answered. "Great is the Heiau of Polihale."

VII. THE RETURN OF LONO
COOK DISCOVERS KAUA'I AND HAWAI'I

Sailing north from Tahiti in search of a northwest passage, famed circumnavigator Captain James Cook is credited with discovering the Hawaiian Islands in January 1778 by landing at Kaua'i. Cook was on his third circumnavigation of the globe. On January 19, after spotting the south and west shores of O'ahu, he sailed on and landed off the Hawaiian village of Waimea, Kaua'i.

There is, to this day, great debate as to whether Cook was the first European sea captain to reach Hawai'i. Through studying 16th-century Spanish maps, some surmise that Cook was preceded by Spaniards.

This account takes Cook from his discovery of Kauai to the Big Island and his death at Kealákekua Bay in 1779, where Cook's presence is still very apparent.

Another modern description of Cook in Hawai'i, The
Curse of Lono, *by "gonzo journalist" Hunter S. Thompson,
is perhaps the wildest, claiming that Cook cursed Hawai'i
forever. Another states that the second Hawaiian to strike
Cook used an iron pahoa, or Hawaiian dagger, forged from
iron traded by Cook's men at Waimea, Kaua'i.*

IN THE MORNING of the 18th (January, 1778), an
island made its appearance, bearing northeast by east; and
soon after we saw more land bearing north and entirely
detached from the former. Both had the appearance of
being high land. At noon the first bore northeast by east,
half east by estimation about eight or nine leagues distant.
Our latitude at this time was 21° 12' N. and longitude
200° 41' E. We had now light airs and calms, by turns; so
that at sunset we were not less than nine or ten leagues
from the nearest land.

On the 19th, at sunrise, the island first seen bore east
several leagues distant. This being directly to windward,
which prevented our getting near it, I stood for the other,
which we could reach; and not long after discovered a
third island in the direction of west-northwest, as far
distant as land could be seen. We had now a fine breeze at
east by north; and I steered for the east end of the second
island, the nearest part being about two leagues distant.

At this time, we were in some doubt whether or no
the land before us was inhabited; but this doubt was soon
cleared up by seeing some canoes coming off from the
shore toward the ships. I immediately brought to, to give
them time to join us. They had from three to six men
each; and on their approach we were agreeably surprised
to find that they spoke in the language of Otaheite and of
the other islands we had lately visited. It required but very
little address to get them to come alongside, but no

entreaties could prevail upon any of them to come on board. I tied some brass medals to a rope and gave them to those in one of the canoes, who in return tied some small mackerel to the rope as an equivalent. This was repeated; and some small nails or bits of iron, which they valued more than any article, were given them. For these they exchanged more fish, and a sweet potato—a sure sign that they had some notion of bartering, or at least of returning one present for another. They had nothing else in their canoes except some large gourd shells and a kind of fishing net; but one of them offered for sale the piece of stuff that he wore round his waist, after the manner of the other islands.

These people were of a brown color, and though of the common size were stoutly made. There was little difference in the cast of their color but a considerable variation in their features, some of their visages not being very unlike those of Europeans. The hair of most of them was cropped pretty short; others had it flowing loose; and with a few, it was tied in a bunch on the crown of the head. In all, it seemed to be naturally black; but most of them had stained it, as is the practice of the Friendly Islanders with some stuff which gave it a brown or burnt color. In general they wore beards. They had no ornaments about their persons, nor did we observe that their ears were perforated; but some were punctured on the hands or near the groins, though in a small degree; and the bits of cloth which they wore were curiously stained with red, black, and white colors. They seemed very mild and had no arms of any kind, if we except some small stones which they had evidently brought for their own defense; and these they threw overboard when they found that they were not wanted. . .

The next morning we stood in for the land, and were met with several canoes filled with people, some of whom took courage and ventured on board. In the course of my several voyages, I never before met with the natives of any place so much astonished as these people were upon entering a ship. Their eyes were continually flying from object to object; the wildness of their looks and gestures fully expressing their entire ignorance about everything they saw, and strongly marking to us that till now they had never been visited by Europeans nor been acquainted with any of our commodities except iron, which, however, it was plain they had only heard of, or had known it in some small quantity brought to them at some distant period. They seemed only to understand that it was a substance much better adapted to the purposes of cutting or of boring of holes than anything their own country produced. They asked for it by the name of *hamaite*, probably referring to some instrument in the making of which iron could be usefully employed; for they applied that name to the blade of a knife, though we could be certain that they had no idea of that particular instrument; nor could they at all handle it properly. For the same reason they frequently called iron by the name of toe, which in their language signifies a hatchet, or rather a kind of adz. On asking them what iron was, they immediately answered, "We do not know. You know what it is, and we only understand it as *toe* or *hamaite*." When we showed them some beads, they asked first what they were, and then whether they should eat them. But on their being told that they were to be hung in their ears, they returned them as useless. They were equally indifferent as to a looking glass which was offered them, and returned it for the same reason; but sufficiently expressed their desire for *hamaite* and *toe*, which they wished might be very large. Plates of earthenware, china cups, and other such things were so new to them that they asked if they were made of wood; but wished to have some, that they might carry them to be looked at on shore. They were in some respects naturally well bred, or at least fearful of giving offense, asking where they would sit down, whether they might spit upon the deck, and the like. Some of them repeated a long prayer before they came on board; and others afterward sung and made motions with their hands, such as we had been accustomed to see in the dances of the islands we had lately visited. There was another circumstance in which they also perfectly resembled those other islanders. At first, on their entering the ship, they endeavored to steal everything they came near; or rather to take it openly, as what we either should not resent or not hinder. We soon convinced them of their mistake; and if they after some time became less active in appropriating to themselves whatever they took a fancy to, it was because they found that we kept a watchful eye over them.

At nine o'clock, being pretty near the shore, I sent three armed boats under the command of Lieutenant Williamson to look for a landing place and for fresh water. I ordered him that if should find it necessary to land in search of the latter, not to suffer more than one man to go with him out of the boats. Just as they were putting off from the ship, one of the natives having stolen the butcher's cleaver leaped overboard, got into his canoe, and hastened to the shore, the boats pursuing him in vain.

The order not to permit the crews of the boats to go on shore was issued that I might do everything in my power to prevent the importation of a fatal disease into this island, which I knew some of our men labored under, and which, unfortunately, had been already communicated by us to other islands in these seas. With the same view, I ordered all female visitors to be excluded from the ships. Many of them had come off in the canoes. Their size, color, and features did not differ much from those of the men; and though their countenances were remarkably open and agreeable, there were few traces of delicacy to be seen, either in their faces or other proportions. The only difference in their dress was their having a piece of cloth about the body, reaching from near the middle to halfway down the thighs, instead of the maro worn by the other sex. They would as readily have favored us with their company on board as the men; but I wished to prevent all connection which might, too probably, convey an irreparable injury to themselves, and through their means to the whole nation. Another necessary precaution was taken by strictly enjoining that no person known to be capable of propagating the infection should be sent upon duty out of the ships. Whether these regulations, dictated by humanity, had the desired effect or not, time only can discover. . .

While the boats were occupied in examining the coast, we stood on and off with the ships, waiting for their return. About noon Mr. Williamson came back and reported that he had seen a large pond behind a beach near one of the villages, which the natives told him contained fresh water; and that there was an anchoring ground before it. He also reported that he had attempted to land in another place, but was prevented by the natives, who, coming down to the boats in great numbers, attempted to take away the oars, muskets, and, in short, everything that they could lay hold of; and pressed so thick upon him that he was obliged to fire, by which one man was killed. But this unhappy circumstance I did not know till after we had left the island, so that all my measures were directed as if nothing of the kind had happened. Mr. Williamson told me that after the man fell his countrymen took him up, carried him off, and then retired from the boat; but still they made signals for our people to land, which he declined. It did not appear to Mr. Williamson that the natives had any design to kill, or event to hurt, any of his party; but they seemed excited by mere curiosity to get from them what they had, being at the same time ready to give in return anything of their own. . .

Between three and four o'clock I went ashore with three armed boats, and twelve marines, to examine the water and to try the disposition of the inhabitants, several hundred of whom were assembled on a sandy beach before the village. The very instant I leaped on shore, the collected body of the natives fell flat upon their faces and remained in that very humble posture till by expressive signs I prevailed upon them to rise. They then brought a great many small pigs, which they presented to me, with plantain trees, using much the same ceremonies that we had seen practiced on such occasions at the Society and other islands; and a long prayer being spoken by a single person, in which others of the assembly sometimes joined, I expressed my acceptance of their proffered friendship by giving them in return such presents as I had brought with me from the ship for that purpose. When this introductory business was finished, I stationed a guard upon the beach and got some of the natives to conduct me to the water, which proved to be very good and in a proper situation for our purpose. It was so considerable that it may be called a lake, and it extended farther up the country than we could see. Having satisfied myself about this very essential point and about the peaceable disposition of the natives, I returned on board; and then gave orders that everything should be in readiness for landing and filling our water casks in the morning, when I went ashore with the people employed in that service, having a party of marines with us for a guard, who were stationed on the beach.

As soon as we landed, a trade was set on foot for hogs and potatoes, which the people of the island gave us in exchange for nails and pieces of iron formed into something like chisels. We met with no obstruction in watering; on the contrary, the natives assisted our men in rolling the casks to and from the pool and readily performed whatever we required. Everything thus going on to my satisfaction and considering my presence on the spot as unnecessary, I left the command to Mr. Williamson, who had landed with me, and made an excursion into the country, up the valley, accompanied by Mr. Anderson and Mr. Webber; the former of whom was as well qualified to describe with pen as the latter was to represent with his pencil, everything we might meet with worthy of observation. A numerous train of natives followed us; and one of them, whom I had distinguished for his activity in keeping the rest in order, I made choice of as our guide. This man from time to time proclaimed our approach; and everyone whom we met fell prostrate upon the ground, and remained in that position till we had passed. This, as I afterward understood, is the mode of paying their respect to their own great chiefs. . .

At sunset I brought everybody on board, having procured in the course of the day nine tons of water; and, by changes chiefly for nails and pieces of iron, about seventy or eighty pigs, a few fowls, a quantity of potatoes, and a few plantains and taro roots. These people merited our best commendations in this commercial intercourse, never once attempting to cheat us, either ashore or alongside the ships. . .

Amongst the articles which they brought to barter this day, we could not help taking notice of a particular sort of cloak and cap, which, even in countries where dress is more particularly attended to, might be reckoned elegant. The first are near of the size and shape of the short cloaks worn by the women of England and by the men in Spain, reaching to the middle of the back and tied loosely before. The ground of them is a network upon which the most beautiful red and yellow feathers are so closely fixed that the surface might be compared to the thickest and richest velvet, which they resemble, both as to the feel and the glossy appearance. The manner of varying the mixture is very different; some having triangular spaces of red and yellow alternately; others, a kind of crescent; and some that were entirely red had a broad yellow border which made them appear, at some distance, exactly like a scarlet cloak edged with gold lace. The brilliant colors of the feathers, in those that happened to be new, added not a little to their fine appearance; and we found that they were in high estimation with their owners; for they would not at first part with one of them for anything that we offered, asking no less a price than a musket. However, some were afterward purchased for very large nails. Such of them as were of the best sort were scarce; and it should seem that they are only used on the occasion of some particular ceremony or diversion. The cap is made almost exactly like a helmet, with the middle part, or crest, sometimes of a hand's breath; and it sits very close upon the head, having notches to admit the ears. It is a frame of twigs and osiers, covered with a network into which are wrought feathers, in the same manner as upon the cloaks, though rather closer and less diversified, the greater part being red, with some black, yellow, or green stripes on the sides, following the curve direction of the crest. These, probably, complete the dress with the cloaks, for the natives sometimes appeared in both together. . .

These people are vigorous, active, and most expert swimmers; leaving their canoes upon the most trifling occasion, diving under them, and swimming to others though at a great distance. It was very common to see women, with infants at the breast, when the surf was so high that they could not land in the canoes, leap overboard, and without endangering their little ones, swim to the shore through a sea that looked dreadful. They seemed to be blessed with a frank, cheerful disposition; and were I to draw any comparisons, I should say that they are equally free from the fickle levity which distinguishes the natives of Otaheite and the sedate cast observable amongst many of those of Tongatabu. They seem to live very sociably in their intercourse with one another; and, except the propensity to thieving, which seems innate in most of the people we have visited in this ocean, they were exceedingly friendly to us. . .

Though I did not see a chief of any note, there were, however, several, as the natives informed us, who reside upon Atooi, and to whom they prostrate themselves as a mark of submission, which seems equivalent to the moe paid to the chiefs of the Friendly Islands, and is here called *haomea* or *moe*. Whether they were at first afraid to show themselves or happened to be absent I cannot say; but after I had left the island, one of these great men made his appearance and paid a visit to Captain Clerke on board the Discovery. He came off in a double canoe and, like the king of the Friendly Islands, paid no regard to the small canoes that happened to lie in his way, but ran against or over them, without endeavoring in the least to avoid them. And it was not possible for these poor people to avoid him, for they could not manage their canoes, it being a necessary mark of their submission that they should lie down till he had passed. His attendants helped him into the ship, an placed him on the gangway. Their care for him did not cease then, for they stood round him holding each other by the hands; or would they suffer anyone to come near him but Captain Clerke himself. He was a very young man, clothed from head to foot, and accompanied by a young woman supposed to be his wife. His name was said to be Tamahano. Captain Clerke made him some suitable presents and received from him in return a large bowl supported by two figures of men, the carving of which, both as to the design and execution, showed some degree of skill. This bowl, as our people were told, used to be filled with the *kava*, or *ava* (as it is called in Otaheite), which liquor they prepare and drink here, as the other islands in this ocean. Captain Clerke could not prevail upon this great man to go below, nor to move from the place where his attendants had first fixed him. After staying some time in the ship, he was carried again into his canoe and returned to the island, receiving the same honors from all the natives as when he came on board. The next day several messages were sent to Captain Clerke inviting him to return the visit ashore and acquainting him that the chief had prepared a large present on that occasion. But being anxious to get to sea and join the Resolution, the captain did not think it advisable to accept of the invitation.

❖ ❖ ❖

VIII. KAUA'I'S FIRST CHRISTMAS
BRITISH EXPLORERS INTRODUCE THE HOLIDAY

Christmas first arrived on Kaua'i's shores in 1786. British explorers Captain Nathaniel Portlock and Captain George Dixon spread Christmas cheer among the Hawaiians of Waimea, as well as aboard their ships.

The sharing of presents, drink and food with the villagers at Waimea also marked the first documented celebration of Christmas in all Hawai'i. Cook missed the Christmas season on his two voyages to Hawai'i, returning in January.

Dixon's and Portlock's ships were the first to visit Hawai'i for commerce. Portlock is today best known in Hawai'i for his namesake Portlock Point, a tony neighborhood on O'ahu's south shore.

It was only decades later that Christmas became an official holiday for Kaua'i's people. The first proper Christmas was celebrated in the mid-1800's. The first New England missionaries who arrived on the island in 1820 followed the Calvinist tradition of the wintertime holiday for they believed that pagan Scandinavian and even Druid influences were at the root of the festive celebrations held during Christmastime.

Today Kaua'i's people wholeheartedly celebrate Christmas with a wide variety of traditional festivities, including the singing of Hawaiian Christmas carols. Midnight Mass in the island's Roman Catholic churches is a highlight of the year for many Portuguese and Filipino communities.

Cutting down Norfolk pines, specially grown as Christmas trees, is a Christmas tradition for some Kaua'i homes.

WINDS BLEW LUSTILY, whipping the deep blue sea into a heap of foam-crested peaks, as the ships of British explorer Captain Nathaniel Portlock lurched and groaned toward the remote Pacific Island of Atooi a few days before Christmas, 1786. Fresh from the wonders of Tahiti, the officers and crew may have been daydreaming of new adventures as the towering pinnacles and verdant valleys of Atooi grew closer, yet surely some were homesick for their own green isle so far away, longing to spend the holiday season with families or sweethearts they had not seen for so many, weary months and might not see again for another long stretch of time.

A day or two before Christmas Eve, Portlock and his second-in-command, Capt. Dixon, anchored their vessels, the *King George* and the *Queen Charlotte*, in the roads off the village of Waimea on the island they called Atooi, later known as Kaua'i. It had been only eight years since the island had been discovered by Portlock's countryman, Captain James Cook, who later met his end in a dispute with warriors on the Big Island. Portlock and his men had no inkling of what kind of welcome they might receive and could not know they had arrived at a most auspicious time—toward the end of the *makahiki* festival, a three-month-long celebration during which the Hawaiians honored the peaceful god Lono by resting from their labors, engaging in sports and entertainment, feasting sumptuously and doing their best to let nothing interfere with their pursuit of pleasure.

As Portlock and his men rowed toward the beach, they were met by dozens of outrigger canoes filled with friendly Kauaians who warmly greeted the pale strangers. Once on shore, Portlock wisely let his sailors mingle freely with the people of Waimea and urged them to share their Christmas celebration with the *makahiki* revelers, thus boosting the crew's morale during their treacherous, years-long circumnavigation and, at the same time, improving relations with the local Hawaiians.

Dixon's classic account of his journey with Portlock, entitled *A Voyage Round the World*, 1789, includes a passage describing what was undoubtedly Kaua'i's very first Christmas. Reading like a page from a Charles Dickens' holiday classic, the entry for December 24, 1786 recalls:

"This being Christmas that season of the year so universally convivial throughout the civilized world, we spent our time as agreeably, and with plenty of as good cheer as we could procure, such as roast pig, sea-pie, &c. &c. and to shew our refined taste, even in our liquor, we no longer dran [sic] grog mixed with simple water, but offered our Christmas libations in punch, mixed with the juice of coco-nut, toasting our friends and mistresses in bumpers of this liquor, which perhaps pleased more on account of its novelty, than from any other circumstances."

Besides imbibing some of the first tropical cocktails ever concocted in Hawai'i, Portlock and his men also rowed ashore for Christmas dinner. In Portlock's historic *A Voyage Round the World*, the event is vividly recalled. The account begins on Christmas Eve:

"We arrived at the house about sunset, and one of chief Abbenoe's men, who had joined us in the course of the afternoon, gave directions for a hog and a dog to be immediately killed and dressed for our suppers, together with a large quantity of taro. The house was well lighted up with torches made of dry rushes, and at eight o'clock supper being ready, it was served up in great order, and I think few people ever ate a heartier supper than we did."

Portlock also acted out the role of Santa Claus to the young children of Waimea village.

He states: "We got up next morning at daylight, and finished the remains of the preceding evening's repast. Previous to our quitting the house, there were near an hundred women about it, most of them with children in their arms; they were very inquisitive to know my name, which they pronounced Popote, and such of the infants as could speak were taught by their mothers to call on Popote; on this I distributed some trifles amongst them, with which they appeared highly satisfied and pleased."

On Christmas Day, Portlock's kindness was repaid sevenfold. Kiana, a chief of Waimea who later sailed with Portlock to China and became the first Hawaiian to intermingle with the Chinese in their homeland, appears in the passage. Portlock recalls:

"In the morning of the 25th, Kiana, the chief whom I saw on shore, came off in a large double canoe, and brought me a present of some hogs and vegetables, which I received, and made him a return that pleased him very much.

"He informed me that the king, accompanied by Abbenoe and a number of other principal chiefs, would be down in a day or two, and in the mean time we should be plentifully supplied with every thing the island produced.

"After many professions of friendship Kiana took his leave and returned on shore. Soon afterwards I sent the whaleboat on shore to Waimea for the sailor I left behind along with Paapaaa and Towanoha; my man returned with the boat, but the other two chose to remain on shore a day or two amongst their new friends, and I understood they were greatly caressed by the natives in general."

Shortly thereafter, the huge north seas and strong trade winds of winter blew Portlock's ships off Waimea's roads toward Ni'ihau. The holiday celebration was soon a fading memory as the men returned to the drudgery of setting sails and keeping careful watch for coral reefs.

Although these early explorers were followed to the Sandwich Islands by successive waves of missionaries, traders and adventurers, Christmas was not celebrated popularly until nearly a century later, when the influence of the New England missionaries, who viewed Christmas as largely a pagan holiday with roots in Celtic and Viking practices, began to wane in the mid-1800's and Christmas was once again observed in Hawai'i with the feasting, merry-making and good cheer that Portlock and his men experienced in Waimea.

The spirit of *aloha* shown to the weary British sailors by the people of Kaua'i two hundred years ago still thrives on the Garden Island and is not so very different from the message of love that gives Christmas its true meaning.

IX. KAUMUALI'I
KAUA'I'S LAST KING

Kaumuali'i, Kaua'i's last king, is considered both a noble and tragic figure. The Kaua'i-born ali'i's birth pre-dated the arrival of Captain James Cook in 1778, and his reign was a peaceful one, but he died in exile in Lahaina, Maui, with his kingdom in the control of alii from the islands of Hawai'i and O'ahu.

More so than the rulers of other Hawaiian islands, Kaumuali'i embraced western ways when they arrived. He welcomed with open arms the missionaries who arrived from Boston in 1820 and the Prussian-led Russians who attempted to take over Hawai'i beginning with Kaua'i in the mid-1810's. However, both these moves proved tragic—allowing the Russians to become a threat to the control of Hawai'i. The Kamehameha's eventually ordered the removal of the

Russians as the island's ruler, and his son George, who returned aboard the missionary brig Thaddeus *from over 15 years on the mainland, died as a rebel instead of becoming the pious leader the missionaries had envisioned.*

Ironically, Deborah Kapule, the wife Kaumuali'i left behind when he was dethroned and removed to O'ahu, became an island leader in her own right. Deborah's compound along the banks of the Wailua River became a gathering place for Kaua'i's foreign visitors and native travelers. Today the Coco Palms Resort stands near the site of her inn, perhaps a more visible reminder of Kaua'i's last queen than any historical site associated with Kaumuali'i.

FAMED THROUGHOUT THE islands for his beauty of face and of person and for his reputation as a surfer, swimmer and canoeman, Kaumuali'i had ruled Kaua'i since his early youth and was the epitome of all the best found in the ruling families of Kaua'i. Believed to have been endowed with the highest *kapu*, or "blue blood," found in all Hawaiian society and possessing a powerful spiritual force, or *mana*, monarchs like Kaumuali'i had been sought out for generations as mates by the nobility of other islands.

The year was 1810—over 30 years after the discovery of Hawai'i by circumnavigator Captain James Cook of the British Navy, and 10 years before the arrival of New England missionaries. The Hawaiian kingdom was still in its formative stages, and Kamehameha stood on the brink of his greatest achievement—the unification of the Hawaiian Islands.

Before Kamehameha's time each island was divided into princedoms, and war was rampant and continual. However, even though battles flared up on Kaua'i and Ni'ihau, the rough, 60-mile-wide Kaua'i channel deterred any outside forces from attacking those islands.

Twice over the past decade Kamehameha had attempted, and failed, to conquer the Separate Kingdom of Kaua'i and Ni'ihau. Each venture had been seemingly struck down by the gods—epidemics, high seas, possibly even dark spiritual powers on Kaua'i had defeated his attacks well before his thousands of warriors and sailing canoes reached Kaua'i.

However, this day would mark the end of both the real and imagined powers of the high-ranking *ali'i*—for the life of Kaumuali'i would now rest in the hands of Kamehameha the Great, a king so low in the *kapu* system that he was forced to approach his own son and heir, Liholiho, stark naked and bowing.

Kaumuali'i's decision to willingly cede his own kingdom and even his own life (possibly as a human sacrifice to Kamehameha's war god Kūkā'ilimoku) was made because he deeply believed that to rule his people was also to serve them. And he knew their safety was at stake, for Kaumuali'i understood that after a decade of grace from attacks from the islands to windward, Kamehameha's thousands-strong army and navy would eventually reach his islands.

In deference to the higher ancestral *mana* of the young ruler's bloodline, Kamehameha symbolically paddled out from shore in a single canoe. The warrior king's powerful strokes soon brought him alongside the schooner. Climbing aboard up a Jacob's ladder, his piercing eyes met those of Kaumuali'i. Without hesitation, the brave Kauaian laid his life on the line.

"Here I am! Is it face up or face down?"

After pausing for an instance the "Napoleon of Hawaii" answered, "There is no death."

Kamehameha then boarded the trading schooner of Captain Winship, the European who had helped convince

Kaumuali'i to make peace. A friendly interview followed and Kaumuali'i offered Kaua'i and Ni'ihau to Kamehameha, who in turn deeded the islands to him for life on the condition that, upon his death, Kaumuali'i would be subject to the sovereignty of Liholiho.

The life of Kaumuali'i since his delivery atop the Birthstones at Wailua, where the demigod Māui once roamed and near the villages of the probable landing site of the first Polynesians to settle Kaua'i, seemed destined for this moment, for only the most royal of Hawaiian kings could make this decision for his people and the people of all Hawai'i.

His high *mana* came from his father, King Ka'eo of Kaua'i, son of Kekaulike, the warrior-king of Maui, and his mother, Kamakahelei, a hereditary ruling ali'i of Kaua'i born of a family descended from the early rulers of O'ahu. This marriage gave Kaumuali'i perhaps the highest *mana* of any ruler in Hawai'i.

Kamakahelei was an especially important Hawaiian ruler. Her strength came in part from the 'Ane'ekapuahi, a powerful prayer she alone knew. The effect of the prayer, which had to do with heat or fire, was feared throughout Hawai'i, especially since Kaua'i was known as "the praying island" at a time when the prayers of *kahuna* and the ali'i could cause death. Incidentally, Kamakau, a Hawaiian historian of the nineteenth century, also claimed that Kamakahelei gave Kaumuali'i's older sister, Lelemahoalani, to Captain Cook to sleep with during Cook's visit to Waimea, Kaua'i.

Kaumuali'i's skill as a diplomat, and ruler, were made known to the western world by British explorer Captain George Vancouver, who sailed into the roads off Waimea on March 9, 1792.

Vancouver comments in his journals about Kaumuali'i: "I was much pleased with the appearance and behavior of this young prince, who seemed to be about twelve years of age. In his countenance was exhibited much affability and cheerfulness; and on closely observing his features, they had infinitely more the resemblance of an European than of those which generally characterize these islanders…His inquiries and observations, on this occasion were not, as might have been expected from his age, directed to trivial matters; but to such circumstances alone, as would have authorized questions from persons of matured years and some experience. He conducted himself with a great degree of good breeding."

The future Kauaʻi king was in turn greatly impressed by Vancouver, and later assumed the title of "King George" and named his own son George, in honor of Vancouver's ruler.

Two years after Vancouver's visit the stage was set for Kaumualiʻiʻs ascension to the throne of Kauaʻi. His father, Kaʻeo, perished at a battle near Pearl Harbor, when opposing forces aided by western sailors in small boats slaughtered him and his men. On Kauaʻi, civil war ensued and Kaumualiʻiʻs stepbrother, an *aliʻi* named Keawe fought against him and took the throne from the young teenager. Keawe favored Kamehameha and looked forward to the conquest of Kauai by him. However, in 1796 Keawe died, and Kauaʻi and Niʻihau at last fell to Kaumualiʻi.

At Keawe's death, 17-year-old Kaumualiʻi established a firm grip on Kauai and prepared for an attack by Kamehameha, who had by then overrun Maui, Molokai, and Lanaʻi and conquered Oʻahu.

In October of 1795 Kamehameha gathered his armies and a navy of canoes and western ships, some armed with cannon, to capture Kauaʻi and Niʻihau, thus completing his conquest of the Hawaiian Islands. He gathered the largest army and navy ever assembled in Hawaiʻi, which, according to western observers, included 1,200 to 1,500 canoes and an army of 10,000 soldiers, half of whom were armed with muskets.

Tradition says the armada sailed from Wai'anae in 1796, but strong winds arose and the lead canoes began to capsize. Chaos reigned in the dark night, canoes sank, men drowned, and the whole fleet was in danger. Recognizing defeat, Kamehameha ordered his canoes back.

The next year, 1804, Kamehameha once again prepared to attack Kaua'i. Ominous warnings from a Big Island prophet followed his decision: "Do not go on this expedition. Live here in Hawaii. There is food in the uplands, there is fish on the seacoast; heaven above, earth beneath," the prophet warned.

Kamehameha boldly replied: "I shall not remain as you advise. I shall go."

To this the prophet retorted: "A man-made canoe you have to sail away from Hawaii, but a god-made canoe it will be that brings you back again..."

Attempting to balance this message from his gods, Kamehameha composed a *ho'ohiki* or vow. "Let us go and drink the water of Wailua, bathe in the water of Nāmolokama, eat the mullet that swim in Kawaimakua at Hā'ena, wreathe ourselves with the moss of Polihale, then return to O'ahu and dwell there."

The conquering king felt confident that his reorganized army of 7,000 Hawaiian warriors and 50 Europeans, many armed with muskets, and eight cannons, forty swivel guns, six mortars mounted on double-hull canoes and 21 armed schooners would bring victory.

The forces gathered at Ka'a'awa, on O'ahu's windward coast, to stage the assault. Swiftly the words of the prophet came true as a devastating typhoid-like disease called *mai 'oku'u*, or the "squatting sickness," spread throughout the camp, disabling and killing scores of warriors. Kamehameha himself contracted the disease, but successfully fought it off. The invasion was stopped.

To make firm the island's future, and to embrace western ways, Kaumuali'i sent his son George to the United States for a western education with a Yankee sea captain. Payment for the education, and passage, was made with a shipload of valuable sandalwood culled from the highlands of Kaua'i. Though accounts of the young Kaua'i prince's life in the United States conflict, most agree that he ended up in Connecticut and worked on a farm and as a carpenter, served in the United States Navy, and returned to Kaua'i aboard the *Thaddeus*, the merchant sailing vessel that brought the first New England missionaries to Hawai'i.

George, who was known to the New Englanders as "Prince George," claimed to have fought and been gravely wounded at Tripoli in the War of 1812. However, some historians claim this story was a fabrication.

When George returned in 1820, he came not as a wise son well-educated in western ways, but as a dissolute man, uncertain of himself and his future role. Indirectly, George did bring lasting change by accompanying the first shipload of missionaries to Kaua'i.

Kaumuali'i was greatly pleased upon his son's return and shed many tears. The accounts of George's schooling in Cornwall, Connecticut, and the many kindnesses shown him by the missionaries and their home churches in New England touched his heart, and he gladly offered them assistance and land to establish a station near his home along the ocean at Waimea.

This openness to outsiders was sincere, for Kaumuali'i had already experienced the dark side of European foreign affairs five years earlier when he was forced to remove the conniving Dr. Schaeffer and a contingent of Russians who built forts at Waimea and Hanalei in an attempt to use subterfuge to overthrow Kaua'i and the entire Hawaiian chain.

Joining Kaumuali'i in welcoming the missionaries was his wife of that time, Deborah Kapule. A generation younger than her husband, Deborah Kapule would go on to become one of the most famous women in Kaua'i's history through her wisdom in advising the island's rulers, her brave stands for what she felt was the best direction for the island, and her great hospitality that foresaw the island's current role as a haven for visitors.

With Kaumuali'i, she kept homes at Waimea and Wailua and served as Queen. She graciously presented missionaries Samuel Whitney and Samuel Ruggles with gifts of shells, mats, *kapa* cloth, food and fine calabashes— all the best the Kaua'i royalty had to give.

Despite the many peaceful overtures of Kaumuali'i and his queen, political intrigue continued and after Kaumuali'i made good his promise to peacefully submit to Liholiho. Following Kamehameha's death in 1819, he was kidnapped in 1821 by the young king aboard *Cleopatra's Barge*, the royal yacht of Hawai'i.

Kaumuali'i accepted his fate, saying: "King Reho-Reho, hear—When your father was alive, I acknowledged him as my superior. Since his death, I have considered you as his rightful successor, and, according to his appointment, as king. Now I have a plenty of muskets and powder, and a plenty of men at command, these, with the vessels I have bought, the fort, the guns, and the island, all are yours. Do with them as you please. Send me where you please. Place what chief you please as governor."

Liholiho fulfilled Kaumuali'i's dreaded wish. He was forced to leave Deborah Kapule and to marry

Ka'ahumanu, one of Kamehameha's wives. Initially the Kaua'i king was also kept in virtual house arrest on O'ahu, while O'ahu *ali'i* began to divide up the lands of Kaua'i.

Kaumuali'i quickly grew accustomed to court life in Honolulu and became a fervent Christian and student of the missionaries. In 1822 Kaumuali'i and Ka'ahumanu—with an entourage of 1,000 *ali'i* and servants—toured the windward islands on a religious crusade of sorts during which Ka'ahumanu preached from the Bible and exhorted her people to follow the missionaries.

Missionary Levi Chamberlin described the royal party in his journal of March 31, 1824. "The stated weekly service…was well attended this afternoon. Kaa rode up in great style in a carriage brought out by Capt. Wildes. The coach was drawn by 10 or a dozen natives by means of a long rope fastened to the tongue of the carriage. She was posted on the drivers seat, Keariiahonui occupied the place of the footman behind and Taumuaiii thus royally attended occupied the interior alone. This is the first vehicle of the kind which has moved on the Sandwich Islands."

During this era the windward *ali'i* gained more control on Kaua'i as their ruler remained in exile and the spirit of the people became broken, resulting in a civil war that erupted in early 1824. The effects of the battle, which focused on the plains between Waimea and Wailua, reverberated throughout the whole kingdom and spelled the end of the royal kingdom of Kaua'i.

Prince George rebelled and violently, but futilely, fought against the O'ahu forces sent to control the island. The last blow perhaps was the death of Kaumuali'i in Honolulu in 1824, leaving his kingdom to Liholiho. His last wish was that the land divisions and *kuleana* of Kauaians should remain intact.

However, unrest continued on the island and on August 8, Prince George mounted a partially successful attack on the Russian Fort at Waimea. He would later die an early death, frustrated and disinherited.

The last words of Kaumuali'i completed the circle of his life, as he acknowledged the new religious power, or *mana,* of the Islands. His last words were to Jehovah, the God of the new western religion, and made to the English missionary William Ellis, who heard the whispered prayer shortly before the king's passing.

Kaumuali'i was buried in the graveyard of the Waiola Church in Lahaina, Maui next to Keopuolani, the "Sacred Wife" of Kamehameha, who had also become a Christian and a close friend of Kaumuali'i following his exile from Kauai. Great mourning occurred throughout the Hawaiian Kingdom following his death.

Today Kaumuali'i's name is still held in high esteem by the kama'āina of Kaua'i as their last monarch, and as the calm, guiding hand that led Kaua'i through a turbulent revolution that began in the days of old and ended with the beginnings of the modern Hawai'i we know today. During the 44 years of his life he had bridged an era, following the flow of the *mana* and his position in the kingdom, with his head high, never losing the regal manner that his heritage had bestowed on him.

X. THE RUSSIAN INCIDENT
THE RUSSIAN FORT AT WAIMEA & OTHER INTRIGUES

The Russian Fort overlooking the Waimea River mouth and a breast work adjacent to the Princeville Hotel are all that remain today of the Russian attempt to take over Kaua'i in the mid-1800's. The Russian agent, a Prussian doctor in reality, told Kaumuali'i, the king of Kaua'i, that he had the support of the Czar of Russia. In return, the Prussian told Russian diplomats that he had the support of Kaumuali'i.

The events surrounding this incident can be confusing. Missionary Sheldon Dibble's gathering of information about the Russian incident includes information gathered from Hawaiians who were alive during that era. In 1909 Honolulu publisher and historian Thomas Thrum elaborated a bit on Dibble's original writings. The following is the result—a short, comprehensive overview based on first-person sources of what happened during Kaua'i's Russian era.

Dibble sparked interest in Hawaiian history in 1838, when he was a history teacher at Lahaina Luna, the missionary school on a hillside above Lahaina on Maui. He interested Hawaiian students David Malo, Samuel Kamakau and others in collecting material about Hawai'i's past. A book of these findings was published by the school press in the Hawaiian language under the title of Ka Moolelo Hawaii. *The students' research was at the core of Dibble's later English-language histories of Hawai'i.*

IT HAS OFTEN been asserted that near the close of Kamehameha's reign the Russians made an attempt to get possession of the Island of Kauai and perhaps too of Oahu, and as reports to this effect have gained credit among many respectable visitors at the Sandwich Islands, it is proper that the facts relative to the subject, so far as they can be ascertained, should be clearly stated.

The Rev. Samuel Whitney landed on Kauai in 1820, when the facts were fresh in the minds of many, and has had good opportunity to collect information on the subject and most of the following particulars are given on his authority.

During the last war between the United States and Great Britain, the ship Attawelpa of Boston, was sold to the governor of the Russian colony at Sitka on the northwest coast of America. Previous to the discharge of the American captain and crew the ship was sent by the governor on a voyage to the Sandwich Islands, where she arrived about the close of the war. Having nearly completed her business at the islands and being about to return, she was unfortunately wrecked at Waimea on Kauai. Most of the cargo and property on board were saved and committed to the care of Kaumualii, the chief of the island, with the request that he would take care of it for the Russians. In the year 1815 the governor of the Russian colony sent an agent to secure the property. The name of the agent was Schoof, a German physician, familiarly called at the islands the Russian Doctor. He came to the islands a passenger on the American ship Isabella, Captain Tyler. He had considerable property committed to his care, consisting principally of powder and clothing, and was accompanied by two servant boys. As the Isabella was not bound to Kauai, he landed at Kailua on Hawaii, where, after a residence of some weeks, he obtained a passage to Kauai in the ship Millwood, Captain Eddes. Kamehameha, the king, sent a messenger with Doctor Schoof with orders to Kaumualii to deliver up the Russian property then in his hands. After landing his merchandise and building a house at Waimea, he commenced trading. Kaumualii soon purchased all his powder, and some other property, for which he was to pay in sandal wood. Not long after the doctor had landed, a Russian ship, the Discovery, arrived with about thirty Kodiack Indians, a part of whom were females. These Indians had been sent on by the governor at Sitka in pursuit of seals, of which he had heard there was an abundance on an island reported to have been discovered a little to the north-west of the Sandwich Islands. The captain of the ship had orders from the governor, in case the island could not be found, to leave the Kodiacks with his agent, Dr. Schoof, on Kauai, and proceed on his voyage; which he did, having failed in his search for the island.

A Russian brig, which was trading on the coast of Mexico, was under the necessity of running down to the islands to repair. The captain of the brig, an American, quarreling with the Doctor, was by him removed from command, but still retained in the Company's service. This brig and a Russian ship, the Myrtle, Captain Young, which had been sent by the Governor to be placed under the Doctor's direction, were at the islands at the same time. The number of the Russians, it is said, was near eighty or ninety men. The Myrtle anchored in Honolulu harbor and the Russians built a block house near the place of the present hotel, mounting a few guns and displaying a flag. The natives and some of the resident foreigners were suspicious of an attempt to take possession of the island and a messenger was despatched to give information to Kamehameha.

The king immediately sent Kalanimoku and other chiefs to Oahu with the following orders: "Go and observe the conduct of the Russians, but be slow to oppose them. If they commit outrage upon the people, exhort the people to bear it patiently. Receive ill treatment with great forbearance, but be ready not withstanding in case of absolute necessity to make a firm resistance." These orders are a specimen of the policy of Kamehameha. He was sensible of the power of foreigners and sought to avoid collision by all possible means.

The night after Kalanimoku's arrival at Honolulu, the Russians sailed for Kauai. The ship Myrtle and the brig were both anchored for a season at Hanalei on the north side of Kauai, where, by the Doctor's order, a slight breast work had been thrown up, and a few cannon mounted.

The Doctor now became anxious to return to Sitka, but either from the fact that he could not bring his business to a close, or from being flattered with the prospect of getting large possessions on Kauai (Kaumualii having given him the valley of Hanalei and two or three other valuable pieces of land), he concluded to stop and superintend the building of a fort at Waimea; the chief being desirous to secure his skill as an engineer in erecting that work. While the fort was being built, the Doctor proposed to Kaumualii to take a lease of the whole island for a certain number of years. He purchased an American schooner, the *Lydia*, and presented it to the chief together with considerable other property, and, as some say, obtained his signature to the lease which he had drawn up. The fort was not completed under the Doctor's direction, but so far finished that a number of guns were mounted on one side, the magazine built and a flagstaff erected on which the Russian colors were seen flying on public occasions. It is proper here to mention a circumstance, which is believed by the natives generally, and by some foreigners, but altogether, as it seems, on too a light grounds.

On a certain occasion he had invited Kaumualii to a feast at his house, together with most of the influential men of the island. The man who had commanded the Russian brig, and who it was well known was anxious to get rid of the Doctor and the Russian service, went to Kaumualii and advised him not to go to the feast, affirming that the Doctor had told him it was his intention to cut him off while there and take possession of the island. Unawed, however, by this information, Kaumualii, well guarded, went to the feast, partook of the entertainment and returned quietly to his home. Probably this circumstance and the fact that the Russian flag was flying in the fort afforded all the evidence that goes to prove an attempt on the part of the Russians to take possession of the island by force. But that this individual, with thirty north-west Indians, a part of whom were women, aided perhaps by the crew of a small vessel (only the brig being at Waimea at the time) should make an attempt to take the island is unworthy of credit. The story about cutting off the chief was doubtless a false report, got up for the sake of hastening the Doctor's departure.

The king, Kamehameha, and Kalanimoku, the chief of Oahu, having heard of the reports relative to the Doctor's proceedings on Kauai, took the alarm and sent a message to Kaumualii to drive off his visitor forthwith. Accordingly the doctor was sent for immediately and told he must get into his boat and be off to the brig, then in the offing, to which he made no objection and took his leave. The next day he sent a boat for his private property and for such articles belonging to the Company as he chose, and departed for Hanalei, whence, with the ship and brig, he took his departure from Kauai and came again to Honolulu.

During the absence of the ship Myrtle at Kauai the chiefs and people of Oahu through the advice and assistance of Mr. Young and other foreigners, took the precaution to erect a fort at Honolulu by which they might be able to command the harbor. On this second arrival of the Russians at Honolulu they were soon desired to depart, which they did without any resistance.

The Myrtle sailed, but being old and leaky, was obliged to re-enter the harbor and soon sunk. The Russians were kindly treated on shore till they had an opportunity to depart.

A short time after the Doctor had left, a Russian sloop of war, the Diana, arrived at Waimea. The captain made some inquiries, respecting the Doctor, his plans, treatment, etc., purchased a few supplies and proceeded on his voyage.

From the above particulars there does not appear sufficient ground for asserting that the Russian government or even the colony at Sitka had any intention to take possession of the islands, though such suspicions at the time were strongly entertained.

▓ ▓ ▓

XI. MISSIONARY ADVENTURES
THE ANTITHESIS OF MICHENER'S ABNER HALE

In this passage from The Missionary Herald—*a popular New England journal in which reports from the far-flung stations of the American Board of Commissioners for Foreign Missions were collected—then youthful missionary leader Hiram Bingham describes his adventures during a tour of Kaua'i in July 1821. The antithesis of Abner Hale, the main missionary character of James Michener's historical novel* Hawaii, *Bingham here enjoys the Hawaiian culture of Kaua'i. He rides aboard a double-hulled outrigger canoe around Nā Pali, hikes dangerous Hawaiian trails, receives a* lomilomi *massage from a Hawaiian woman, and even defends surfing as a worthy sport.*

Bingham's comments on the disastrous effects to the Hawaiian ohana, *or family, system wrought by forcing*

Hawaiian commoners out of taro *ponds and surfing spots to collect sandalwood for the* aliʻi *is ironic in that the missionaries are generally the scapegoats for ruining the Hawaiian culture.*

Bingham's adventure takes place mostly on the north side of the Waimea River, near the supposed location of Cook's landing. At the time Kauaʻi's last king, Kaumualiʻi, was encamped nearby. Missionary Bingham leaves Waimea to climb to the forest highlands of Kōkeʻe, and then apparently traverses a dangerous, and now lost, trail down to Wainiha, an isolated valley near Hāʻena on Kauaʻi's north shore. From there the party travels to Hanalei and sails back along the Nā Pali Coast to Waimea.

AFTER A QUICK passage of 20 hours, we came safely to anchor in Wimaah roads, and the king immediately sent a double canoe to take us ashore. Highly gratified to meet our good friends, the king, on the beach, a few rods from the place of landing, I saluted him with a hearty aloha, and with a kiss, as I took his friendly hand. He replied, "I very glad to see you."

THE MISSION HOUSE

The mission house is large, 54 feet by 24, and commodious, having a good floor, doors, glass windows, five bed-rooms, and two large rooms, which are not only convenient for the two families, but the answer for a school-room, dining hall, and place for public worship. It stands at the place of landing, near the water's edge, and but a few rods east of the mouth of the Wimaah river. On one side it is enclosed by the king's dwelling house, and by a heavy semi-circular wall 10 feet high; and on the other, by the ceaseless waves of the vast Pacific. In front is a small battery; and back of the wall, which encloses nearly an acre of ground, stands the fort, on the high bank of the river, covering the village. The mountains rising in the north, the ocean on the south, the moon beheld over the eastern part of the island, and the sun setting behind the western, or behind Oneehow, which lies in sight, or sinking, as it were, into the ocean, seen between the two islands, present a scenery truly grand; but now possessing a degree of familiarity to the brethren and sisters residing at Wimaah, which gives to that place something of the charm of home.

ARRIVAL OF KANEO

Soon after noon, Kaneo, with her attendants, landed just in front of the mission house, where the king and queen, with their attendants, met her, embraced, and joined noses, with loud crying, many tears, and other expressions of emotion. After some minutes, all sat down together on the sand for a considerable time, till the first bursts of feeling had subsided, when the king conducted his guests to the house, which he had prepared for their reception, by removing a quantity of imported goods lately purchased, and spreading his best mats, both in the house, and the court in front. Having ordered the slaughter of hogs, dogs, &c. for the purpose, he prepared a full repast for the company. At evening, he resigned his own dwelling house to his guests, and retiring to another, sent out a crier to prohibit the common people from entering the enclosure, where Kaneo and her ladies and servants were lodged, and set a guard also at the gate. The king's company, this is, his wife Tapoolee and particular friends, Kaneo and her attendants, spent much of the day in decorating themselves with a kind of temporary ornaments, which they call *laualla* beads; and in a favorite amusement of playing in the surf, or which a pretty good description is given in *Trumball's Voyages*. All engage in it, without distinction of rank, age, or sex; and the whole nation is distinguished by their fondness for the water, and the dexterity and facility with which they manage themselves in that element.

THE SURF BOARD AND THE MANNER IT IS USED

The surf-board, or the instrument used in playing in the surf, is of various dimensions, from three feet in length, and eight inches in breadth, to fourteen feet in length and twenty inches in breadth. It is made of light wood, thin at the edges and ends, but of considerable thickness in the middle, wrought exceedingly smooth, and ingeniously adapted to the purpose of gliding rapidly on water. The islander, placing himself horizontally on the board, and using his arms as oars, paddles out into the sea, meeting the successive surges, as they roll along towards the shore. If they are high, he dives under them, if they are low, or smooth, he glides over them with ease, till he is ready to return, or till he gains the smooth sea beyond where the surf breaks. Then choosing one of the highest surges, adjusting his board as it approaches him, directing his head towards the shore, he rides on the fore front of the surge, with great velocity, as his board darts along swifter than a weaver's shuttle, while the whitening surf foams and roars around his head, till it dies on the beach, and leaves him to return or retire at pleasure. Often several of them run at the same time, as in a race, and not unfrequently on a wager. The board moves as down an inclined plain, and the art lies principally in keeping it in its proper position, giving it occasionally an accelerating stroke with the hands, so that it shall not lose the propelling force of the wave, and thus fall behind it or retying it with the foot when liable to shot forward too fast. Sometimes the irregularity or violence of the water tears their board from under them and dashes it on the rocks; or threatening to carry them into danger, obliges them to abandon it, and save themselves by diving and swimming. I informed the king, as he sat on the beach witnessing the sport, of the desire of building a church, or a house for the public worship of the true God, at Waihoo. He expressed his approbation, and also his intention to send his brig to Taheite.

VARIOUS NOTICES

By the help of Samoo, a pupil of the Taheitan missionaries, who has been in America, and experienced personal kindness from our friend and patron, Dr. Worcester, and who now lives with me, I have commenced a comparison of the languages of the Sandwich Islands with that of Taheite, which I hope to be able...to pursue hereafter, as I am pleased to find many words in both, precisely alike and many others radically the same.

SABBATH

To-day I have been allowed to preach to a small congregation composed of this branch of the mission, a few other white people, and a few natives. The king, who was present, and who tarried a short time after service, said he understood a little of the discourse, some parts of which I endeavored to make still more plain to him, by more familiar, illustration. All our intercourse with him hitherto has been pleasant. We long to see him adopted in the Redeemer's family, to embrace him as a Christian brother, and to look at him with social gratitude and confidence as possessing the pious feelings of nursing father to the church, as well as friend and paternal regard to the missionaries. The king appears to be pleased with George Sandwich. He says he is like the other missionaries, and that he must remain here, and he will give home land, clothes, &c. He would rejoice to see his own son exhibit as much sobriety, and says, if George Tamoree were like George Sandwich, he would hold him fast, to give him a great deal of land, and a plenty of goods. Young Tamoree might be a very great comfort to his father. To-day his wife, daughter of Isaac Davis whom he took at Owhyhee before he had seen his father, brought to our house a little babe very sick, to seek for it some medical aid. Every instance of this kind makes us feel more deeply our need of a faithful and devoted missionary physician in this land of pollution, disease, and death.

ARRIVAL OF REHO-REHO

At about 3 o'clock, A. M. a small boat arrived, bringing from Woahoo his majesty Reho-reho, king of the windward islands, Boka, the governor of Woahoo, and Nike chief of Karakakooah, with about thirty men and two women. A most singular and hazardous adventure, and as mysterious as in its design, as it was hazardous in its nature, and singular in its manner. It appears, that, previous to the return of the Cleopatra's Barge to Hanaroorah, the king and his company left that village by Pearl river, a place 12 or 15 miles distant. But, coming down to the lee ward part of the island, and having a fair wind, he thought he could fetch Atooi; and, contrary to the wishes and expectations of his landing chiefs, refused to land at Pearl river. Strengthening his heart with such spirits as his beloved bottle afforded, he commanded his boatman to steer for Atooi. All were afraid, and all remonstrated; but in vain. They were without water, provisions, compass, chart, or mariner; embarked in a small open sail-boat, built by a native of the islands, crowded with passengers, stretching out to sea, under the brisk trades, with the presumption, that riding over the rude waves, they might possibly reach Atooi, one hundred miles distant. But the king, half intoxicated, fearless of danger himself, and regardless of the reasonable apprehensions of others, would hear to no advice or remonstrance; neither the perils of the ocean, nor the hostility of supposed enemies, could alter his purpose to proceed. He assumed the character of greater of his little home-built vessel; and, in his merry mood, considered his fingers spread out as representing the different points of the mariner's compass, which he attempted to express in broken English, and directed the doubtful course of his bark. When the boat was twice nearly capsized and ready to fill with water, the chiefs and company said, "We must go back;" but the king said decidedly, "No bail out the water and go on," and with something of that spirit, which dictated the proud, artful, and animating address of the dauntless Roman, "Fear not, for thou carriest Caesar," he added, "If you return with the boat, I will swim to Atooi in the sea." At his command they speedily bailed out the water with their calabashes, and continued their course, steering well to the northward (as the king had a pretty good idea of the bearing of Atooi) til just before dark, when they saw this island far under the lee bow, then veering to the westward and southward, with great hazard and much inconvenience from the successive breaking of the sea upon them, they reached this place, before the break of day; but in a condition as powerless and defenseless, as the poor missionary, who passes unmolested from island to island. No roaring cannon opposed or welcomed the king's approach.

His Reception by Tamoree

Tamoree, being early apprised of his arrival, rose, and with apparent composure dressed himself, and in a small canoe, with two or three attendants, went out quietly on board the king's boat, gave him his friendly *aloha,* and the customary salutation of joining noses (while the company expressed great joy at seeing Tamoree) then conducted him ashore, and appropriated to his use a large and convenient house, well fitted for his reception, spread with the beautiful Oneehow mats; and, at the young king's earnest request, lest his people at Woahoo should conclude that he was drowned in the sea, or killed at Atooi, dispatched two of his vessels, a brig and a schooner, to inform them that he had escaped the dangers of the ocean, and landed here in security, where he waited for two of his wives to join him, as he had left all five of them behind. Thus has the king effected what he long ago proposed, and what he has repeatedly declared to be his intention; but what the friends of both kings, and of the people, desired might not be accomplished. The result is still doubtful as the nature of the design. Such, however, is the pacific disposition of Tamoree, that, although Reho-reho has put himself completely in his power, we are persuaded he will not hurt a hair of his head, but will pay him due respect as a superior. What could we ask, on this occasion, better than that these two kings should agree together to give their kingdoms to Christ, the rightful proprietor.

ARRIVAL OF BOKA'S WIFE FROM WOAHOO

It was interesting to witness the safe arrival of governor Boka's wife from Woahoo, this morning, in a single canoe, with a small canvas sail, aided by four men with paddles. Tired and hungry, they put in yesterday at Hanapapa, a valley six or seven miles from this, where lies the farm given to Mr. Ruggles, and tarried there a night; having spent the night before in pursuing the wayward course of the king, upon a rough sea. It is not a very unfrequent case, that natives pass from one island to another in a single canoe, though they often have a fresh breeze and a heavy sea. The contrivance used to prevent the canoe from easily upsetting, consists of a large stick of light wood, about two thirds the length of the canoe, turned up at the ends, somewhat like a sleigh runner, lying on the surface of the water, parallel with the canoe, at the distance of 9 or 10 feet, and connected with it by two smaller sticks, lashed at one end firmly to the top of the canoe, and at the other, bending down to meet the buoyant stick, that runs upon the water. Still such canoes must be considered very unsafe at sea, for any but the natives. If a sea breaks over them with much violence, they must fill with water, which not unfrequently happens when there is much wind or surf. In such a case, all on board have recourse to their dexterity at swimming; and while some of the number sustain and preserve the articles liable to be lost, others, placing their weight on the very hindermost part of the canoe, elevate the fore end, so that a considerable part of the water flows out; then, casting themselves suddenly off, the canoe becomes more buoyant and manageable, and one of them springing into it bails out the remaining water with a calabash, while the rest resume their places with their little effects, and joyfully pursue their course again, ready, as soon as rested, to encounter another overwhelming sea. Reho-reho expressed a high degree of sudden, strong, agreeable emotion...(for) Boka's wife had followed him...in a canoe.

An Old Treaty Renewed

Tamoree proposes, in a very formal manner, to surrender himself, his island, and all that he has to Reho-reho; and, with some agitation, addressed him to this effect, "King Reho-reho, hear, when your father was alive,

I acknowledge him as my superior. Since his death, I have considered you as his rightful successor, and according to his appointment, as king. Now I have a plenty of muskets and powder, and plenty of men at command, these, with the vessels I have bought, the fort, and guns, and the island, all are yours. Do with them as you please. Send me where you please. Place what chief you please as governor here." Nike, the Karakakooah chief, addressed the council in few words, and referring to the treaty made between the two kings, confirmed the fact, that Tamoree had held this island under Tamahamaha. A solemn silence pervaded the house for some time, while all waited, with deep solicitude, to hear the reply of the young king, on which as much appeared to be suspended. Then, with a mild and manly aspect, he addressed Tamoree as follows, "I did not come to take away your island. I do not come to take away your island. I do not wish to place any one over it. Keep your island and take care of it just as you have done, and do what you please with your vessels." To this succeeded a shout of cheerful and hearty approbation from all parties, and Tamoree retired from the council, with a peaceful smile. Thus, without noise or bloodshed, the treaty, made with the late king, is recognized and ratified with his son and successor—a treaty which allowed Tamoree the peaceful possession of the lee ward islands, as tributary king.

JOURNEY ACROSS THE ISLAND

Mr. Whitney and myself set out to go across the island. Our reason for undertaking this tour at this time, was principally, to explore the country, to see the inhabitants at their dwellings and employments, to meet the two kings on the opposite side of the island; to seek their proper attention to them; to express to them our wishes that our proposed expedition to the Society Isles might not be too long delayed; to obtain, if possible, Reho-reho's express approbation of our desire to teach the people at large to observe the Christian Sabbath, and other duties of the Gospel. We hoped to cross the island in a day, and took a few cakes, two bottles of water, and a little wine for our refreshment during the day. Attended by my Taheitan youth, the faithful Samoo, a native domestic of brother Whitney's, as our guide, and Mr. Chamberlain, we set out pretty early in the morning, traveling on foot, and crossed Wimaah creek, and ascended on the west side of it, by a circuitous path, to the high and mountainous parts, which extend through the whole island. We found no inhabitants residing in the upland country, but met several natives, some bringing down sandalwood upon their shoulders, others firewood. The former is brought in this manner, the distance of from 10 to 20 miles. I attempted to raise up one man's burden from his shoulder, which I should say was not far from what is called a picul, equal to $133\frac{1}{3}$ lbs. weight. The king requires each man, woman and child on the island, to furnish a picul of sandalwood, whenever he has occasion for it in the purchase of vessels, or cargoes.

ASPECT OF THE COUNTRY

The land, as it rises several miles from the sea shore towards the forests, is not well watered, except in the narrow valleys, where the streams descend from the mountains, and where the principal productions are found; nor does it produce trees or shrubbery; and though generally covered with grass it appears like a barren waste. On the east side of Wimaah creek, several thousand acres have, this summer, been overrun with fire, divesting it of the little verdure, which had appeared in the old grass.

The face of the country exhibits marks of former earthquakes and volcanic eruptions. A variety of forest trees, besides the sandal-wood, are seen, all different from any that I have ever known in America. Some appear to be suitable for building timber, and some would make very pretty cabinet furniture.

ADVENTURES ON THE WAY

About one o'clock, P.M. it began to thunder, and we were soon enveloped in a cloud, that hung upon the mountains. At two, a heavy shower or rain commenced. We took shelter in a temporary booth, built by the sandal-wood cutters, where we experienced, and had occasion to record, the preserving care of Omnipotence, who made his lightnings play, and thunders roll, harmless around our heads. At three, as the shower appeared to be principally over, and we were anxious to reach the opposite side, if possible, before dark, we passed on; but, to our disappointment, the clouds gathered more thickly over our heads, and the rain came down copiously upon us, and poured in torrents from the points of our half sheltering umbrellas, as we trudged along in a narrow, winding, slippery foot path, on sharp ridges, ascending and descending rugged steeps, till we came to two little temporary sheds of the woodcutters, unoccupied, and cheerless as the wastes of desolation, situated in the midst of this inhospitable wilderness, surrounded with dreary mountains and deep solitudes, on the bank of a swift mountain torrent, swelled by the rain. Into these we crept to seek a partial shelter. The principal one, about 30 feet in length, and 8 in breadth, consisted chiefly of a few poles, resting partly on the ground, and supported in front by little crotches, four feet high, thatched with leaves on the top, but entirely open in front. Solitary, damp, and cheerless, as the temporary sheds appeared, we thought it expedient to make them our lodgings for the night, as we could not proceed, with safety, to the nearest settlements on the other side, without day light; and the day was now too far spent to attempt it. Our attendants struck up a fire, and collected fuel to feed it. We dried part of our clothes. The rain abated. The thunder ceased. The stars appeared. By the light of our fire, we read a portion of Scripture, and united in offering our evening sacrifice to him, who had hitherto preserved us; and having spread down upon the damp leaves a large cloak, which served as a bed for three of us, we laid ourselves down to our slumbers, under the care of the Watchman of Israel. We had no fear of beasts of prey, or poisonous reptiles; of highway robbers, or hostile bands of savages; nor did the unusual degree of cold in the atmosphere, the uncomfortable dampness of the ground where we lay, nor the plague of the flies, which every where infests the land, produce a sigh for the comfortable dwellings, the downy beds, and the full spread tables, of our native country.

Passage Over a High Table-land

The rising day dawned upon us in peace, and invited us to proceed. Our path was still wet, and rugged, and slippery, leading up and down successive steeps, and through many, many places, especially as we passed over a tract of high table land; while the singing of birds cheered the rude forests around us, which never feel the frosts of autumn, nor the chilling blasts of winter. About 9 o'clock a.m. we came suddenly to the verge of Mounahena, a high and steep mountain, which overlooks the northern part of the island, where the clouds were literally spread under our feet, completely bounding the view below us, though we had the clear and bright sun shine where we stood;

but, breaking away occasionally before we began to descend this giddy height, showed us the white surf of the Pacific, rolling upon the shore, at the distance of six or seven miles; while the majestic mountains on the right and left, added peculiar grandeur to the novel scene, and spoke the greatness of him, who weighs the mountains in scales, and the hills in a balance, who taketh up the isles as a very little thing, and holds the waters of the ocean in the hollow of his hand. Down this awful steep on which we stood, several thousand feet in its perpendicular descent, with the toil of three long hours, we descended on a very sharp ridge, running from the top to the base of the mountain, and so nearly perpendicular, that, in many places, we were obliged to go backwards, clinging to roots of trees, and shrubs, and crags of rocks, our guide going before, and showing us where to place our feet, and where to hold with our hands. Our path was, for the most part, shaded and cool, and, much of the day, our progress was neither tardy nor unpleasant; but, in some places, attended with danger, particularly to Mr. Whitney and Mr. Chamberlain, as they were more liable than myself to distressing giddiness from our situation. The vapors condensing upon the rocks and cool earth, trickle down, and form numerous little streams and cascades in different parts of this mountain, and of Soomahae on the right, and Makana on the left, which, being augmented by frequent showers, descend and unite in forming the river Wineha, and thus, with short and rapid course, roll to the ocean.

THEY ARRIVE AT THE DWELLINGS OF THE NATIVES

Descending a little way from the verge of the mountain, the border of the tableland, we came below the cloud, which usually hangs a little below the top of the Monnahune, and enjoyed a more clear and full view of the country, the rivers, villages, plantation and settlements of the heathen inhabitants, in this part of Atooi, where the joyful sound of salvation now echoed. Finding ourselves, at length, safely arrived at the foot of the mountain, but almost exhausted, we gladly cast down our weary limbs on our mat, in the first house to which we came. There friendly natives, apparently glad to see us, kindly rubbed and pressed with their hands, the muscles of our legs, quite sore and lame, in order to relieve them, or to prevent them from becoming worse. This operation, which they call *lomelome,* they almost always perform in cases of extreme wariness. This family was the first we had met with, after leaving the settlement of Wimaah, where we started. After resting here a little, we ate the remaining morsels of our cakes, read a portion of Scripture, and, with the consent of the family, lifted up our prayers and thanksgivings to God, who had preserved us amidst "the perils of the wilderness," and who, we believe, has abundant blessings in store for the needy heathen around us. Following down the river Wineha, we were obliged to cross it five times, without a bridge or a boat, sometimes leaping from one large stone to another, which rose above the surface of the water, and sometimes wading. The inhabitants along the banks, in a friendly manner, saluted us with aloha, adding the compliment, *ma-ma,* (nimble,) with reference, doubtless, to what we had achieved, rather than to our apparent activity. Near the head or formation of this river, as in many other mountainous parts of these island, are found bananas of spontaneous growth, and a sort of wild apple, and a plant somewhat resembling hemp, especially in...bark, which the natives manufacture into excellent twine, fish lines, nets, &c. The bananas grow along up the sides of the mountain, and, though very luxuriant, appear to be far less fruitful, than when cultivated in the valleys. The trees, called in the language *Ohea* but by foreigners, for convenience, apple, were generally in full blossom; but here and there a tree exhibited fruit in different stages of maturity.

COME TO THE ENCAMPMENT OF THE KINGS

Dragging our weary steps along till just before night, we came to the place, on the sea shore, about half a mile west of the mouth of the river, where the two kings and their suit were encamped. Tamoree was sitting with his family in his wagon, placed on the ground, and defended from the fresh trade winds, by a large mat suspended by poles. Reho-reho, in one of the houses of the little cluster, was slumbering, in the paroxysms of drunkenness. Tamoree very kindly ordered a good supper of tea, sea-bread, baked pig, and taro, as he set before us, which we set down on green grass to receive, giving thanks to God, for this seasonable refreshment; while a multitude of the inoffensive natives was attentively observing us. Tamoree told us he had no house for us, or for himself to sleep in, as the houses at that place were all occupied by Reho-reho and his company; but that a temporary boot, (composed of slender poles, ingeniously covered with green leaves) was a building for himself and family, where he politely offered us a lodging place with him. Spreading down their mats on the green grass, they made us a comfortable bed, then five sheets of tapa for bed clothes, were presented each of us, according to the custom of the country when visitors tarry through the night.

VISIT TO HENERAE

As we wished to improve the present opportunity to explore the district of Henerae, a place of primary importance in this part of the island, and five or six miles distant, Tamoree sent a canoe to carry us, and a messenger on foot to see that a dinner should, be provided for us there. Henerae has a small fort, built of clay [probably the Russian Fort at Puu Poa at Princeville, *ed.*] on a verdant hill, eligibly situated, but of little value; a considerable harbor, which is said to be tolerably safe for vessels most of the year; a pleasant river, 70 or 80 yards wide, but which, like most of the rivers, has a bar at its mouth; several thousand acres of valuable land, little cultivated, though watered with frequent showers, and apparently fertile; together with a small population who might, with Christianity, be happy.

They Return to the Two Kings

Taking our leave, we embarked in a double canoe, with the aid of a sail run briskly before the wind, and, in less than an hour, landed at the place where we left the kings in the morning. Reho-reho encamped for the night in a grove of laualla. The leaves of the trees being from four to six feet in length, and very thickly set, form a very dense and cool shade by day, and a pretty good canopy by night, in this climate. Some parts of this grove bear a resemblance to an orchard of apple trees in a meadow ground. In the evening, large torches made of *tootooe* (oil-nut) illumined the king's camp, and presented a novel and truly romantic scene The inhabitants treated us hospitably. Coming thirsty to the foot of fort hill, I asked the natives, whose huts line the shore, for a *neoo* (cocoanut). One of them ran to a tree and brought me a large one, containing nearly a quart of milk. He tore off the thick, fibrous husk with his teeth, and cracked the shell for me, and I walked along, up and down the hill, draining the milk, and eating the meat of my cocoa-nut, and sharing it with my companions. We then sailed up the river a mile or two, gathered from a large tree a few oranges, con versed a few minutes with some of the natives, on our great object, and walked back to the river's mouth.

▨　▨　▨

XII. WAR ON KAUA'I IN 1824
THE TRAGIC FALL OF GEORGE KAUMUALI'I

The sweeping changes brought about in Hawai'i between 1815 and 1824 altered the course of Kaua'i's history. Kaumuali'i, Kaua'i's last king, died in 1822 as an exile on Maui. His son George—who, though not a mission follower, returned to Hawai'i in 1820 aboard the brig Thaddeus *with the first missionary party from New England—failed to regain his father's kingdom and died a tragic death at an early age, also in exile.*

Known in the early 1800's as the leeward islands, Kauai and Ni'ihau were still somewhat removed from the windward islands of O'ahu and those beyond. However, the war of 1824, when George Kaumuali'i attempted to regain his birthright to the island, perhaps forever brought the island chain under one central rule, both on paper and by threat of force.

The battles in this bloody passage in Kaua'i's history took place on the upland plains near Hanapēp'e, close to Wahiawa, a town now lost to time since the demise of the sugar plantation village that once stood there.

This selection is from missionary leader Hiram Bingham's A Residence of Twenty-One Years in the Sandwich Islands, *a well-written account of the upstate New Yorker's life as a missionary in Hawai'i, written after his return to New York after over two decades in Hawai'i.*

Bingham was thrust into critical events in Hawai'i's history during his tenure as the mission leader in Hawai'i. He seemed to have had a special interest in Kaua'i, having toured the island extensively during his first years in Hawai'i.

BEFORE THE DAWN of the next morning, August 8th, 1824, the confused noise of the battle of the warrior was heard pealing through the valley, from the fort. The malcontents, surprising the little garrison, had commenced the work of blood.

Roused by the noise of battle so near, and hearing the balls whistle over us, what was our surprise and anguish to hear that George and his coadjutors were attempting to take the fort! We trembled for our friend, Kalanimoku, and his party, and for George, too. For ourselves and little ones, we looked to the Lord as our defence, while hostile insurgents were passing and repassing our door; and we were not forsaken.

Some of the insurgents entering the fort, and hoping for a rush of the neighboring inhabitants to ensure the victory over the garrison, one of them stood on the walls and called aloud to the two divisions of the valley on either side of the river, "Ho Waimea!—Ho Makawele!—come on—the Hawaiians are beaten—the Kauaians have the fort!" Some of both parties rushed to enter, amid balls and bayonets. Kahalaia and Niau, a royal chief, being on the opposite side of the river, started to cross the river to defend ·the fort. The former was dissuaded by the latter on account of the personal danger. But rushing into that danger himself, and meeting with Kiaimakani, he demanded if he were a friend, and was instantly shot down by an insurgent, who was then cut down by an attendant of the fallen chief. Kiaimakani fled.

The noise of the battle continued about thirty minutes. Meantime, Kalanimoku sent for Mr. Whitney and myself to come to him, then on the sand beach, a little distance west of the fort. As we left our habitations, Mrs. B. and Mrs. W. watched the steps of their husbands till they passed near the fort, when the firing, which had ceased, was renewed. That was to them a moment of deep solicitude. Their flesh and hearts trembled, as they looked one on the other, and on their sweet babes, and dared not ask, "Where are our protectors ?" Then they thought of the care of the Watchman of Israel, and found support.

Crossing the river, we came to the chief, and asked, "What is all this? He replied, "This is *war.*" In a few minutes, his trusty aid, Kalakoili, a very stout, athletic native, came from the scene of battle, and with unusual energy of manner, reported to the chief that the insurgents had fled towards Hanapepe. We asked Kalanimoku for a guard for our house and family. He replied, "I have but few men, and the Kauaians I cannot trust." Willing to do what he could, he issued a tabu, forbidding any to approach our house unbidden. At his request, we united in prayer. Mr. W. and myself then repaired to the fort, to dress the wounds of the bleeding, and to bury the slain. As I ascended the walls amid these new scenes, how was I shocked and my soul filled with grief as I lifted a mat from a fallen victim, and saw young Trowbridge whom, the evening before I had attempted to rescue from the toils of infidelity, now lying, dead on the rampart. Covered with wounds, he lay in his blood. He seemed to have fallen in close combat, hand to hand, and the death stroke appeared like that of a hatchet. Another Englishman, named Smith, we found mortally wounded in the fort, as if white men had been special marks for the assailants, as needing first to be disposed of.

In a few hours, Kalanimoku, Kekauluohi, and her husband, Kanaina, Kapule and others, marched into the fort, armed. We were struck with the martial appearance of the females, Kekauluohi, Premier, carrying a heavy pistol, and the ex-queen, Kapule, walking with a drawn sword in her hand. Kalanimoku, on account of his strait, despatched a small schooner for Oahu, offered our families a passage, and advised us to go. They knew not the strength and numbers of the insurgents. They knew not whom to admit into the castle and whom to keep out, and the force was obviously small. Even the captain of the garrison was suspected of disloyalty or great mismanagement in allowing the insurgents to scale the walls. The approaching darkness of night might be the signal for a renewed attack. They dared not send-out to pursue the insurgents or to meet them in the field, and unless they could get help from the windward soon, Kapule and others considered their situation exceedingly perilous, and manifested unexpected concern as to the effect of our departure. Trowbridge, and the mortally wounded young native, who expired while we were there, were buried within the walls with funeral solemnity. We encouraged our friends to trust in the Lord, to seek His providence, and obey his will, believing that he would not forsake those that forsake not him.

The mind of Kalanimoku seemed to be looking intently to see what Jehovah, the Christians' God, would do with him. He does not appear to have taken any part in the contest, till he had called the missionaries to lead him in prayer, after which he left his sand bank, where he had slept, crossed the river, and took on himself the charge of the fort, and the business of restoring order.

Here the value of a trustworthy chieftain could be appreciated, and here I saw, for once, the reason which had not before been so fully obvious, why the women of rank bore arms in war, in such a country, where neither the intelligence, nor the virtue, nor the established customs of the nation would shield them from violence, if unarmed and separate from their husbands or warrior friends.

Towards night, we entered a double canoe, in the river, with our wives and little ones. Hurrying towards the schooner in the roadstead, we were well nigh swamped in the surf, through which we had to pass. Our children shrieked aloud as the waves dashed over us, threatening to engulf us like the raging of the rebellious multitude. Our small stores were damaged, our water for the voyage injured; and for a moment we felt ourselves to be in the "perils of the sea," as well as in "perils among the heathen." We, however, reached the vessel drenched with salt water, and set sail, but our solicitude for our friends behind us, and our apprehension of an attack from the insurgents before, was scarcely diminished. For as we passed Hanapepe and Wahiawa, we had reason to suppose that if the insurgents still meant to conquer, they would deem it of material consequence to them to capture this vessel, and thus prevent Kalanimoku's appeal to the windward islands for aid. Had this been done, it is not difficult to conceive how perilous would have been the situation of our families, and that of Kalanimoku and his party.

A captive, Kamakakini, was regarded as an instigator of the revolt, was put on board this schooner, and placed on the hold, and closely bound with ropes to a stanchion, to be conveyed, as we supposed, to Oahu. On the following morning, we went to the hatchway to see and converse with him, but his place was vacated. In the silence of the night, he had been called on deck by the captain, stabbed, and thrown into the sea.

No necessity appeared for this heathen execution. It was said the captain had orders not to land the prisoner. But this was different from Kalanimoku's subsequent treatment of known and acknowledged leaders of the insurrection.

We had an unusually speedy passage, as if the Lord had heard us at once, and we quickly found ourselves "at the land," in Honolulu. If a strife, commenced without a preamble, manifesto, or any declaration stating the cause, and the object proposed, can properly be called a war, the news of the war was quickly proclaimed, not only through Oahu, but through the group.

Great sympathy for Kalanimoku and his friends was manifested when his perilous situation was made known. The startling expression, often repeated, "*Mai make Kalanimoku ia Humehume ma*–Well nigh slain is Kalanimoku by George and his party," not only called forth the sympathy of relatives, friends, missionaries, and foreign residents, but roused the spirit of war in many a Hawaiian breast, and that of revenge, it was feared, in some, and avarice in others. Thousands were ready to rush to the field of contest. Of these, every one seemed politician enough to decide what must be done in this emergency. "*He kaua, he kaua*–War, war" rung through the village and valley of Honolulu; and in a few hours a thousand men were ready to join and defend their chieftain, and bring the Kauaians under the same government with the windward islands. Governor Boki was then in England,

and his place was well supplied by Namahana. This reinforcement embarked the next day, and quickly reached Waimea, to the relief of Kalanimoku, while the insurgents were rallying at Wahiawa, the estate of George.

Through a merciful arrangement of providence, the insurgents did not renew the attack on the fort or on Kalanimoku, but while rallying, allowed him time to obtain a reinforcement which would make such an attack useless, or destructive to their cause. Nor is it less wonderful that, after that reinforcement arrived, the leaders of the insurrection did not then hasten to propose peace on some terms rather than risk another battle. The citadel being in full possession of an experienced general, who had the resources of the nation at command, and an armed force now with him greater, probably, than ever the insurgents brought together, it was madness for the rebel chiefs to strike again for victory, or to insist on independence. But, perhaps through ignorance of the art of war, they had failed to know the strength of Kalanimoku when thus I reinforced, or, through desperation, some of them preferred rather to die in battle than to submit to the government of Liholiho; and perhaps the feelings of revenge towards those chiefs of Kauai who stood by Kalanimoku impelled them to hold out for another trial of strength and military skill.

During the pause or the mustering of the forces of the two parties, Kalanimoku received from the infatuated George the following singular specimen of diplomacy, embracing a partial profession of respect to the windward government, and a strong desire to punish the chiefs of his own island who had not favored him and his party according to his wishes.

"Dear Sir,—We wish not to hurt any of the people from the windward islands, but those chiefs belonging to Kauai. Therefore I hope you will separate your men from them, and let the Atooi chiefs fight the battle, for we wish not to hurt any of you from the windward. Our lives have been threatened by Tapule, by Haupu, by Kumakeha, and by Wahine. These are the chiefs we want to go against. But your people we wish not to trouble. Send me answer as soon as you can.

Yours, &c., G. P. T."

Kaahumanu being detained at Maui, after her husband's interment, Kalanimoku's express schooner hastened thither from Honolulu, to report to her. It approached Lahaina with a signal of distress, and as the captain sprung on shore, he cried out, *"Ua kaua o Kauai*! *I kii kanaka mai au*—Kauai wages war! I have come for men;" then gave the particulars to the queen. She thought the trouble had arisen because her late husband [Kaumualii, ed.] had not taken proper measures to secure the quiet submission of his son and other chiefs and people. She was ready to prosecute the war, and subdue the insurgents, and required a reinforcement of soldiers to embark at once from Maui to succor Kalanimoku, but hesitated to send any high chief. But Kaikioewa, an old chief of high rank, in a spirited address of some eloquence, said,

"I am old, like Kalanimoku. We played together when children. We have fought together beside our king, Kamehameha. Our heads are now alike growing grey. Kalanimoku never deserted me; and shall I desert him now, when the rebels of Kauai rise against him? I will not deal thus with him. If one of us is ill the others can hasten from Kauai to Hawaii to see the sick. And now, when our brother and leader is in peril, shall no chief go to succor him. I will go; and here are my men also."

Asking Mr. Richards what they should do with the rebels, he was referred to the divine rule, "love your enemies." He rejoined, "We do not go to kill Kauaians; we go to put an end to fighting. We will take the rebels and bring them to the windward, and put them to farming." Hoapili was also inquisitive as to the accordance of war with Christianity. They both asked questions difficult for a Christian missionary to answer, and some which different missionaries would, if obliged to speak at all on the subject, be likely to answer differently, respecting the lawfulness of war, and the manner of conducting it if compelled to engage in it; but questions which showed that their consciences were awake to consider what was Christian duty in this case of insurrection. Hoopili, Kaikioewa, Kahekili (thunder), a stern warrior chief, and two companies of men, embarked immediately on board two schooners, and hastened to the scene of strife.

Soon after the sailing of this reinforcement, Kaahumanu spontaneously, like the king of Nineveh, proclaimed a fast, in order to seek God's favor. This was observed by many, with apparent propriety, on the 27th August. At Lahaina, an uninterrupted Sabbath stillness prevailed from morning till evening. Amusements and labor, and the kindling of fires for cooking, seemed to be entirely suspended; and the chiefs and a concourse of the people attended public worship, and united in presenting their confessions and supplications before the throne of mercy.

Arriving at Kauai, Hoapili united his force to that of Kahalaia, embracing the loyal warriors of Kauai, and the reinforcements from Oahu, who had joined Kalanimoku, at Waimea, and chose to lead them to battle.

On the 18th of August, a force under Hoapili marched from Waimea towards Hanapepe and Wahiawa, where the enemy held a position overlooking the valley of Hanapepe, nearly two miles from the sea-shore. Like other astrologers, Gov. Hoapili claimed some superiority over his countrymen, and doubtless supposed he could produce some impression on their minds by appearing to consult the heavenly bodies, in respect to the course to be pursued, the time and the result of the contest. He gazed much at the stars. He noticed the relative position of our principal planets, then visible, and fixed stars in the zodiac; probably more for the purpose of inspiring confidence and courage in the soldiers, as a means of victory, than for any information supposed to be derivable from the stars, as to the result of the battle, or the fitness of the time for commencing it.

Heathen leaders doubtless know that the belief that success is practicable, whether that belief be encouraged by interest, experience, martial skill, astrology, or prophecy, is a powerful means of union, strength, and success in war. When Hoapili, after his repeated observations, predicted that if the loyal party should be beaten by the insurgents, the whole group of islands would be overcome by them, and there would be no place to flee to for safety, not even their own homes, he put a spur to their courage and constancy, and assumed a position not likely to be proved false.

Though the distance from the fort at Waimea to the encampment of the Kauaians was scarcely more than eight miles, the army, on the way, halted and rested on the Sabbath. The next day they proceeded, crossed the river, and ascended the heights on the east side of the valley of Hanapepe, and were drawn up in the order of battle. Silence was commanded before the onset, and prayer was offered to the Great Jehovah. Then, in a curved line or semicircle, they advanced, the right and left extremes intending to pass the enemy's lines, and capture the whole force. As they drew near, the insurgents, who had taken a station behind a wall with a small field piece, discharged it a few times with some apparent effect; for Hoapili's men, who were in its range, prostrated themselves before it at each discharge, then rose again and advanced. Some supposed at the moment that this engine of foreign war was doing the work effectually, though it was neither weakening the strength nor daunting the courage of the government troops who returned the fire and pressed on. The insurgents, unable to stand, were beaten and routed; some forty or fifty were killed, the rest fled chiefly to the woods and taken. Kiaimakani, their boldest leader, attempt to conceal himself by holding up grass between himself and the passing pursuers, one of whom perceiving a motion of the grass; fired a musket ball into it "at a venture," by which the unhappy old warrior chief was killed, and his violent dealing returned upon himself.

George and Betty, and their infant daughter, fled on horseback to the mountains. The two latter were soon captured and treated with kindness. The child was, however, by Kaahumanu named Wahine-kipi, Rebel-woman. George eluded his pursuers for a considerable period. A party of men were sent by Kalanimoku to find and take him, and being led by Kalaiheana, a head man from Oahu, went into the mountains in pursuit of him. They occasionally called aloud, "O Humehume, show yourself to us. You shall not be slain, if you will make your appearance. Come, let us return to the sea-side to your father, Kalanimoku." After some weeks spent in the search, he was found and captured, and brought in a pitiable state into the presence of the dignified Kalanimoku, who, at his father's request, had been disposed to befriend him, and had commiserated him from the beginning of the contest. This noble, victorious, semi-civilized chieftain took off his own mantle and threw it over the poor, misguided young chief, thus saying, most significantly, "*Live.*" He was restored to his wife and child, and for the safety of Kauai, sent to Oahu, where he remained several years, until his death.

George, in his childhood, had been sent by his father to America, partly from apprehensions of danger to the child from jealous or aspiring relatives. He was supplied with the means of support; but Capt. R., who took the charge of him, lost both his own property and that of his ward. George labored as a carpenter's apprentice for several years, then for a time in the service of a farmer; but feeling homeless, or restless, or disposed for the scenes of war, he enlisted in the U. S. navy. He was in the engagement between the Enterprise and Boxer, and, in the act of boarding, was wounded in the side by a British pike. He afterwards went up the Mediterranean as one of the crew of the Guerriere, under Com. Decatur, and was in an engagement with an Algerine frigate. Then returning to Charlestown, he was, at the solicitation of Christian friends, released and sent to school for a season. On the sending forth of a mission to these islands, he accompanied it, not as a missionary, or as under the control of the Board, who had paid for his academical instruction and his passage home. Of course, neither the Board nor the mission was implicated in his political or seditious proceedings. He took a course contrary to their wishes and counsels, and the tendency of their instructions, though, as a son of a king, he thought he had rights to maintain by force. But how clear it is that education and civilization, without a firm belief in God's Word, will accomplish little or nothing for the heathen.

After the decisive battle, one of our promising pupils, Laanui, a chief from Oahu, who had taken part in the war, wrote back to Namahana the following brief report, which showed some advancement from the late barbarism of the country, of which Kahalaia and some others were not yet wholly cured:

"I have no captives. I regard implicitly the Word of God–of Him by whom we live, who warded off the balls from us, who is our Lord and yours; and on whose account we are without captives. In the midst of the battle, when the enemy fled, then I ceased. I went not to search for captives. I remained with your brother, Hoapili. When your brother returned to Waimea, we returned. And when we reached Waimea, there we abode, at the mouth of the river. Therefore, I have no captives at all to send up to you."

XIII. CLEOPATRA'S BARGE
Hawaii's Royal Yacht wrecks at Hanalei

I interviewed researchers from the Smithsonian Institution who conducted the first major underwater archaeological search in Hawaiian waters during the summer of 1995 in hopes of uncovering the wreck of Cleopatra's Barge. *They found copper sheeting, pieces of leather and other items that confirmed the location of the long sought-after wreck and presented their findings at an informative slide show at the Princeville Hotel.*

The 83-foot-long yacht is perhaps the most famous in America's maritime history and was wrecked in Hanalei Bay in 1824. Built by the wealthy New England shipping merchant family the Crowninshields, Cleopatra's Barge *was the first deep-water cruising yacht built in the U.S. and the first royal yacht of the modern era, after its purchase in 1820 by Liholiho—Kamehameha II. It caused a sensation in its day and was toured by thousands of curious early 19th-century coastal residents of America who wanted to see a ship used for pleasure rather than for trade or war.*

Renamed Haaheo o Hawaii, or "Pride of Hawaii," by Liholiho, the yacht was used to move the royal family from Lahaina to Honolulu, when the O'ahu city became the new capital of the Hawaiian kingdom. In Kaua'i's history, the sleek yacht is part of a dark passage, as it was used to transport Kaumuali'i, Kaua'i's last king, to exile on O'ahu and Maui in 1821. The yacht met its end in Kaua'i's Hanalei Bay, when it went aground on a reef near the Wai'oli Stream's mouth in April 1824.

The overview of Cleopatra's Barge by W. D. Alexander, missionary descendant and avid historian of Hawai'i during the early twentieth century, and missionary leader Hiram Bingham's first-hand account of an attempted salvage offer a concise look at the past and end of this most colorful vessel. Alexander was a frequent contributor to the Hawaiian Historical Society's Papers and played a leading role in the historical world of his day.

THE FAMOUS YACHT, Cleopatra's Barge, which was destined to play an interesting part in Hawaiian history, was built for Captain George Crowninshield of Salem, Mass., the first American yachtsman. Like his father and grandfather before him, he had made his fortune as a shipmaster and merchant in the China and East India trade. The family had also fitted out three privateers during the war of 1812, one of which, the "America," was very successful. A brother of his, Benjamin Crowninshield, was Secretary of the Navy under President Madison. In 1815, having retired from active business, he determined to build a yacht that should be the finest example of ship-building afloat, and to make a pleasure trip in her to the Old World. To carry out this purpose, he employed Retire Becket, a famous shipwright of Salem, who had turned out many vessels noted in their time for speed. The work was commenced in the spring of 1816, and the yacht was launched October 21st, of the same year, with her masts in place and fully rigged, in the presence of an immense concourse of people. Her fame had been heralded far and wide, but it was not till December 6th that she was ready for inspection by the thousands who were anxious to go on board.

The first day that she was on view, 1900 women and 900 men are said to have gone on board, and for many days an average of 900 visitors a day inspected the vessel. Her registered tonnage was $191\frac{1}{2}$ tons; she was 83 feet long on the water line, 23 feet beam and $11\frac{1}{2}$ feet deep. In rig, she was a hermaphrodite brig, i.e. fore-and-aft rigged on the main, with square rig forward, and carried a large outfit of all the different kinds of "kites" that could be carried on a vessel of her rig. Her main cabin measured 19x20 feet, and was paneled in mahogany inlaid with bird's-eye maple and other fancy woods.

The furniture was mahogany, upholstered in red velvet, decorated with gold lace. There were two large sofas with gilt-bronze ornaments, a chandelier, a sideboard, two large mirrors, etc., and an elaborate service of silver and china.

She had five staterooms off the cabin, while the forecastle had had accommodations for ten men and three boys. The total cost of Cleopatra's Barge was said to be $50,000, a large sum for those early days.

On January 15th, 1817, Captain Crowninshield took his yacht out for a trial trip, sailing from Salem to Gloucester, and returning the next day. After his return, the weather having turned cold, the yacht was frozen in her dock, and many people drove over the ice in sleighs to visit her. On the 30th of March, 1817, she left Salem for the Mediterranean, under the command of Captain Ben. Crowninshield, a veteran of Bunker Hill, who was a cousin of the owner, Captain George. The captain's son, Benj. Crowninshield, Jr., called "Philosopher Ben," kept a full record of the voyage, illustrating it with water-color drawings, which have been preserved. We have only time to give a brief sketch of the voyage. They first visited the Azores, arriving at Fayal, April 24, where great numbers of the inhabitants came on board, and a ball was given at the American Consul's house in honor of Cleopatra's Barge. Then they proceeded to Funchal, Madeira, where the yacht was visited by thousands of people. The log stated, "About 1500 persons came off to see the vessel, a large proportion of them ladies, who were nearly all seasick, after being onboard a few minutes."

From Madeira they sailed for Gibraltar, where they found the American frigate United States, Captain Shaw, as well as several Dutch and Austrian men-of-war, whose officers were entertained on board of the yacht. Next they visited Malaga, Cartagena and Port Mahone, having a close race with the frigate United States, for two days and nights, in which the yacht came out slightly ahead.

She was twice chased by Moorish pirates, but outsailed them. Their experiences at the various Mediterranean ports were very similar, but their reception at Barcelona capped the climax. The crowds of visitors became so great that the yacht was hauled out into the stream to avoid them, but even then she was followed by hundreds of boats. "No less than 8,000 people visited her in one day at this port." Philosopher Ben writes: "We rise at 5 o'clock and dress before strangers. We take our breakfast standing, and then crowd among the visitors. This condition of things continues till night, and we go to rest between 12 and 1 o'clock." At Marseilles Cleopatra's Barge was repainted throughout, refurnished and decorated regardless of expense. Three musicians were hired to remain on the yacht as long as she was in the Mediterranean. Their next port of call was Toulon, where the French naval officers were much interested in the yacht, and became very friendly to Captain Crowninshield and his officers. At Genoa they had many visitors of distinction, among them Baron von Zach, a distinguished German astronomer, who published in French at Genoa, in 1820, an account of his visit. He was delighted to learn that young Ben Crowninshield was a neighbor and pupil of Dr. Bowditch, the eminent mathematician, and proceeded to catechise him. When he expressed surprise at the statement that the ship's longitude was obtained by lunar observations, "Philosopher Ben" replied: "Why, our cook can do that." The cook, a negro, was found in the galley, and asked: "By what method he calculated longitude by lunar distances." He said, "It's all one to me. I use the methods of Maskelyne Lyons, Witchel and Bowditch, but on the whole I prefer Dunthorne's-I am more used to it, and can work it quicker." The cook had a bloody chicken and a knife in his hands. These he was ordered to lay down, while he was put through an examination by the astronomer. He answered all questions put to him, and showed his private log-book, with his day's work in navigation for the voyage.

From Genoa they continued their voyage to Leghorn, and then the Isle of Elba. As Captain Crowninshield was a great admirer of Napoleon, he entertained many of the ex-Emperor's adherents at the three ports he visited, and secured a number of souvenirs of him which are still preserved as heirlooms by his family. From Elba he sailed to Civita Vecchia, and traveled thence to the Eternal City. There he had interviews with the mother of Napoleon, his sister, the beautiful Princess Pauline, and Prince Lucien Bonaparte. On leaving Civita Vecchia for America, they received on board as two passengers two followers of Napoleon, the captain of the vessel in which he escaped from Elba, and a surgeon of his staff. This circumstance led to the yacht's being chased by one of four small French war vessels stationed off the port, which they easily outsailed.

They finally arrived at Salem October 3rd, 1817, and the yacht was laid up. The owner, George Crowninshield, while planning another voyage, died suddenly on the 26th of November, 1817. In settling the estate, the yacht was sold at auction. She made one voyage to Rio Janeiro, after which she was sold again, and run as a packet between Boston and Charleston, S.C.

In 1820, in fulfillment of a previous agreement with Kamehameha, she sailed from Salem or Boston on June 18th, 1820, and arrived at Lahaina, Maui, on November 6th, of the same year.

CLEOPATRA'S BARGE IN HAWAIIAN WATERS

On the 16th of November, 1820, Liholiho, Kamehameha II, and his prime minister, Kalaimoku, purchased Cleopatra's Barge of Captain Suter, for $90,000, to be paid for in Sandal-wood, in installments. Her name was then changed to "Haaheo o Hawaii," "Pride of Hawaii."

During the next three years she made frequent voyages between the islands. One of these deserves special mention in this place. I have elsewhere related how King Liholiho, either from drunken whim or to carry out a crafty design, sailed from Honolulu, July 21st, 1821, professedly for Ewa, in an open sail-boat, and compelled his attendants to continue the voyage to Waimea, Kauai, Arriving there the next day, he threw himself, entirely helpless, into the power of King Kaumualii. That noble chieftain, instead of taking any advantage of Liholiho's defenseless condition, gave him a hospitable reception, and sent his own brig to Honolulu to make known the king's safety, and to carry his commands. In two days, the five wives of Liholiho arrived on board of Cleopatra's Barge. The two kings then spent several weeks in a tour of the island of Kauai.

What return did Liholiho make to Kaumualii for his generous hospitality? On their return September 16th, Kaumualii was invited on board of the Cleopatra's Barge in the evening. While the unsuspicious prince was seated in the cabin, orders were secretly given to make sail, and he was torn from his kingdom, to remain thenceforth a virtual prisoner of state. Soon after his arrival in Honolulu he was induced to marry the imperious queen dowager, Kaahumanu. "In her chains," wrote Stewart at the time, "and I am told they are far from being silken bonds, he is still securely held." He died May 26, 1824.

WRECK OF CLEOPATRA'S BARGE

As the Rev. H. Bingham relates: "Through the mismanagement of a drunken captain and crew, the beautiful Cleopatra's Barge was wrecked in the bay of Hanalei, Kauai, and lay not far from the beach dismantled and ruined." This occurred towards the end of April, 1824. Mr. Bingham's History, pp. 221-2, contains a graphic description of an attempt made to haul the brig ashore.

Three immense cables, each composed of twelve ropes of hau bark were attached to the mainmast, a few feet above the deck. "The brig lay in about 10 feet of water, and partly on her side, which was farthest from shore, and close to a reef which rose nearly half way to the surface. Over this reef they proposed to roll the vessel." After the multitude had been marshaled along the ropes and instructed as to what to do, an old Kaukau, chanted an ancient mele, addressed to Lono, used when a tree for a canoe was to be dragged from the mountains to the shore. "The multitude quietly listening some six or eight minutes, at a particular turn or passage in the song, indicating the order to march, rose together, and as the song continued with increasing volubility and force, slowly moved forward in silence, and all leaning from the shore strained their huge cables, tugging together to heave up the vessel.

The brig felt their power-rolled up slowly towards shore and there instantly stopped; but the immense team moved unchecked, and the mainmast broke and fell with all its shroud being taken off by the cables drawn by unaided muscular strength. The hull instantly rolled back to its former place, and was given up as irrecoverable.

The interest of the scene was heightened by the fact that large man by the name of Kiu, who had ascended the standing shrouds, being near the main-top when the hull began to move was descending when the mast broke, and was seen to come down with it in his fall. Many hastened from the shore to the wreckage to see the effect of their pull, and to look after Kiu. He was found swimming about on the seaward side of the wreck, where he had plunged unhurt when in imminent danger."

❖　❖　❖

XIV. HANALEI
HALELE'A'S CAPITAL

*Hanalei* Valley and Hanalei Bay are perhaps the most beautiful sites in the Hawaiian Islands, perhaps in all the Pacific Islands. In reference to the incredible beauty, an ancient Hawaiian proverb states: "See Hanalei, then die!" Complementing this beauty is an intriguing history of Hawaiian ali'i, shipwrecks, missionaries, ranchers and reckless visionaries who attempted to tame the beauty for profit, only to fail over and over.

Halele'a, the ancient Hawaiian name for the Hanalei District, roughly translates as "house of the rainbows" or "house of pleasure." Both names are apt. The tradewind-borne rainbows are literally a daily occurrence at Hanalei, and pleasure is a priority for the surfers, beachgoers and escapists of modern society who are today the modern-day dwellers of Hanalei.

Rich in history, both Hawaiian and Western, the waters of Hanalei Bay hide the remains of Cleopatra's Barge, *the first royal yacht in the world which went aground here in the 1820's. Today researchers from the Smithsonian Institution are studying artifacts from the wreck, the site of which was rediscovered in the summer of 1995.*

TWENTY-FIVE YEARS ago, carrying my old nine-foot surfboard, a pack of rice and beans and a wallet full of dollars earned hawking the fun house for a traveling carnival on O'ahu, I hitched out to Hanalei Bay from the airport at Līhu'e with an elderly Hawaiian man in a vintage panel truck full of vegetables. Kūhiō Highway was a ribbon of quiet concrete with barely a car on the road in either direction as we drove north, past old plantation camps and sleepy villages.

The *kupuna* dropped me off at the lookout above the valley of Hanalei. The sun was just about to set and the lavenders, reds and oranges lit the square, mirror-like patches of *taro* below. Expectantly, I trotted under the load of my gear to the lower lookout for a view of the surf. Powerful, six-foot waves peeled along the point and behind me, a full moon rose in the direction of Kīlauea.

Things were simpler then. The plateau of Princeville was still a working cattle ranch—a descendant of R.C. Wyllie's 10,000 acre spread of beef, sugar cane, coffee and cotton started by that gentleman planter in 1853. A Club Med stood on the traditional hotel site above the river mouth, the latest in a long line of rustic lodging houses that began with Captain Kellet's Lanihuli and included the Deverill's Hotel, the Birkmeyer's Beach and Sea Ranch and the Guslanders' enchanted Hanalei Plantation Hotel.

I assumed the beach and the sea surrounding it had always been a laid-back picture of tranquility. But one day, as a part-Hawaiian friend and I were scanning the horizon for wave signs off Puʻupōā (the cliff of the night fire) near the spot where the Princeville Hotel now stands, I stumbled upon what looked like the crater of a huge bomb.

"Russians," he said. "Oh, long time ago; no need worry," he reassured me and pointed out another probable encampment site on the far side of the river.

"Hey, no big thing; my ancestors drove 'em out maybe hundred, hundred fifty years ago," he laughed. Then his face turned serious. "The heavy kind, the real heavy kind, over there," he said pointing to Makahoa Point on the seacliff at Waikoko, the western border of the bay. "One *heiau*, you know, old 'kine temple, *kahuna*, spooky stuff."

His respect for Hawaiian ruins was a trait I found common in local residents. Hanalei is the site of many events in Hawaiian mythology and the location of several *heiau* of importance. *Moʻo*—those giant, fire-breathing geckos that could take many forms and be a friend or foe to a Hawaiian family—are still rumored to exist in isolated spots, and the deeds of the legendary hero Kawelo can be heard from old-timers.

Kawelo was a *kupua,* or a part-human, part-god whose domain extended from Hanalei Bay to Kaʻula Rock south of Niʻihau, an easy jaunt for the giant-size man-god. Legend says he slew a rival 120-foot giant who lived at Hanalei with only his war club. The enemy giant was as strong as 320 men, but not as smart. Tripped up in a snare set by Kawelo's wife Kaʻākauhuhimalani, he was clobbered and torn in two by our hero.

With *moʻo* and Kawelo on my mind, I made a short pilgrimage to Honolulu to take advantage of the musty archives there that hold many of the secrets of Kauaʻi's historical past. I found a slim, yellowed booklet titled *The Russians on Kauai* and I discovered that in 1816 the Russian flag had flown over Hanalei. In fact, its name had been changed to Schefferthal after a German physician in cahoots with Russians attempting to dominate the Hawaiian Islands. Indeed, the entire valley had once been deeded to Tsar Alexander I, Emperor of Russia, by King Kaumuali'i of Kaua'i in exchange for a schooner!

At Pu'upōā, cannons had aimed out of the crater at the protected bay and the seacoast to the north. They had come off the Russian brigs *Myrtle* and *Ilmen*, which had spent a few seasons anchored below. Thankfully, the encounter ended in a victory for the Hawaiians who routed the Russians and their twenty or so Aleut confederates, killing two and forcing the invaders back to O'ahu.

I shared my findings with my friend and the following weekend I was awakened at dawn by him and an old Hawaiian man of at least 90. We walked the beach from Black Pot to Waipā, almost to the rise at Waikoko that leads to Lumaha'i. Time had not dimmed the *kupuna's* memory and he spun pidgin-accented tales of the area, reciting the Hawaiian names for the *ahupua* (land divivisions) along the way.

"Wai'oli-the singing waters; Waipā-the touched water; Waikoko-the blood water," he said, alluding to ancient signs and double-meaning words that hid obscure stories about each spot.

Sitting on a driftwood stump along the banks of the Wai'oli Stream, he used his *koa* wood cane to illustrate the finer points of life in the old days at Hanalei.

"Right here," he said, jabbing his cane into the sand, "was one village called Kalema. Here my people like follow the God of the missionaries; it is named after Bethlehem in the Bible. The old gods died long before, they get one new God."

"Bingham, he went learn about the old Hawaiian ways during the wreck of *Cleopatra's Barge*," said the *kupuna* after a gap of five still minutes.

My friend glanced at me, raising his eyebrows as if to say it was a new story for him, too.

"Bingham came 'round Kaua'i for his second visit to Hanalei; first time was by canoe from Wainiha, this time on foot. Coming down one hill, he see Liholiho's royal ship *(Haaheo O Hawaii–*The Pride of Hawaii) on its side, right off one reef in about ten feet water. More than thousand Hawaiians from Nā Pali, Ko'olau, Waimea and Hanalei sat along shore ready to pull boat up."

(Later I learned that the yacht had been wrecked by a crew of drunken Hawaiian sailors while the King himself was on a fateful trip to London where he died from a case of measles.)

The old man continued: "Eighteen chiefs direct the salvage. Even Deborah Kapule was here; she one favorite *wahine* of Kaumuali'i. Swimmers and divers brought in pieces of cargo and weavers stripped *hau* bark for make strong cable. Three strands, twelve layers thick and hundreds of feet long were fixed to the mainmast. A chief named Mamakani–the Windwatcher–helped the men and began one old chant. Bingham, the missionary, he not know what for say—he knew the Hawaiians were asking the god Lono for help them pull. But the old black coat, he wrote down the chant in his book when he saw the practical purpose of it, a Yankee, yeah?"

"Anyway, the ship, she came up but Kiamakani no could stop the pull in time; she tilted back for shore and snapped her mast; *pau*! The chiefs gave up. Went for one Budweiser," he laughed.

The story of Hiram Bingham, a staunch Calvinist missionary, amidst thousands of Hawaiians at Hanalei intrigued me and I sought out his writings.

Bingham offered a good description of the hardships and victories of early Wai'oli missionaries William Alexander and Edward Johnson, noting that the establishment of the station nearby the landmark Wai'oli Hui'ia Church in Hanalei also marked a change in shipping activity on Hanalei Bay. Quarterly packets bringing fresh goods from O'ahu and the mission base in Boston, sparked a boom in trading among the Hawaiians along the north shore. Bibles, calico, slate tablets, tools and other New England manufactured goods were traded for local produce and livestock. The practice also spilled over into secular trade when the occasional whaling vessel pulled into the bay for supplies.

The sea off Hanalei also brought its share of tragedy. The Alexanders lost a son off Waipā who drowned after a six-hour ordeal in heavy surf; later, the Johnsons also lost a son when the inter-island packet *Kalihiwai* sank off Hanalei Point.

The increased trade served to add another class of newcomers to the growing population of the bay. Veteran sailors from England, France and ports along America's seaboard began to settle in Hanalei, and they applied their labors to planting crops.

Charles Titcomb, John Kellet, Godfrey Rhodes and John Bernard all landed along the balmy shores of Hanalei in the 1830's and 1840's and started small plantations. They raised orchards of local oranges from trees first brought to Kaua'i by Vancouver in the 1790's, and Titcomb even experimented with silkworms, but blamed heavy taxation for his failure to succeed with his wriggly crop. They also grew tobacco of the finest Hawaiian variety, and claimed to have rolled some 200,000 cigars from one harvest.

In 1840 the Hawaiians, missionaries and early planters were joined by Capt. Charles Wilkes and the crew of the

U.S. Exploring Expedition who made a stop in the bay's calm summer waters to record its geography and natural wonders for the outside world. Wilkes referred to Hanalei in his book on the expedition, as Halele'a—the House of Rainbows—a name the Hawaiians used for the entire district.

Tragedy struck the planters as it did the missionaries, when one of their number was lost at sea just outside the bay. Frenchman John Bernard was returning home aboard the Hawaiian schooner *Paalua* on April 18, 1845, when the vessel was hit by a heavy squall and was washed into the bay by a large swell. Except for a Hawaiian crewman, all perished, including Bernard and a family of New Zealanders.

In the 1850's, the first mechanically-powered boats appeared in the bay, when California river boats with giant paddlewheels along their sides took up inter-island trade. But, side-wheelers made for a rough trip across the channels and failed to become permanent fixtures. In the 1870s, steam-powered schooners began regularly scheduled service from Honolulu to Hanalei. The *James McKee*, named after the founder of the Kealia Sugar Plantation on Kaua'i's east side, was the most popular ship, charging $6 for cabins and $2 for deck passage.

In 1874, a month after becoming the first elected king of Hawai'i, David Kalākaua sailed into Hanalei aboard the steamer *Kilauea*. A battery of 21 'ohi'a logs stuffed with powder were ignited to salute the Merrie Monarch as he arrived, bursting off irregularly and leaving behind stacks of firewood for the rural Hanalei inhabitants.

The ships also brought Chinese immigrants to the bay to work the growing sugar plantations, and a few probably smuggled in cargos of opium as well. The immigrants eventually outlasted their *luna* in the Hanalei fields and planted rice when the sugar plantations opted for drier fields in Kīlauea.

By 1911, rice had supplanted *taro* and sugar in Hanalei, and the need for a pier to load the heavy burlap bags of grain aboard waiting ships became pressing.

The ships had also grown, and loading them from small fleets of row boats was too cumbersome. The legislature agreed with the Hanalei rice growers and funded the landmark Hanalei Pier in 1911.

World War II brought a company of soldiers and sailors to Hanalei who occasionally took local kids down the coast to Nā Pali's valleys aboard fast patrol boats, prefiguring today's commercial tours. The image of Hanalei Bay filled with WWII servicemen carried over into the movie world when the classic film *South Pacific* was shot along its shores in 1957 and the view of Mount Makana—better known now as Bali Hai—became an internationally recognized symbol of the mystery and romance of the Pacific Islands.

Today, the people who were born and raised in these parts and the outsiders who have been around a while, are trying once again to get a grasp on the rapid changes taking place in Hanalei. While *taro* again fills the valley, tourism has become the big business of the day.

◈ ◈ ◈

Gorham D. Gilman

XV. NĀ PALI CANOE VOYAGE
FROM HANALEI TO WAIMEA IN 1845

The Nā Pali Coast stretches for over 15 miles from Keʻe Beach at Hāʻena, on the North Shore, to just before Polihale on the northern end of the west-side beaches known as Barking Sands. Na Pali is accessible only on foot from the trailhead at Keʻe to the wide mouth of Kalalau Valley, about 12 miles distant. Hawaiian trails that once dropped down from the Kōkeʻe forest highlands to some of the valleys are now lost. Otherwise, kayaking, Hawaiian sailing and paddling canoes, and powerboats are the only way in for a landing, and then usually only during the calm summer months from late May to early September. Peopled by Hawaiian taro farmers, fishermen and cattle ranchers until about 1920, Nā Pali is now uninhabited, except for transient campers.

Joining Honolulu judge Gorham D. Gilman for his trip down Nā Pali the day of August 19, 1845 would be an invitation readily accepted by the thousands of visitors who each year venture along the deep, blue waters fronting the majestic pinnacles and valleys. Today touring Nā Pali is done in modern-era rubber inflatables and fiberglass-hulled motorized catamarans. Gilman sailed aboard a traditional Hawaiian sailing canoe for a unique look at the isolated life of Nā Pali's Hawaiian dwellers. To Gilman the trip was very adventurous as he entered a world very few haole *of his day had seen.*

Gilman's at-times-comic fear of climbing the vertical ladder at Nu'alolo, and of riding west-side surf in the canoe, points out the dividing line that most haole *cringe in fear at crossing—a line that strong,* akamai *rural Hawaiians don't even see.*

I WAS AWAKENED this morning by the clock's striking three, and, as it was the hour that I had set for my departure, I prepared myself to leave. I found the table spread with refreshments for the voyage, of which I was glad to avail myself, after which I left the house silently, not wishing to disturb my kind friends too early. The full moon was flooding with its light the grand mountains, the valley and the bay. Not a sound broke the stillness save the gentle splashing of the waves as they broke on the beach. A short walk brought me to the house where the crew of my canoe were sleeping. It was with some difficulty that I roused them up, and got them to move along. I had given them explicit orders the day before to have everything ready when I should come down, but when I arrived, expecting to find the canoe rigged, they were anything but ready. The canoe was not loaded and the men were not together, but part in one place and part in another.

After a delay of an hour and a half, we shoved off through the surf and directed our course toward Waimea.

A light breeze sprang up, and the houses and beach of Hanalei were soon lost in the distance. The coast which we were passing was too dim for us to distinguish objects on shore, but as I had ridden past it shortly before, I did not particularly regret this. The sun was just rising when we reached the point where the great palis or precipices begin. These precipices are one of the grandest wonders of the Islands, but the danger of examining them on the passage deters many persons from visiting them. There are those who will travel by land sixty miles around rather than sail these fifteen by canoe, and I was warned not to try. But with me curiosity was stronger than caution.

I must confess that when we passed the last landing, and were fairly entering on the dangerous part, I felt a little timid, for if any accident should happen, there was no help for us. The rocks rose perpendicularly from the water without any landing place, and if upset, the only hope would be the chance of being picked up by some passing canoe. In fact a canoe making the passage was capsized a few days before and her cargo lost. The natives, however, are so expert that they have little or no fear at such times; the canoe was soon righted, and the man's escape with his life was considered hardly worth talking about.

We had not sailed far along the *pali*, when we came near sharing a similar fate. By some careless maneuver of the natives, the outrigger, which serves to balance the canoe, rose clear out of the water. In a moment more, if all hands had not thrown their weight on that side, we should have been in the sea. The native, however, did not seem to notice it, and they took the scolding that I gave them with a most provoking indifference. As the canoe passed on, the cliffs grew more and more lofty. The sea was smooth and there being no wind, our passage was pleasant, giving us an opportunity to examine the varying appearances of the *pali*. The sea was dashing up against the base of the precipice, and roaring through the caves, which have been worn by the constant action of the waves. The summit of the mountain took the most wild and fantastic shapes. Sometimes sharp spires shot up hundreds of feet, and again a rounded battlement would present its front like a turreted citadel of feudal days, and then a deep valley but a few rods wide might be seen, shut in by steep walls. It is no wonder that the natives give credence to the wild legends which are connected with various parts of this range. A few of these I will relate as they were repeated to me, while we sailed along, and served to beguile the tediousness of the voyage.

As the canoe was passing a rock that seemed blackened by volcanic fires, the captain gave orders to stop, and to paddle close in to the rocks. As we drew near, he pointed out an arch large enough to admit a small canoe. The water within, being confined, was agitated so that I did not care to venture in, but went near enough to see that it was a kind of volcanic chimney. Its inner walls showed the effects of the mighty fires, and from an aperture on the top of the bluff, the light came straggling down, giving the place a weird look. The tradition is that Pele came to these Islands from some foreign land, that Kauai was the first island that she visited, and that she landed at the very spot that I have just describe. She tried the foundations of the Island, to ascertain if there was a sufficient quantity of food to be obtained, and this pit or chimney is the place where she descended. She commenced her operations, but soon found that the water was in too close proximity for her convenience. For she and old Neptune were deadly enemies, and in their contests exhibited the fiercest rage, to the destruction of all who might be involved in it. Not liking this situation, she moved on from island to island, till she finally settled on Hawaii.

In another place two small, upright rocks are called *The Children*, who, it is said, wandered up to the heights, and there perished from thirst, were deified, an became objects of worship.

One place is pointed out as the scene of a comparatively recent occurrence. The old Governor, Kaikioewa, was on this side of the island, and arrived (I believe) by an inland route on the summit of a very precipitous peak, and there sat down to drink *awa*. While enjoying his cup, he decided that he must have a drink of water from a spring some hundred feet below and   dispatched a native to get it. The native knew better than to offer any objection. He could but die either way. A comrade offered to go with him, and together they descended the precipice, and climbed back again in safety. Any one looking at the place would pronounce the feat next to impossible.

When we had passed about two-thirds of the pali we came to a little bay making in between two arms or points of land, on the shore of which we noticed several canoes, and a few miserable huts. As the morning was well advanced, I consented that the men should land to refresh themselves with rest and food, and while they were doing this I strolled around to see the place. It would answer well for a place of detention, for there is no visible way of ingress or egress except by water, and yet there is a way for those who have sufficient nerve to brave the danger. As we came along, I had noticed a sort of ladder placed against the face of the cliff, for the purpose of reaching the heights above. A native presented himself as a guide, and I let him lead the way. Starting off, I had no doubt that I was going to ascend the ladder at once, but I had taken but a few steps before I found myself halting and reconnoitering. The way which had appeared so easy, now showed itself full of danger. The path has been excavated by the natives with their rude tools, from the face of an overhanging cliff. It is not a level, but if formed like a gouge turned edgewise, so that one's hold is very precarious. It is also too low to admit of any other than a stooping posture, and I was obliged to shuffle along with the utmost caution. My guide seemed quite at home, as he stood upright outside of me, with his body projecting beyond the surface of the cliff, and encouraged me on. I had taken off my shoes, and by degrees had worked myself two-thirds past, when I rested for a survey. There I was, my chief support a little projecting stone, not sufficient to afford a hold for my whole foot, and my hands clinging with a death grasp to the rock, and in this situation overhanging a gulf, that was foaming and boiling, as the surf broke over the rocks some sixty or seventy feet below me, and which would have proved my death place, if I had made the least mistake or slip. I had strong curiosity to go forward, but discretion prevailed, and I returned. I was then told that few white men had gone as far as I had, and that none had ever passed up the ladder. Taking a less dangerous standpoint, I took occasion to examine the ladder. It is made of trunks of two cocoanut trees, one of which stands against the cliff, and the other out from it, like planting the side of a ladder against a house. The outer stick is well secured with ropes, and is the only means of communication between above and below. The natives pass up by it, even with a load, as unconcerned as if passing the best bridge. It is surprising to see even the children pass it free and unconcerned, as if on level ground. I can only wonder that there is not an accident every day.

A few rods back from the beach rise the cliffs, in some places perpendicular for 500 feet, forming an amphitheater. Along the base on one side are ranged the houses, which form a striking contrast with the black mass of rock rising behind them. All their food comes from above, where it is said there is a fine valley, (Nualolo), which the feet of white men have never profaned. Here, shut out from all intruders, they live in peace and happiness, such as it is—pleasure today—borrow no thought for tomorrow.

When His Majesty passes around the island, he stops here for a part or the whole of the night, to see an exhibition of fire works, got up for his entertainment. It consists in throwing light poles, which have been set on fire, from a lofty peak (Kamaile) overlooking the sea. If skillfully thrown, they will go a long distance, making a pretty show. The natives sometimes take a large bird, and set it off with a burning substance attached to it.

This little bay is the gathering place for canoes passing between Waimea and Hanalei, as well as for those that go over to the island of Niihau, which can be seen here at a distance of about 25 miles.

Having spent about an hour at this place, we again took our seats in the canoe, and continued our voyage towards Waimea. Our company was now increased to four canoes, ours being the largest, and there was something of a contest as to which should lead, but I believe that when so inclined, we could distance the others. The three other canoes were bound for Niihau. One of them was quite small, containing only three persons, a man and two women, who handled their paddles like professional rowers. The top of the canoe was covered with mats firmly secured, with openings left just large enough to admit their bodies, but at best it was a slight affair to stand the rough seas in the channel.

As we were passing by a very high bank, I noticed the figure of a native sketched upon it. This was very distinct, its limbs, its brown skin and a white cloth wrapped around its loins, and reminded me of rocks found at home, which had been marked by the Indians. I was quite surprised when a shrill whistle and a beckoning movement of one arm dispelled the illusion. It was a young native who was standing against the face of the rock, watching us.

After paddling five or six hours, including stops, we passed the further extremity of the *pali*s in safety, and the whole appearance of the land immediately changed—from lofty and fantastic peaks and precipices to a barren, uninteresting sand beach, on which we tried to land for water, but found the surf too heavy. The canoemen had shirked their work and we were much behind the usual time for the passage. Meanwhile there was not a breath of wind, the sun was pouring down his scorching rays, and the sea like a mirror reflected them with blinding intensity. The men, however, seemed perfectly indifferent as to the length of the voyage. For an hour we had a most disagreeable sail along a monotonous sand flat.

At last we came in sight of the cocoanut trees near Waimea, and I urged the men, but in vain. Suddenly a strong wind arose. The sea was soon running very high and covered with white-caps, and every few minutes it broke over us, half filling the canoe. It did no good to talk to the men, although I offered them a reward—they were criminals, and seemed indifferent to life or death. It having become dangerous to proceed, I ordered that the canoe should be beached, which was done with difficulty and danger, but we were safe. Waimea was nine miles away, and the distance had to be walked.

About 4 o'clock p. m. I arrived, tired and hungry, at the hospitable residence of Rev. S. Whitney, the missionary of this station, where a most cordial welcome, a good bath and a warm supper did much to refresh me. I had been twelve hours in the canoe, where I could neither lie down nor sit up with any degree of comfort, and as I had expected to be at Waimea to breakfast, I had not brought any food with me except a few dry crackers. Besides, after the wind rose and particularly in getting ashore, I was wet through.

But after a good night's rest I rose quite refreshed. After breakfast Mr. Whitney showed me his vineyard, which is the best on this island. The first plants were introduced by the Russians.

XVI.   KAUA'I IN 1840

THE UNITED STATES EXPLORING EXPEDITION

The United States Exploring Expedition circled the globe from 1838 to 1842 as the United States' first scientific voyage of exploration. Under Commander Charles Wilkes of the U.S. Navy, and following guidelines set up by Captain James Cook and other circumnavigators and explorers, the expedition stopped over in Hawai'i in 1840, during which time team members spread out to explore Kaua'i with the assistance of Hawaiian men.

In this selection from Wilkes' journal, he has arrived at Kaua'i aboard his flagship Vincennes. *Five other vessels, with a total expedition count of over 500 men, were spread out in Hawai'i. He begins a tour round Kaua'i at Ladd & Co.'s sugar mill. The site is near the present-day town of Kōloa. A monument at the entrance to Kōloa town commemorates the company and the industry it sparked across Hawai'i.*

In touring Kaua'i, Wilkes and his men gathered
information on the social conditions and opportunities for
agriculture and became familiar with the flora, fauna and
climate.

Hanapēpē, another stop for Wilkes' team, is today a sleepy
west-side town, with a main street lined with art galleries,
though it was once a center of life for Kaua'i's businesses.
During World War II and prior, the town was a bustling
center of activity. With the development of Nāwiliwili Harbor
outside of Līhu'e, nearby Port Allen has all but shut down.

Wilkes was an authority on oceanography and spent four
years exploring the Pacific, recording scientific and cultural
information at over 280 islands. His observations drew
interest in Hawai'i from the political and scholarly worlds of
the East Coast.

THE SUGAR-MILLS of Ladd & Co. are said to be
doing a good business. They are turned by water. The
sugar is of a fair quality, and has been sold in the United
States at a profit. The natives are induced to raise the
sugar-cane, which is sometimes ground, or
manufactured, on shares, and is also bought. The labour
of the natives, in raising the cane, costs twelve and a half
cents per day. This, however, is paid in paper currency,
issued by Ladd & Co., redeemable at their store;
consequently the price of the labour is no more than six
and a quarter cents; for the sale of goods is rarely made
in these islands under a profit of one hundred per cent.
The want of a native currency is beginning to be much
felt, both by the government and people; a fact that will
tend to show the advance they have made and are making
in civilization.

The sugar, I understood, could be afforded in the
United States at from four to four and a half cents the

pound. This, however, I think is rather a low estimate, to include growth, manufacture, freight, and charges...

...The district in which Waimea is situated, is called Hanapepe, and extends to Napali on the west, and Hanapepe on the east. The former is about twenty miles distant from Waimea, and the latter six. At Napali a part of the central range of mountains meets the sea, and shuts in the plain near the sea-shore by a perpendicular precipice, between fifteen hundred and two thousand feet in height.

The sandy plain that skirts the southwest side of the island is from one fourth of a mile to a mile wide, and lies one hundred and fifty feet above the level of the sea; the ground rises thence gradually to the summit of the mountains. This land is fit for little except the pasturage of goats, and presents a sunburnt appearance, being destitute of vegetations in the distance of eight or ten miles from the sea. The plain above spoken of, therefore, has little to recommend it. There is a strip of land just before the mountain ascent begins...

...The basaltic rocks and strata, as it will be seen, have been much reversed and upturned, an present their columnar structure very distinctly to view, inclining in opposite directions. Although the volume of water in this cascade is not great, yet its form and situation add very much to its beauty: it falls into a quiet basin beneath, and the spray being driven by the wind upon each bank, affords nourishment to a variety of ferns which grow there. At its foot it forms a small river, which passes down through the centre of the valley. This whole scene is very striking, the banks forming a kind of ampitheatre rich in foliage, and with rills of water coursing down them in every direction.

The water of this stream is used by the natives to irrigate their taro patches, and the soil of the valley is exceedingly fertile, producing sweet-potatoes, pumpkins, cabbages, beans, &c. the whole district is almost entirely supplied with food from Hanapepe and Waimea valleys, which occasions the population for the most part to centre in these two places: throughout the remainder of the island, the huts and inhabitants are but sparsely scattered.

The district of Hanapepe forms a mission station, and is under the care of the Rev. Samuel Whitney. He states the population in 1838 to have been 3,272. Mr. Whitney informed me, that for some years past he has kept a register of births an deaths, which shows that the latter is to the former as three to one. Other late authorities make the decrease in this district as eight to one for several years; but a resident of such standing as Mr. Whitney must be reckoned the best authority.

Mr. Whitney imputes this rapid decrease to former vicious habits, and both native and foreign authorities attribute the introduction of the venereal to the visit of Cook. This infection, brought to these islands by the first voyagers, may now be said to pervade the whole population, and has reduced the natives to a morbid sickly state; many of the women are incapable of child-bearing, and of the children who are born, only a few live to come to maturity.

Mr. Whitney assigns as another cause of the decrease in the population, the recklessness of human life, brought about by the despot government under which they have been living, which has destroyed all motives to enterprise and industry, rendered precarious the blessings of life, and produced a corresponding recklessness as to the future. Much of the sickness is owing to over-eating and irregularity in meals: for the inhabitants fast sometimes for days together, and then germinate to the greatest excess.

There has been no case of infanticide, to Mr. Whitney's knowledge, during the last ten years, and he does not believe that the law interdicting sexual intercourse is promotive of this crime; for from all his inquiries, he has not been able to learn a single fact that will tend to warrant such a conclusion: on the contrary, he thinks that the law in question has rather acted to prevent its commission.

Intoxication certainly forms no par of the cause of diseases, for Mr. Whitney bears testimony, that he has not known six cases of intoxication within the last thirteen years. A spirit, however, is distilled from the ti, potatoes, watermelon, &c.

The marriage law has had a good effect in this district, and will probably be the means of arresting the desolation that is now sweeping over the land. From thirty to forty marriages have taken place yearly. I have been thus particular in the population of this district, as it is generally reported to be that wherein the causes of decrease are most active. This cannot be owing to the climate, which is very similar to that of the leeward portions of the other islands, and the atmosphere is considered dry and healthy. Can it be owing to the fact, that the original virus of the disease was here first spread, and that it has continued to be more virulent here than elsewhere?

As respects agriculture, there being no market for the sale of produce, the supply seldom exceeds the wants of the district. Some attempts have, however, been made to produce cotton and the sugarcane; but, for want of encouragement, the produce has not yet been sufficient to clear the expenses.

The improvement in the morals and instruction of the natives is very considerable. There are sixteen schools, all taught by native teachers, at the expense of the people. Two-thirds of the adult population read, and many of them can also write. The instruction is now confined to the youth and children, of whom about three hundred attend the schools regularly, and six hundred more occasionally. Much improvement has lately taken place in their habitations, and in the manufacturing of their wearing apparel, consisting of tapa, &c.

There is one church, and one hundred an fifty-nine communicants: the number that attend worship in the morning is about a thousand, and in the afternoon about half that number.

The island of Niihau was not visited by any one belonging to the squadron; but is seems proper that in giving an account of the Hawaiian Islands, it should be spoken of. It is situated sixteen miles southwest of Kauai, and is eighteen miles long by eight broad. There is an anchorage on its western side, but no harbour. Its eastern side is rocky and unfit for cultivation; the inhabitants therefore reside on its western side, on the sea-shore, and are for the most part miserably poor. They cultivate, principally, yams and sweet-potatoes, the former of which succeed much better here than at any of the other islands. Water is very scarce, and they suffer occasionally from droughts, from which cause they are not able to raise the taro. This island is celebrated for the beautiful mats manufactured by its women. It is also said to be a favourable place for the manufacture of salt.

The number of inhabitants is one thousand; and what is remarkable, although but a few miles removed from Waimea, on the island of Kauai, they show an increase, in the proportion of births over deaths, of eight to six. The climate cannot be very different, and both would be equally subject to drought, if it were not for the rivers and the irrigation dependent on them. On this island there are two hundred children, about one-third of whom read: these are divided into twelve schools, under native teachers.

The district of Koloa on Kauai is twelve miles long by five broad. The face of the country is much broken into hills and extinguished craters. The land is good along its whole extent and half its breadth, and they have a sufficient quantity of rain to enable them to dispense with irrigation, of which but a small extent only would be susceptible.

The climate is generally mild and equable, the range of the thermometer being usually from 60° to 80° F.; but during the summer months it is occasionally found as high as 90°, and in winter as low as 50°. Sugar-cane grows in luxuriance, as well as cotton; the mulberry, both Chinese and multicaulis, Indian corn, sweet-potatoes, yams, and taro also flourish.

This has been the seat of the operations of some foreigners (Americans), and although, as has been before remarked, the natives derive but little pecuniary profit from their labour, yet the influence of a steady occupation has produced a striking improvement: they are clothed in foreign goods, and are generally found employed, and not lounging about as formerly. The comforts of their habitations have, however, as yet undergone but little change.

The population in 1840, was one thousand three hundred and forty-eight. There is a church, with one hundred and twenty-six members, but no schools. The teachers set apart for this service were employed by the chiefs, who frequently make use of them to keep their accounts, gather in their taxes, &c. The population is here again increasing, partly by immigration, whence it was difficult to ascertain its ratio. This district, it will be observed, lies immediately on the east of Hanapepe. Infanticide is not known, and drunkenness rarely if ever happens. There are no epidemics; asthma and ophthalmia are the diseases most prevalent: the later is ascribe to the strong winds which blow constantly, and irritate the eye with the minute particles borne on them.

There is no western route from Waimea to Halelea; it is therefore necessary, in getting to Napali, to take a canoe and coast along the shore. As this would not have answered the purpose of our gentlemen's visit, they determined to take the path directly across the island, and were provided with two guides by the kindness of Mr. Whitney. They left his hospitable mansion the next morning, having noted the standing of the sympiesometer. Shortly after starting they were joined by a native, laden with provisions and cooking utensils, which the kindness of Mr. Whitney had provided, and sent for their use. They at once commenced a very gradual ascent over a barren surface to the half-way house, about twelve miles. At first they found nothing but withered grass, then a few ferns, where goats only could find pasturage, and , a mile or two before reaching the halfway house, some stunted acascias and sandalwood. The route was along the river the whole distance, though in a deep gorge beneath them. All the wood used at Waimea must be brought from this distance. Their guides carried them about a mile beyond the half-way house, to a deserted hut, intending to stop there for the night; but our gentlemen found it so infested with fleas and vermin, that, although it rained, they returned, and passed the night comparatively free from these annoyances. The height of the half-way hut, as given by the stympiesometer, was three thousand four hundred feet. The sea was a sight the whole distance, and the coast was seen as far to the west as Napali. The country thus seen appeared similar to what they had passed over: it was furrowed in places by ravines, but yields no water except when rain falls abundantly upon the mountains.

At half-past 5 p. m., the thermometer stood at 69°, and the next morning at half-past six at 72°.

After sending the native back to Waimea who brought the comforts which Mr. Whitney's kindness had provided them with, they began their journey across the island, and entered into a very luxuriant and interesting botanical region, passing through several glades, which appeared well adapted for the cultivation of wheat and Irish potatoes (which have never been tried here). Large tracts were free from wood and level, on which was growing a sort of wild cabbage in great abundance. Wild hogs were evidently numerous, for many were started in the bush, and their rooting was to be seen along the whole route. Wild dogs are said also to exist in bands. During the day, a storm of wind and rain came on. After passing this fertile region, they reached the table-land, which is a marshy district, filled with quagmires, exceedingly difficult to travel through, and in which they frequently sunk up to their knees in mud and water. This tableland was supposed to be upwards of twenty miles square. Here the natives were inclined to turn back; but, as they afterwards said, they considered themselves bound to proceed "on so unusual an occasion." Their fears arose from the report that natives had been lost in crossing by this path. At about 3 p.m., they reached the Pali or precipice, which is like that of Oahu, having a very abrupt, though not dangerous, descent. Many interesting plants were gathered on this route, such as Acaena, Daphne, Pelargonium, Plantago, Drosera, with several interesting grasses.

At the Pali they neglected to make observations with the sympiesometer, but their impression was that the height was six or seven hundred feet more than the situation of the half-way house, which would given an altitude of about four thousand feet. Mr. Alexander, the missionary at Halelea, informed them that he had made it that height by triangulation.

The descent of the Pali was found to be very steep and fatiguing: but by slipping, tumbling, scrambling, and swinging from tree to tree, they reached the margin of the river Wainiha, at its foot. The stream was in this place about six hundred feet above tide. They were obliged to ford it; and in consequence of the heavy rain of the day before, it was so much swollen as to be almost impassable, the water reaching to their breasts. This, together with floundering through the taro-patches, as the darkness set in, made them consent to take up their lodgings in a native hut. In the morning they passed down the valley of Wainiha, which here forms a glen. The sides of the mountains, that rise abruptly about fifteen hundred feet on each side, are covered with vegetation in every variety of tint; whilst the tutui tree (Candlenut), the bread-fruit, orange, banana, plantations of Broussonetia papyrifera, and taro-beds, together with pandanus trees, whose blossoms scent the air for miles, filled the valley with luxuriance. This prolific vegetation, with numerous cascades falling over the perpendicular sides of the rock, combine to form one of the most picturesque scenes on this island.

About noon they reached Halelea, most of the distance to which was travelled along the sea-shore. On their way they crossed the Lumahae, a river similar to the Wainiha, and running parallel with it. The foot of the Pali is about five miles from the coast.

The extensive sugar plantations, with a few neat cottages, with verandas and thatched roofs, and throws of small cabins forth labourers, give the place the aspect of the tropical plantations of European nations.

Mesrs. Peale and Rich, being furnished with horses and a guide by the kindness of Mr. Burnham, took the eastern route to Halelea through a fine level country, cultivated in sugar-cane and affording good pasturage. The natives here use the plough, and it was said at Koloa that there was an instance of two of them having netted one hundred and forty dollars by their crop of sugar the last year.

The principal trees were acacias (*koa*), pandanus, the *tutui* (Aleurites). The latter is the largest and most conspicuous, from its white leaves resembling blossoms at a distance. The plain over which they passed was two hundred and fifty feet above the level of the sea. There are in it many gullies, formed by the small streams that run down from the mountains; all of these are, however, blocked up by sand-bars, through which the water filtrates, forming quicksands, which it is somewhat dangerous to pass over. The immediate shore along this route is rocky and susceptible of little cultivation, except near the mouths of the rivers, where taro-patches are to be found.

At noon they reached Lihue, a settlement lately undertaken by the Rev. Mr. Lafon, for the purpose of inducing the natives to remove from the sea-coast, thus abandoning their poor lands to cultivate the rich plains above. Mr. Lafon has the charge of the mission district lying between those of Koloa and Waioli. This district was a short time ago formed out of the other two.

The principal village is Nawiliwili, ten miles east of Koloa. This district contains about forty square miles, being twenty miles long by two broad. The soil is rich: it produces sugar-cane, taro, sweet-potatoes, beans, &c. The only market is that of Koloa. The cane suffers somewhat from the high winds on the plains.

Mr. and Mrs. Lafon are very industrious with their large school, to which some of the children come a distance of five miles. Our gentlemen were much pleased with what they saw, and were satisfied that good would be effected by their manner of treating the natives.

The temperature of Lihue has much the same range as that of Koloa, and the climate is pleasant: the trade-winds sweep over it uninterruptedly, and sufficient rain falls to keep the vegetation green throughout the year.

As yet there is little appearance of increase in industry, or improvement in the dwellings of the natives. There are no more than about seventy pupils in this district, who are taught by natives. There are two houses of worship, and about forty communicants. No decrease is apparent in the population within a few years.

On the fertile places, although the pasturage was good, yet no cattle were to be seen.

From Lihue, they pursued their way to Hanawale, which is a small fishing village at the mouth of a little stream. The country on this route was uninteresting, until they reached Wailua, the residence of Deborah, a chief woman of the islands, readily known as such from her enormous size, and the cast of her countenance. She has a person living with her called Olivia Chapin, who speaks English, and has learned how to extort money. Deborah has about forty men in her district; but they were absent, being employed in the mountains cutting timber to pay the tax to the king.

Near Deborah's residence are extensive fish-ponds belonging to her, which have been made with great labour: they are of different degrees of saltness. The fish are taken from the sea when young and put into the saltiest pond; as they grow larger, they are removed into one less salt, and are finally fattened in fresh water. While our gentlemen were there, Deborah received young fish in payment of the poll-tax, which were immediately transferred to her ponds.

Wailua, (two waters,) was formerly a place of some importance. It is situated on a small stream of the same name, in a barren, sandy spot.

Deborah furnished them with a double canoe, to carry them up the river to visit the falls. Taking the western branch, they ascended it for two and a half miles.

There are many good taro-patches and sugar plantations on its banks. They landed in what appeared to have been an old crater, in form of a basin, with high perpendicular banks. The low grounds along the river are extremely fertile, producing bread-fruit, sugar-cane, oranges, &c. The latter, however, are suffering from the blight, and some of the trees were covered with a black smut, produced by a species of aphis.

In ascending, an insulated black rock is passed, known as the "Muu," which has been detached from a high rocky bluff, that is remarkable for the dikes visible in it.

They afterwards ascended the bank, two hundred feet high, and crossed about half a mile to the falls, over a plain covered with grass and wild sugar-cane. The stream was very small, running sluggishly, and passed over a precipice of barren rocks, one hundred and sixty feet in height. Although there is neither tree nor shrub along the stream above the fall, the valley beneath is filled with them; the most conspicuous was the pandanus. The whole scene is picturesque. Below, the falls present a very curious appearance, the wind continually breaking and dispersing the water in heavy showers over a great variety of ferns, which are growing in the crevices of the rocks. The volume of water does not exceed ten hogsheads a minute. In the basin beneath were found many fine specimens of Neritina granulata, and two other species were found further down the stream, about four feet below the surface: these were procured by diving. Mr. Rich obtained specimens of the plants. Mr. Peale found but few birds; ducks were abundant on the river's banks, some of which were killed. Rushes were growing along the banks from eight to ten feet in length, four or five feet under the water; besides these, the banks were covered with hibiscus and ricinus (castor-oil trees), growing wild.

Returning to Deborah's, where they remained for the night, they met Messrs. Dana and Agate. Deborah entertained them in "white style," at a table set with knives, forks, &c., and gave them tea and sugar. Their bed was native, and composed of a platform of about twelve feet square, covered with mats. This proved comfortable, with tapa as a covering in lieu of linen.

The next morning, they started for Waioli and Halelea. The country on the way is of the same character as that already seen. They passed the small villages of Kupau, Kealia, Anehola, Mowaa, and Kauharaki, situated at the mouths of the mountain streams, which were closed with similar sand-bars to those already described. These bars afforded places to cross at, though requiring great precaution when on horseback. The streams above the bars were in most cases deep, wide, and navigable a few miles for canoes. Besides the sugar-cane, taro, &c. some good fields of rice were seen. The country may be called open; it is covered with grass forming excellent pasture-grounds, and abounds in plover and turnstones, scattered in small flocks.

On their way they passed through a beautiful grove of *tutui*-nut trees, in which the Rev. Mr. Alexander is in the habit of preaching to the natives. There trees are large, and form a delightful shade. There are few places in the open air so well calculated to hold divine service in, and it is well fitted to create feelings of religion. The view, by Mr. Agate, will give a good idea of it.

These nut-trees grow with great luxuriance on this island; and an excellent oil is expressed from the nut, which already forms an export from these islands. We heard here, that at New York, it was pronounced superior to linseed-oil for painting. There is a manufactory of it at Honolulu; but I understood that it dried with difficulty. It is said to bring one dollar per gallon on the coast of South America. The native candle is made of these nuts strung upon a straw; they are likewise roasted and eaten.

Before reaching Waioli, they passed through a forest of pandanus trees. Waioli is a mission station, the residence of the Rev. Mr. Alexander, by whom they were very kindly received. This district is called Halelea. Waioli is on the north side of Kauai. The plain on which it is situated is only six or eight feet above the level of the sea, and lies between the Halelea and Waioli rivers. Though of small extent, it is one of the most fertile spots of which these islands can boast.

The Halelea district comprises a large proportion of arable land: it extends to the distance of twenty miles to the eastward of Waioli; the portion, however, which lies to the westward is of a totally different description, being broken up into precipices and ravines, affording no inducements to the agriculturist, and having very few spots susceptible of cultivation; its extent is about fifteen miles. The eastern portion is watered by at least twenty streams; many of these are large enough to be termed rivers, and might be employed to turn machinery. It is elevated from three to eight hundred feet above the sea, and comprises about fifty thousand acres of land, capable of producing sugar-cane, cotton, indigo, coffee, corn, beans, the mulberry, and vegetables.

⬙ ⬙ ⬙

XVII. WAILUA c. 1852
OLD WAILUA & DEBORAH KAPULE

George Washington Bates, an early travel writer, visited Kaua'i in 1852. Bates enjoyed Kaua'i, traveling across the island, stopping for a leisurely trip up the Wailua River, just as many Kaua'i visitors do today.

Bates' mid-19th-century travelogue of the Hawaiian Islands is one of the earliest Hawai'i travel books. Interesting details of Kaua'i during its transition from an ancient kingdom to an island dotted with sugar cane plantations make the book a valuable source of historic information. Except for asides in quoting Byron and other English authors, Bates' experiences as a Kaua'i traveler are noteworthy.

Of special interest is the writer's interaction with such famous Kaua'i figures as Deborah Kapule, who in her youth was the queen of Kaumuali'i, Kauai's last king; and in her dotage, the progenitor of Kaua'i's visitor industry, with her friendly hospitality at an inn at Wailua, near the site of the Coco Palms Resort.

During Bates' sojourn, the United States was considering the annexation of Hawai'i, a fact which he considered in writing the book. His detailed account, written for an American audience, described agriculture especially well, including coffee-growing and silkworm-farming at Hanalei.

The drawback to the book is a steady stream of illusions to classical and English poetry and a bit too much of rah-rah American flag-waving. He tells of a Fourth-of-July trip up the Nāwiliwili Stream: "a few American citizens gliding along beneath the ever-glorious beacon of true empire—the 'stars and stripes!'"

THE FIRST VILLAGE of any importance after leaving Lihue is Wailua (two waters). I was informed it was the property of Kapule—better known by her baptismal name Deborah—an ex-queen, and formerly the consort of Kaumualii, the last king of this island, who died at Honolulu in 1824.

Wailua is a small and scattered village, located on either side of the river bearing the same title. The only interest it now retains is its having once been the abode of royalty. Every thing was going rapidly to decay. The canoes that were once occupied by her majesty an her friends I found rotting in a shed that stood near the banks of the stream. The only interest the natives seem to cherish is the cultivation of their taro plantations, and in taking care of their numerous fish ponds. It was difficult to conceive that the village had ever been honored with a "royal presence."

Having ranged among the decaying dwellings, I entered the old building used by the villagers as a house of divine worship, and exchanged a few solitary words of compliment with the girls and women—for the uncomplimentary men returned with nothing but significant grunts and sundry gesticulations—I began to make preparations to ascend the river. It was with a keen sense of disappointment that I learned that the old queen Kapule, the steady friend, through many long years, of every visitor who had been there before me, had removed to the other side of the island. I had promised myself a sail up the beautiful stream in one of her large canoes, that had been formed out of solid log by a canoe-maker of a past generation. But as this gratification was impossible to procure, I submitted to the loss of it with becoming resignation.

A large canoe, however, was procured, with a sufficient number of men to paddle it, and a youth of eighteen, who spoke good English and Hawaiian. We had our little vessel launched just above the heavy sand-bar at the mouth of the stream, and quietly proceeded on our way. The mouth of the river is easily forded at low tide, but a few yards above this bar there is water enough to float a first class line-of-battle ship. The scenery up this river is second to none in the tropics. It wends its way through scores of taro plantations, orange and cocoa-nut trees, plantains and bananas. Its banks are densely clothed with the screw-pine, and the native mamaki and hau, the latter of which extend their picturesque branches until they droop and kiss the bosom of the gentle waters. Again, and on either hand, the unruffled bosom of the river, with the clearness of a vast mirror, reflects every object that crowds its banks with wild and romantic beauty. At every few yards the scene change, and the eye becomes delighted with the charm of a continuous panorama.

The Wailua River stands associated with the very genius of romance and superstition. Every object on the banks, every rock in the stream, and every cliff by which it is overlooked, has attached to it some legend of lovers, warriors, priest, and kings. About three miles above the village, and within a few rods of the left bank, there stands a singularly-shaped rock. Its form is a well-defined sugar-loaf, sixty feet high, and twenty across the base. The natives have invested it with every attribute which can constitute a ghostly character, an it is known to them by the name of Kamalau.

The origin of this ghost's existence—accepting the native legend as authority—is simply this:

At a very early period, the site occupied by this gray rock was, as it is now, a fine banana grove, sacred only to the gods. On numerous occasions, some daring natives, impelled by thievish propensities, appropriated the productions of this grove to their own use. At length the gods became highly incensed at the frequency and extent of these outrages, and a supreme council was held to devise measures to arrest and punish the aggressors. Kamalau, who was the presiding deity of this awful synod, was unanimously appointed supreme guardian of the sacred grove. He descended from a lofty cliff—the site of the council—on the other side of the stream, and, alighting on the spot he now occupies, transformed himself into the rock described above.

Kamalau had a favorite sister whose name was Kulai. Her bosom was filled with sorrow when she saw her brother forsake the home he had occupied so many ages. Not being able to sustain this wholesale desertion, she took a leap similar to that just taken by her brother. Whether it was owing to a want of greater elasticity, or to some other legitimate impediment, tradition does not specify: but the lovely and forsaken goddess fell into the river, and immediately became petrified for her presumption in daring to follow her brother. At this day, the superstitious natives take a peculiar pleasure in pointing the traveler's attention to this rock, submerged about two feet below the surface of the stream.

Tradition says that Kamalau succeeded in his guardianship of the sacred fruit. No more thieves ever again attempted to disturb its repose. The rock Kamalau stands today, and the banana grove, forming a dense mass of vegetation, that has continued to spring up from decayed matter during unnumbered generations, yet flourishes around it. No compensation however valuable, can induce a native to visit this spot during daylight, much less in the darkness of night.

A short distance above the *Ghost* is another rock, whose sharp summit just peers up above the placid bosom of the stream. It is termed the *Canoe-breaking Rock*, from the legend that, in early days, when this valley was densely peopled by savage warriors, the canoes of their enemies who came hither were dashed to pieces, and their rowers put to death...

Our canoe stopped at the foot of a hill two hundred feet high. It formed one of the sides of an ancient crater, the bottom of which was composed of a rich soil covering about fifty acres. Through this wild and deep ampitheatre the picturesque stream was gliding musically over its rocky bed. And in this spot, covered as it was with *taro* and various kinds of foliage, there were hundreds of wild ducks, which could be easily approached within shooting distance.

Climbing the steep banks, and crossing over an elevated plain about half a mile, accompanied by my guide, I at last reached the object of my search. For some distance before arriving at the falls, I saw clouds of vapor ascending toward the sky, and heard the solemn tones of their undying music. On reaching the brink of the abyss, the sublime scene bursts at once on the vision of the astonished and delighted visitor, and for a time chains him to the spot. As my eye endeavored to follow the huge sheet of water as it went hissing and foaming into the *hell of waters* below, my limbs trembled under me, and I instinctively clutched the limb of a solitary tree under which I stood.

After contemplating the scene before me in solemn silence for some minutes, I resolved on reaching the foot of the falls, where I should obtain a better view. Descending the rocky banks about a quarter of a mile below the cataract, and carefully climbing over a slippery masses of basalt which had tumbled down from the heights above, I at length found myself enveloped in the warm spray of the foaming torrent. At this spot the scene assumed a terrific sublimity. On the night previous to my visit a heavy rain had rapidly raised the waters of the river, and at this moment, the view was unusually grand and imposing. The brow of the cataract was sixty feet wide, the depth of water six feet, and its entire length of fall one hundred and eighty feet to the pool by which I stood. The basaltic rocks bounding this huge abyss rather overhung the vast masses of rock piled rudely below.

DEBORAH KAPULE

Soon after my arrival at Waimea I had the honor of an interview with Kapule, an ex-queen, and once the favorite wife of the last king of Kauai. She had removed her residences from Wailua, and taken up her permanent abode at this village, once the seat of her ancestors. I found her occupying a neat stone house, handsomely matted on the floor of the apartment; for there was only one, and that served for every purpose. There was something about it that indicated ease, comfort, and dignity. Although not so immense as formerly, Kapule's physical bulk was pretty solid. In height she was nearly six feet, and her weight between two and three hundred pounds. Her age was above sixty. Her countenance was the very seat of perfect good-nature, and her conversation was exceedingly cheerful. Her *maids of honor* were two or three of the handsomest girls I saw on the group. In 1824 she bore arms in the old stone fort against the insurgent warriors. She has always retained the reputation of kindness to foreigners—a report which her deportment toward myself amply sustained.

But Kapule's history has been an eventful one. When her husband had ceded this island to Kamehameha the Great, it was thought that she exercised too much influence over him. By royal authority he was admonished to put her away; but she was his favorite wife, an his heart clung to her with an intense affection, an the order was disregarded. Soon after the cession of the island, the conqueror was summoned to the world of spirits. The imperious Kaahumanu was almost inconsolable at the loss of her royal husband. Suddenly she bethought herself of the King of Kauai. He was the handsomest man on the group, and his own son ranked next with him in this particular. But the bereaved woman was a queen! So she sent an order to Kauai for the king and his son to await her pleasure at her royal apartments in Honolulu. They obeyed the summons, and on the 9th of October, 1821, both fate and son were secured to her conjugal bed by the tie of marriage! Subsequently she was expelled from the Church for an indulgence which would have been legitimate had not her liege lord been snatched way from her to share the couch of a royal paramour.

CAPTAIN COOK'S LANDING PLACE

About a mile west of Waimea village is the spot where the first English boat landed from Cook's expedition. It is opposite a couple of cocoa-nut trees, which were pointed out to me by the natives as the only memorial of that event. But on such a spot, and strictly in keeping with the surrounding scenery, they seemed to be the most fitting monuments. I first saw them at the hour of noon, when the sun was at the hottest, and shedding an ocean of light on the fair sand beach. Regardless of the crowd of natives that surrounded me, and of the noon-day hour, I walked along the same shore, and bathed in the same clear waters that had witnessed the landing of the distinguished navigator seventy-five years ago! It was here that the Hawaiians first saw the face of a white man; here, that they looked upon him as a god. Little did Cook think, at that moment, that he would find a grave on the shores of this far-distant archipelago.

Kumalu

The estate called Kumalu, one side of which is bounded by the Falls of Wailua, is, in point of beauty, surpassed by none on the group. It is located immediately between the junction of the Kukemakau and Koheo Rivers. The commodious dwelling-house stood on the very brink of the crater formed valley I have already referred to, and behind it was a garden covering two or three acres, beautifully interspersed with a large variety of flowers of every hue and odor; and on the gentle slopes that stretched away to the right of the mansion, handsome acacia groves were flourishing, with all the magnificent tinge which the climate of the tropics imparts to foliage.

But the principal charm of the estate, an especially of the mansion itself, was gone. The family that once occupied it had departed for a distant land; had left with it an eternal adieu. There was that about the spot which spoke of that family, and seemed to whisper that they had but just gone on a neighboring visit. And yet there were gentle memorials that told the stern truth—that from this enchanting abode—this Elisium in miniature—that lovely family had gone forever...

...The then owner of it was Lieutenant Turner, an English gentleman. He had purchased it entire for the small sum of $4,050—an immense sacrifice to its former proprietor, Mr. Brown, also an Englishman. The estate contained one thousand acres. It had formerly been conducted for the support of the dairy business, and Mr. Turner designed following the business of his predecessor...

◈ ◈ ◈

XVIII. PRINCEVILLE AND R.C. WYLLIE

PRINCEVILLE'S VICTORIAN BEGINNING

Princeville is a tableland set at the center of Kaua'i's north shore. Majestic ocean and mountain views, two world-class golf courses, luxurious homes, a world-class hotel and vacation accommodations make it a leading resort in Hawai'i.

Princeville and the life of Scot Robert Crichton Wyllie, a foreign minister of the Hawaiian kingdom, are forever entwined. Wyllie founded Princeville in 1860, setting in motion an ongoing story of development of one man's dream amidst incredible beauty. Wyllie's dream continues to draw those with similar goals—a luxurious life in paradise.

Wyllie's life story is one of the most interesting of all the characters that were drawn to Hawai'i in the nineteenth century. He was advisor and host to Hawaiian monarchs, prominent Victorian visitors and early Kaua'i pioneers from Europe and America.

Had Wyllie's grand plantation along the Hanalei River succeeded, the face of the north shore would be quite different today. Unwisely trying to profitably grow coffee and sugar on lands ideal for taro patches ruined Wyllie's venture, keeping the population of the Halele'a District—the House of the Rainbows in Hawaiian—limited to its long-time Hawaiian families, early Chinese merchant families, adventurous Western settlers and missionaries, rather than the plantation villages that grew up around mills across Hawai'i.

"I NEVER SAW such a romantically beautiful spot in all my life time. Were I forty years younger . . . I would throw the Foreign Office with all its musty papers, into the King's hands, and spend the remainder of my life here."

So proclaimed Robert Crichton Wyllie, the founder of Princeville at Hanalei, as he began building his Kaua'i retreat there in 1860. Then the powerful Foreign Minister of the Hawaiian kingdom, the thin, aging Scot longed to recapture his lost youth through this idealistic project, which also entailed constructing what he hoped would be the most successful sugar mill in all Hawai'i.

Wyllie's Honolulu home was known as Rosebank and set in a lovely spot in the verdant valley of Nu'uanu above the bustling port of Honolulu. But, like many successful men, Wyllie had a dream. And into his dream he brought King Kamehameha IV, his wife Queen Emma and their young son Prince Albert Edward Kauikea'ouli, a dark-eyed two-year-old and the pride of the Hawaiian kingdom. During a visit by the royal couple Wyllie grandly named his new estate Princeville after the young prince and set off on his quixotic quest.

The land selected for Wyllie's north shore Kaua'i plantation faces perhaps the grandest backdrop in all Hawai'i. A spectacular view of the mountains of Hanalei ringing crescent-shaped Hanalei Bay flows naturally into the majestic forms of Mount Makana, a ridge best known to filmgoers as Bali Hai in the musical *South Pacific*.

The Princeville estate was pieced together from holdings of rich bottom land along the meandering Hanalei River and from flat grazing lands on the plateau above and east of the river. Wyllie's design included a magnificent estate home and a world-class sugar mill to be bought and imported all the way from Glasgow, Scotland.

Some of the land reportedly was sold by John Kellett, an old hand on the Hanalei River who had come from England years before and married a Hawaiian woman of Hanalei. The couple's home on the rise between the river and the plateau became a gathering place for visitors, including Wyllie and his guests. Kellett was known as a pilot along the rivermouth, too, plus he kept a warehouse for outgoing produce of the valley.

Rare etchings from Wyllie's era show the remains of a Russian Fort at Puʻupōā Point near where the Princeville Hotel now stands. The fort was a sister to the better-known and larger one at Waimea, and constructed by the infamous Dr. Schaffer, who planned to conquer Kauaʻi in the 1810's in the name of the Russian Czar. His plans were thwarted by Kauaʻi's last King, Kaumualiʻi, and the rough, mud-walled fort at Puʻupōā overtaken by Hawaiians from nearby Hanalei Valley.

Wyllie's vision for Princeville was a culmination of his life of seeking fortune and beautiful places. At birth, as at his death in 1865, he was squarely in the midst of court society. Born in Scotland in 1798, the son of a low-ranking lord, the tall, thin lad studied to be a doctor. However, upon turning 20 he departed from Scotland for good, embarking on a life sparked by a quest for the ideal and romantic.

After a misadventure in attempting to settle in Russia, he sailed to the South American port of Valparaiso, Chile. After two years of service in Chile as a doctor, a quest for riches made in the trading business of merchandise going around the Horn led to Wyllie moving up the coast to Lima, Peru, and becoming a successful merchant. He eventually moved on to Mazatlan, Mexico, where the Scot prospered, enabling him to return to Great Britain in 1830 a millionaire.

Wyllie settled in London, joining a counting house, and became a London clubgoer. However, a dozen years of London Victorian life was enough for him and he again left for the New World.

Returning to Mexico, he met Santa Ana, the Mexican general best known for his victory at the Alamo. There he dreamed up a proposal to purchase a sizeable piece of land near Sacramento, California, as a site for a British colony. The plan failed but, when Wyllie journeyed back to Mazatlan, he met General William Miller, a friend from his days in Chile who was now to be the British consul general in Hawai'i.

Wyllie entered Hawai'i as Miller's aide, arriving in Honolulu in February 1844. The United States, France and Great Britain were then eyeing Hawai'i as a colony or protectorate, and diplomats were busy wooing Kamehameha III. When Miller was dispatched to Tahiti, Wyllie became the British proconsul.

The Hawaiian court quickly took to the adventurer. His British heritage also helped. A lingering, idealistic view of Great Britain by the Hawaiian royalty, a carryover from the visits by Captain James Cook and Captain George Vancouver, the first western leaders to visit Hawai'i, made Wyllie a symbolic link to the British monarchy. Wyllie introduced court protocol to the Hawaiian monarchs and suggested creating links with European royals.

One of Wyllie's most important suggestions was to create agricultural societies to diversify Hawai'i's economy away from the waning business of providing supplies to whaling ships. This plan included Hanalei's rich lands, where he wanted to establish "the great business place on this island," according to the diary of Lucy Wilcox, the matriarch of the Wai'oli missionary family at Hanalei.

Wyllie discovered Hanalei on a passage across the Kaua'i Channel aboard one of the infrequent inter-island schooners of the early 1850's. His first view of Hanalei's towering mountains and cascading waterfalls from the railing of the brig eased his wandering spirit; he had found the earthly paradise that had eluded him on four continents. Wyllie set his heart and part of his fortune on making Halele'a (the "House of the Rainbows," as the Hanalei District was then known) his hideaway from the rigors of city life and his last resting place.

His first step was to secure the lease on coffee lands in Hanalei Valley owned by early settler Godfrey Rhodes. To run the plantation, Wyllie hired Godfrey Frederick Wundenberg, a German who had settled in the 1840's at Hanalei. Two years later Wyllie bought out Rhodes' financial interest in the land and added plantation owner to his long list of titles.

Alternate problems of drought and floods in the 1850's led Charles Titcomb and other coffee growers in the verdant valley to abandon their crops and turn to growing sugar; Wyllie followed suit. Seeing the need for a mill to process his sugar, Wyllie sent off to his homeland to obtain the state-of-the-art machinery.

While waiting for the equipment to arrive from the industrial-age factories of Glasgow, Wundenberg oversaw the construction of a towering brick smokestack that rose 110 feet above the east bank of the Hanalei River. He also acquired a fleet of 11 scows to bring the cane from the growing fields deep in the valley down the river to the mill, which was located about midway between the river's mouth and the current Hanalei Bridge.

The price for the completed mill alone exceeded $40,000—enough money to buy all of Hanalei in those days—and it was the wonder of its age across the entire kingdom. Instead of a team of laborers, a conveyor belt carried the raw cane into the factory. Heavy, finely tuned rollers efficiently extracted the juice, and the bagasse waste was carried out again by conveyor, saving hours of manual labor.

Titcomb, along with the other sugar planters in the valley, realized after harvesting several crops that Hanalei was too wet for the sun-loving cane. Selling his 750 acres in Hanalei Valley to Wyllie for $29,000 in the early 1860's, he moved his operation east, founding Kīlauea town and the Kilauea Plantation.

Wyllie disregarded Titcomb's decision to move and instead expanded his sugar-growing operations, wistfully naming Titcomb's acreages "Emmaville," after his departed king's widow.

Princeville Plantation was further expanded in 1863, bringing it to the size that it is today, by adding *kuleana* made up of *taro* fields at Kalihi Wai and Kalihi Kai, the present-day 'Anini.

In spite of his sizeable investments in land and commercial buildings, Wyllie never built his own house at Princeville, but preferred to rent half of Lanihuli, John Kellett's home located on the hill above the Hanalei River.

Lanihuli became a second home for the diplomat-cum-sugar planter, and he placed Koka, a Chinese steward, there to care for the many off-island guests who visited remote Hanalei while Wyllie was occupied with court business in Honolulu. The guests included an overflow from his diplomatic and aristocratic contacts—travelers, celebrities, painters, musicians, archaeologists and scientists known to have visited him at Rosebank. Wyllie's estate became a quiet, peaceful retreat for the upper crust.

An account found in the July 1861 issue of the Hawaiian-language newspaper *Hae Hawaii* offers a look at the infusion of royal life Wyllie brought to the isolated Hanalei District he loved. Written by his plantation manager's 13-year-old daughter, Josephine, the account tells of a celebration held on May 20 of that year: "At Mr. Wyllie's request, father had a big celebration in honor of the little Prince of Hawaii's fourth birthday. . .The celebration consisted of a parade of two hundred Hawaiian men and women on horseback dressed alike, the men in red and white shirts and blue pants, and the women in red and yellow pau's and maile *leis*. They rode through the valley, crossed the river and rode to the top of the hill, where a feast and games had been prepared for them and in which the family joined. In the evening the large bon fires were lighted in the low lands, and on the hill tops, making a fine display and discharging bombs which resembled cannonading."

The arrival of Lady Jane Franklin, the widow of Northwest Passage explorer Sir John Franklin of England, was cause for a grand celebration the year after Princeville was named, and 60 years of bachelorhood nearly came to an end for Wyllie, a life-long avoider of commitment to anything but his investments and his kingdom, when Lady Jane visited Lanihuli.

Several years before her visit, Wyllie had noted his feelings about women in one of his voluminous journals, "For what are called fine and fashionable Ladies, I have always liked them better as Partners for a Waltz, than as Partners under the same roof for life."

But a spark was struck inside Wyllie, perhaps for the first time, and his desire for a partner for his last days heightened when the 69-year-old, tiny, gray-haired noblewoman arrived in Honolulu. He insisted that she and her niece, who was traveling with her, cross the channel to Hanalei and stay with him at Princeville to share in his glory there.

Following an excursion to view the volcanoes on the Big Island, Wyllie booked passage for the ladies and himself. They were met by Wundenberg, who paddled out to the bay in a long boat to pick them up. The burly German rowed the trio upstream to a landing shaded by weeping willow trees situated below Kellett's hillside house.

Walking past whitewashed, red-roofed plantation manager houses and across a wide lawn dotted with blooming orange trees and fragrant tropical flowers, Lady Jane came upon a small metal memorial to a sailor who had sought her long-lost husband. The iron tablet's raised letters said: "Sacred to the Memory of WM. LUXFORD, Late Quartermaster of H.B.M. Ship Enterprise." The sailor had died at Hanalei in the winter of 1850 while his ship wintered following a search for Franklin in the Arctic.

For 12 days Lady Jane and her niece Sophie sojourned at Princeville, watching the sunsets over Mt. Makana, the ever-changing waters of the bay and the misty, mystical mountains that reach up beyond the valley. On a Sunday they ventured across the river to attend a service at the Wai'oli Mission conducted by Rev. Johnson and attended by Abner Wilcox and his son Albert, who would one day take over Wyllie's holdings at Princeville.

The aristocrats scoffed at the humble service offered by the New England missionaries, and Lady Jane suggested

Wyllie build an Episcopal chapel to go along with his dream estate. Wyllie promised a piece of land overlooking the bay known as the "Crow's Nest" to Lady Jane for the chapel, but after his death she was unable to find any documents fulfilling the grant.

After their short stay the women left Princeville, and Wyllie's life, forever. The aging Scot didn't forget the grand lady, though, and suggested to his king that she become ambassador to Japan, with the authority to negotiate a treaty with Hawai'i. He wrote Lady Jane, asking unsuccessfully for her portrait, and later had to hush a court rumor (which he admitted starting) that the two were to wed. Back in Honolulu, Wyllie turned again to his duties as foreign minister, never to see the love of the autumn of his life again.

Upon Wyllie's death on Oct. 19, 1865, at Rosebank, the threads of his holdings began to unravel. Having no direct heirs, Wyllie had willed his estate to his nephew Robert Crichton Cockrane, who had arrived by invitation three months before. The one hitch to the will was that Cockrane take the family name of Wyllie, which he readily did. The surviving Robert Wyllie took up residence at his late uncle's estate at Princeville and soon began delving into the books of his new-found fortune. He quickly realized that the impressive sugar mill was an extravagance built as a showpiece rather than as a wise investment. Hawaiian farmers also showed him that the climate of Hanalei was ideal for *taro* or rice, but too wet for commercial sugar-growing.

The titles to Princeville's lands, according to Mary Sophia Rice, whose family owned Lihue Plantation, were "encumbered with so many mortgages and prohibitions of selling that the inheritance was like coming to possession of a drove of elephants."

Young Wyllie became depressed over this rude awakening and, during a Saturday evening musicale at the Hanalei home of plantation manager John Low, he slipped away from a crowd of men and slit his throat. Remarkably, he lived through the suicide attempt, although Abner Wilcox recorded the wound as being wide enough to insert four fingers and a thumb.

A rider was sent at breakneck speed to Kōloa to fetch Dr. James Smith, and a whaleboat was dispatched to Honolulu for a doctor.

Young Wyllie regained consciousness and scribbled, "Oh! My poor mother, don't tell mother. Fix it up so she won't know." At the suggestion of Low, Wyllie hastily wrote a will in which he left Princeville, in equal shares, to his mother and to his fiancée, Ida von Pfister, of Honolulu. Dated "Princeville February 4, 1866," the blood-stained document carries a wavering signature that still illustrates his condition.

Dr. Smith and Rev. Johnson arrived, barely finding a pulse in Wyllie's arm. For three more days the 25-year-old man held on, at times rational, at times delirious. Finally, he died at 6:05 a.m. on Wednesday, and Dr. Smith wrote in his journal, "I pray I may never see another (such) case."

He is believed to be buried in an unmarked plot surrounded by an iron fence just west of the Wai'oli Meeting Hall at Hanalei. Along with him was buried the dream of his uncle—to build the family estate above the crystal waters of the bay.

Princeville Plantation was sold on Oct. 2, 1867, by S. N. Castle & Attorney, executors of Wyllie's will, to Elisha Allen, a judge for the Supreme Court of Honolulu. Still owing were two mortgages totaling $38,150. The vast estate, from Hanalei Valley to Kalihi Wai, sold for $40,050. It had cost Wyllie $200,000. Five years later Allen sold a one-eighth interest in the plantation to Captain John Low, who took over management. Several months later Allen further divided the plantation and incorporated Princeville in 1867.

Sugar was still Princeville's main product, with Honolulu's C. Brewer & Co. as agents, when a German, Carl Koelling, bought an interest in the plantation in 1889. He sold stock, forming the Hanalei Sugar Mill Company.

Unable to adjust to Hanalei's wet climate, the company failed in 1892 and was sold to Abner Wilcox's son Albert in 1895, in part to pay off C. Brewer's debt.

Albert Wilcox was able to acquire all of Princeville in 1899, when the Allen family sold out to him. He rented out the lower lands to Chinese rice growers and planted the upper lands in elephant grass for cattle ranching.

In 1916 Lihue Plantation bought Princeville Plantation from Wilcox, keeping it as a cattle ranch until Denver's Consolidated Oil and Gas bought it through its Eagle Development Corp. in 1969. Renamed Princeville Development Corp. and spun off as a publicly traded corporation, the development company has since gone through the hands of Australian investor Christopher Skase and his ill-fated Qintex empire. It is now owned in the majority by Suntory, the privately-held Japanese distiller.

Pushing ahead with Wyllie's grand dreams, a new Princeville Hotel offers elegant suites and rooms and an ambiance rivaling Europe's grander hotels. Guests from across the globe marvel at the combination of natural wonder and elegance that Wyllie envisioned over 130 years ago.

As happens to so many famous men in history, Wyllie's foresight and dreams became reality only after his death. His imagination and vision were the seeds that spawned today's fabulous resort and, indeed, Princeville is the commercial hub of the north shore.

The beautiful homes, exquisite hotel and condominiums, and expansive golf course are jewels in Wyllie's crown. Offering world-class amenities to international visitors and overlooking the still majestic lands and waters of the "House of the Rainbows," Princeville is Wyllie's dream come true.

❖   ❖   ❖

XIX. NI'IHAU
FROM A HAWAIIAN-POLYNESIAN VIEW

Ni'ihau *seems shrouded in mystery outside the island of* Kaua'i. *On Kaua'i the island is not so removed from daily life. The Hawaiian-speaking shoppers at local grocery stores at Waimea or Kekaha are probably from Ni'ihau, and fine Ni'ihau shell lei necklaces are displayed in shops across the island.*

However, learning more about the Hawaiian people of Ni'ihau is difficult. To gain an understanding of Ni'ihau—and its people, culture and past—Rerioterai Tava, a Tahitian woman raised on the mainland United States and now living on Kaua'i, and Moses Keale, a native Hawaiian from Ni'ihau, have written Niihau-Traditions of a Hawaiian Island. *The book describes, from an insider's viewpoint, life on the "Forbidden Island" of Ni'ihau.*

Tava and Keale introduce the reader to the simple, Hawaiian ways of Niʻihau, offering an overview of life past and present on the arid island located 17 miles due northwest from Kauaʻi's west side.

The authors succeed in writing an engrossing book that covers a subject that is fairly obscure. Presented from the viewpoint of the Hawaiian, with much oral and scattered written information collected on the island's place names, language and society, Niihau-Traditions of a Hawaiian Island *is considered by many to be the best single book on Niʻihau.*

FOR MORE THAN a century, the Hawaiian island of Niihau has been forbidden to outsiders. The owners are the Robinson family, descendants of the Sinclairs who originally purchased the island in 1864. Keeping the privacy of Niihau as a way to protect the Hawaiian lifestyles of the residents, the Robinson family has restricted visits over the years to an occasional invited guest, a few public officials and physicians. To add to the mystique of life there, the family will not grant any interviews to discuss aspects of life on Niihau. Most information about the people and their lifestyles has been gathered from Niihau residents themselves.

According to the 1980 census, there were 226 persons living on Niihau. Approximately two thirds of the residents are Hawaiian, comprising the largest colony of pure Hawaiians in the state. The remaining part-Hawaiian residents are a mixture of Japanese, Portuguese, Chinese or other ancestry. The Niihauans are free to travel to and from the island whenever they wish. What little information that outsiders have received suggests that the lifestyle of Niihau retains a special native Hawaiian spirit that resembles the rural Hawaii of a fading past.

The physical remoteness of Niihau from mainstream Oahu life contributes to this sense of time standing still. Situated 17.5 miles southwest of Kauai, Niihau is believed to be the oldest of the eight major islands in the Hawaiian chain—its age is estimated to be five to seven million years old. Seventh in size in the Hawaiian chain, it is relatively small-the island comprises seventy-two square miles and is approximately eighteen miles long and eight miles across at its widest point. It is shaped something like a foot. Of the island's 47,217 acres, 46,705 acres are privately owned. The state and federal government each own 256 acres of land, which was ceded either by presidential proclamation or governor's executive order. In 1983, the State Department of Taxation assessed the value of the entire island at $7.20 an acre.

The island of Niihau is a remnant of a once-substantial shield volcano. Geological evidence suggests that the volcano's summit was at a point about a mile or so east of the present island, and that the ocean eroded most of the ancient volcano peak, particularly from the east side. Some experts believe that the disappearance of much of the shield's eastern side was due to vertical faulting. Should this be true, a substantial portion of the volcano separated and slowly sank into the ocean, leaving only one side to form the low mountains that are on the east side of Niihau. Volcanic cones stand at each end of the island: Kawaihoa at the southern tip and Lehua, now an island, at the northern end. Both a'a and pahoehoe lava are found on Niihau. Niihau rises 13,000 feet above the ocean floor, the highest point above sea level is 1,281 feet at Paniau, although seventy-eight percent of Niihau is less than 500 feet in elevation.

Niihau has a coastline of 200 miles, of which 110 miles are prone to tidal-wave action. The coastline terrain can be quite dramatic-there are three miles of sea cliffs of 1,000-foot elevation or more. The fringing reef to the north and south of the island is, in many areas, exposed at the sea's surface. Some of these limestone masses are residuals of large size that were islands when the reef was growing around the island. Beaches on the east shore collect ocean debris and are dotted with glass Japanese fishing "balls," or floats—now a rarity elsewhere.

An extensive geological survey of Niihau conducted in 1921 by Norman E. A. Hinds indicated a significant submerged mountain and a bench or reef ledge. Dr. Hinds received permission from Niihau's owner, Aubry Robinson, to conduct an eight-day study of the island, collecting fossils and making offshore soundings. From these studies he concluded that the mountain forming Niihau is mostly submerged, with its base 2,000 to 2,500 fathoms deep (a depth which makes further study difficult). Judging from the present sea cliffs, he suggested that Niihau must have originally been forty miles in diameter; today, wind, rain, wave erosion and downward faulting have reduced the island to less than thirty-two miles in diameter. More than half of the eastern six miles of land is now also submerged. Soundings conducted 1.5 miles off the southern point of Niihau showed a submerged reef ledge forty fathoms deep. Another reef shelf sixty feet below sea level was found to extend eastward six more miles.

The land features of the island are also diverse. There are essentially four types of geography, each in equal parts: mountain range, pastureland, marginal pastureland that is fertile only during the rainy months and sand, rocks and ponds. The uplands and most of the pastureland are covered with five feet of rich red dirt, which is common in old volcanic lands. The southwest coast has cemented sand dunes up to 150 feet high. Of Niihau's seventy-three square miles, sixty-nine are dry land or temporarily and partially covered by water. Niihau has an arid climate. The high mountains of Kauai block rain clouds from reaching Niihau. In addition, the island's low elevation causes little precipitation. In fact, the island gets so little rain that there are no permanent forests. Despite the aridity, there are 3.4 square miles of permanent water, lakes and reservoirs. Niihau also has the largest natural lake in the state, Lake Halulu, which comprises 182 acres. A U.S. Geological Survey in the 1920s documented the presence of about fifty freshwater punawai. There may be others that are hidden or secret.

Puuwai is Niihau's principle town or settlement. The original name of the settlement was Kauanaulu. However, when another church was opened at Kauanaulu, the name of the town was changed to Puuwai Aloha o ka Ohana. With time, it was shortened to simply Puuwai.

The manner of life on Niihau today has not changed much since the turn of the century—a unique rural setting has been preserved that might well be envied by some discontents of modern life. Life simply moves more slowly on Niihau. It was believed by many in the days of old and remains true today: Niihauans are superior in many ways to other Hawaiian islanders. They are hard working, sober and well-taken care of. Idleness is rare, and free time is spent sharing life with friends and family. They live off the produce of the land, relying only on a few store-bought foods. Transportation is by bicycle or walking; sometimes horses, which are owned by the Robinsons, are used by the cowboys. The serenity of this island paradise is disturbed only by the frequent screeching of peacocks.

> *Puuwai kau mai iluna, hooheno ia nei e ka ua*
> *naulu –*
> "Looking up to Puuwai, caressed by the rain of
> the naulu wind."

The town of Puuwai is a picturesque scene of small houses, quiet roads and the church. The homes are widely scattered throughout the town amid large *kiawe* trees, cactus and rocks. There is a short main street approximately three-quarters of a mile in length. Many of the homes are more than 1,000 feet apart from each other. Each home is surrounded by a rock wall that forms a private yard, which is used mostly to keep out the sheep and pigs. Many of the rock walls are covered with night-blooming cereus, *pikake* and bougainvillea. Most yards are cleared of rocks and cactus. Most water for daily use is obtained by catchment in 1,000-gallon wooden or concrete storage tanks.

All of the people on Niihau today speak English, but since Hawaiian is their first language, they often prefer to speak the language of their forefathers. There are no Hawaiian textbooks, so children learn Hawaiian by studying the Bible and singing Hawaiian church hymns at home. By studying the Bible, they learn the symbolic phrasing and poetry of the Hawaiian language. A favorite pastime of the children is trying to stump each other by reciting phrases from the Bible. The others must try to guess not only the chapter, but the verse. The months of the year on Niihau, as they are said in Hawaiian, reflect the differences between this Hawaiian island and all others:

Ikuwa	January	Kaelo	April
Welehu	February	Kaulua	May
Makalii	March	Nana	June

Welo	July	Hinaiaeleele	October
Ikiiki	August	Hilina	November
Kaaona	September	Hilinehu	December

In the middle of the town stands the only church on Niihau. It sits majestically among large, old *kiawe* trees and is surrounded by a stone wall covered with night-blooming cereus, with a quaint cemetery on the church grounds. The schoolhouse is within the churchyard. The influence of Christianity on Niihau lifestyle has been pervasive for the last one hundred years. In the nineteenth century, Francis Sinclair decreed that everyone on Niihau would go to church—even visitors. He went so far as to keep meticulous track of those who did not attend church and then punished them!

Sundays on Niihau are truly reserved for the Lord and observed as a day of rest. Early in the morning the church bells toll the hour at Iubile Church, and the rest of the island is quiet. During the service, some of the most beautiful choral singing in the Hawaiian chain can be heard. The voices are for the most part untrained, but their harmony and unrestrained quality are reminiscent of choral music heard throughout the South Pacific. The unique hymns heard on Niihau, however, are known only to the islanders. Their hymnal, *Buke Himeni Hawaii*, can be purchased only on Niihau, and there is no music notation, only lyrics. Melodies of familiar church hymns are used, with the islanders' own words.

Fishing, games and many other daily activities stop on the Sabbath. On Sunday evenings, the entire island listens to the "Gentle Moke" radio program from Kauai, which features Hawaiian music, talks, messages to Niihauans from off-island and a half hour of religious music.

A typical weekday on Niihau begins at five in the morning. The entire family participates in the morning ohana prayer service before the father leaves for work. Breakfast usually consists of the famous "Hawaiian pancakes" made from flour, water and sugar, or coffee and Saloon Pilot crackers and leftovers from the night before. Being a patriarchal family, much attention is given to the needs of the husband or father.

The Niihau man, usually dressed in jeans and boots, enjoys his work even if it takes from dawn to midnight. A work day is not measured by an eight-hour day, but rather until a task is done. Boys begin working at fifteen or sixteen years of age. On an average, men work three days a week, mostly as paid cowboys for the Robinson ranch. The rest of their time is spent in gardening, fishing and similar work. If there is no work on Niihau, the men, sometimes with their families, can go to the Robinsons' business operations on Kauai. On Kauai, the workers live in camp-like areas called Pakala, Kapalawai, Kaawanui and Kekupua.

The men of Niihau make the most-desired charcoal in the state, so much so that supplies fall behind demand. Cutting down the kiawe trees, the men split them into short logs. The logs are put into large tile ovens, where they burn to coals and remain until cool, a process of several days. Once cool, the charcoal is broken into chunks and bagged for commercial use. The smaller chips are also gathered, bagged and sold for gardening purposes.

The women of Niihau attend to all of the usual household chores while raising the children in the old Hawaiian way. Children are obedient, and when not in school, they attend to their own chores as well as helping with the cooking and cleaning. As soon as children are able, they are given small duties and responsibilities. Great respect is shown by the younger generation for their parents and elders. When there are guests, the children sit to the side, often helping to serve the visitor. They are silent until spoken to, as was the old way. Usually the head of the house and the guest are served first, with the women and children eating later. Although the housewife has a kerosene stove in her kitchen, at times such as luau and parties, much of the cooking is often done in the traditional style-outside in the *imu*. The family often enjoys *kalua* pigs, sweet potatoes and other Hawaiian foods. Considerable flour is brought to the island, along with a few other food and grocery staples such as poi, salmon, Saloon Pilot crackers, taro, rice and soap. Few green vegetables are available on Niihau, so the housewife must order them from the store a week in advance.

At certain times of the year, the women will take the younger children to the beach for the day to search for the prized *pupu o Niihau*, the famous Niihau shells. Off-season, women spend a good deal of the day sorting and piercing shells, and making shell leis to sell. The additional income helps supplement the family budget. The majority of Niihau women dress in the traditional muumuu, although some women wear pants. There is no "women's movement" on Niihau—women serve to please their husbands and appear happy and content with their roles. When their husbands return home in the evenings after work, the women and children are there to greet them.

At the end of the typical day, the Niihau family is once again together. Making their own entertainment, the guitars and ukuleles are tuned and the songs begin. Before retiring for the night, the *ohana* prayers are repeated.

There are no airports, taxis, liquor, hotels, jails, post offices, cars, highways, bridges, harbors, shopping centers, tall buildings, theaters, beauty parlors or mongoose on

Niihau. All mail to the residents of Niihau is sent to Makaweli, Kauai. There is, however, electricity, and politics. Niihauans are conscientious voters with 166 residents registered to vote in the one voting precinct. Traditionally a conservative Republican district, Niihauans voted Democratic in 1982 for the first time in their history.

Other signs of the outside modern world are becoming apparent. When Niihauans visit Kauai to see *ohana*, or to market their exquisite shell leis, they get a taste of change. Through their ingenuity, the men of Niihau have found other ways to tap into the "luxury" of things electric. They go off-island to seek motors from old lawn mowers. These are connected to alternators for electric lights. Solar energy lights some homes. Televisions are also powered by the home-made generators. Stereo radios and tape recorders connect families to the music and news from other islands. Some homes even contain such modern conveniences as sliding glass doors, louvered windows, wall paneling and carpeting. There are also five trucks on the island used for ranch work. Some of the inhabitants smoke tobacco, although the Robinson family has always tried to discourage the habit. Niihau is arid, and a serious fire could mean the destruction of the island plus no one wants to see cigarette stubs littering the land.

Settled into their island home with these few changes, Niihauans are healthy and happy. They are rarely motivated to gain more material possessions beyond their basic needs. They have no worries about paying the mortgage on time; their homes are provided by the Robinson family, in keeping with an agreement with Kamehameha V at the time of the sale of the island to the family.

It is little surprise, then, that the Niihauans' most outstanding trait is friendliness with a smile and a handshake, a heritage they can be justly proud of. Though they may seem shy to outsiders, the islanders truly understand and express the aloha spirit and the ohana tradition, living and caring for one another. To a Niihauan, the entire island is ohana, and their usual greeting is the traditional Hawaiian sniffing kiss, touching nose to nose. Indeed, as one walks along the road passing their homes, voices call out from the dwellings, "*Hele mai ai*". It is a greeting to share the bounty that is the blessing of the land, the family and the spirit.

XX. THE CHINESE OF KAUA'I
OVER 200 YEARS OF ISLAND HISTORY

The heritage of the Chinese of Kaua'i dates back to the first decades following Captain Cook's discovery of the island in 1778. The Chinese were the first migrant workers to arrive on Kaua'i's shores during the sugar cane boom in the mid-1800's and brought a diverse and interesting Asian culture to the island.

Today, though as a percentage of the population their numbers may be small, descendants of Chinese immigrants of the nineteenth century continue to play leading roles in Kaua'i politics, real estate and many businesses. Some of Kaua'i's most renowned artists, such as the late Ruben Tam, are of Chinese heritage.

Following my graduation from the University of Hawai'i, I was fortunate to have spent time in Taiwan with my

Mandarin Chinese-speaking sister and her husband, who as the son of an American medical researcher had spent much of his youth in Taipei. My sojourn in Taiwan—which included surfing trips to unexplored beaches and coastlines, plus an acting role in a Kung Fu movie as a dark-suited drug smuggling haole *villain—combined with a stopover in Hong Kong gave me a greater appreciation for the Chinese culture. Credit must also go to Li Ling Ai, a close family friend and author of the Hawai'i classic* Life Is For A Long Time *about her life as the daughter of Hawai'i's first Chinese doctors, and as the former Asian representative for Robert Ripley. Her discourse on Chinese culture and ways under a shade tree on a hot summer afternoon in New Jersey was particularly enlightening.*

I'D BEEN IN Taiwan for months, living in a hillside home north of Taipei, which was my base for touring the Chinese island nation. The visit was my introduction to Asia, made in the years after my graduation from the University of Hawai'i, a time when I was free to travel the world.

High in the inland mountains of central Taiwan, I sipped a cup of tea laced with home-brewed rice whiskey and thought about how little I really knew about the Chinese of Hawai'i. It was spring and the air was warm for all the altitude. Taiwanese aborigines gently stroked the blond streaks in my hair with curiosity, debating in their ancient tongue what the *kwai-lo* (foreign devil) had done to deserve such adornment.

The mountain tribe had some Cantonese blood in their veins, but mostly they were descended from a clan of canoe voyagers from Southeast Asia, first cousins of a people group that had roamed the Pacific from Fiji to Tahiti, from New Zealand to Hawai'i—the Polynesians.

And what I was gleaning were insights into how the Chinese, people of the heavenly Middle Kingdom (the only civilized nation on earth, according to their sages), interacted with native inhabitants on an island to which they migrated in search of a better life.

This encounter parallels the story of the Chinese who first arrived in Hawai'i some 200 years ago. How apt that this arrival came in 1789, during the "Year of the Rooster," a lunar year symbolized by a loud, fighting sign that foretold the two centuries of struggle and change the Chinese would undergo in Hawai'i.

Those first arrivals were kinsmen of the Cantonese who ventured to Taiwan in the 1500's, and they sailed through the Sandwich Islands about a decade after famed circumnavigator Captain James Cook of Great Britain opened the islands up to the western world. Working their passages on a British schooner as sailors, cooks and carpenters, the first 40-or-so men of South China to lay eyes on Hawai'i were on their way to the Pacific Northwest, contracted to build a ship and, while there, hoping to gain a fortune through fur trading on their own time.

About 18 months before this very crew sailed, a young Hawaiian king of Herculean build walked their dusty, dirt-packed streets, perhaps the strangest human apparition to appear in China since the pale Venetian, Marco Polo, trekked and wrote his way across the massive empire in the late thirteenth century.

Standing head, shoulders and feathered cape above the thousands of Chinese peasants in the market of the Kwantung Province coastal city of Macao, the *ali'i* Kaiana of Kaua'i proudly strutted along, clearing the way with a tall, sturdy hardwood spear probably honed from a Kōke'e *koa* tree. The year was 1787 and the handsome, young chief, cloaked in a brilliant red and yellow cape fabricated from thousands of feathers plucked from Kauaʻi forest birds, was a stranger in a strange land, the first native of Hawaiʻi to ever encounter the people of China.

Kaiana sailed to Canton aboard the *Nootka*, a trading ship captained by John Meares of England, who plied the China fur trade from America's northwest to the Orient and across to South America. Promised passage to Pretane (Great Britain), the Kauaʻi chief was stranded for months in the South China province from where, decades later, thousands of migrant workers would sail, seeking their destinies in the sugar fields of Hawaiʻi.

Never deviating from the powerful, but kindly, demeanor that so clearly marked those of royal blood in Hawaiʻi, Kaiana became known by every class of people in the thriving ports of Macao, Canton and what is now Hong Kong.

During a sojourn in Hong Kong, I walked those same streets Kaiana had trod. A world away from the quiet mountains of central Taiwan, I was shopping at midnight in antique shops sandwiched together amidst the flashing red and green neon of Kowloon. My quest was for a *fung shui* instrument, a compass-like Chinese tool used by Taoist soothsayers in geomancy to foretell the most propitious direction in which to travel, or to align the rooms of a new home.

The glitter, crowds and earthiness on the streets of Hong Kong was a magnification of the stereotypical Chinatown—a lens through which most people view the Chinese. I recalled walking through Honolulu's Chinatown during a Chinese New Year's celebration and, as a youngster, gawking at the herbal shops and eating *wor gau gee* for a late dinner in lower Manhattan's teeming Mott Street district. Now, after years in Hawaiʻi, and a half year among the Chinese in their native land, I was beginning to see beyond this flashy surface, picking out the meanings of Chinese characters, ordering a simple dinner in my broken Chinese and understanding some of the sources of the traditions, and business acumen, that lay beneath the century-long history of Hawai'i's Chinese.

Native Chinese English-language students also opened my eyes to the many subcultures of China. "All *kwai-lo* look the same to us," they told me, echoing the cultural myopia of most westerners. They pointed out that although Chinese read a similar written language made up of thousands of characters, their spoken languages vary from province to province. And, they admonished me, there are many social and physical differences between the Punti, Hakka, and Tuichow or Hoklo—the people groups from which Hawai'i's Chinese descended.

The first Chinese settler in Hawai'i was probably a craftsman from one of these peoples who jumped ship along with English boatswain John Young (later, a naval advisor and favorite at the court of Kamehameha the Great).

Although the fortune of this first "China Man" in the Islands is uncertain, the lasting influence of China in Hawai'i came as a result of the insatiable desire of Chinese merchants for the aromatic white heart of sandalwood, the small-leafed tree found in the highlands of Kaua'i that became the symbol both of great wealth and of great loss in the Sandwich Islands in the early nineteenth century.

The first cargo of sandalwood was probably taken to Canton as early as 1790, but the earliest recorded shipment came from the forests of Kaua'i in 1792, when Captains Kendrick and Douglas sailed with two shiploads. Rebuffed in Canton by traders who refused the yellowish *nalo*, or false sandalwood, which they had unwittingly transported thousands of miles, they returned to Hawai'i angry, but wiser.

The captains soon educated the Hawaiians about which trees to select, and trade boomed. Asian artisans—as they still do in Taipei, Hong Kong and other capitals of Southeast Asia—carved the richly scented wood into idols, boxes, temple carvings, and from its oil made medicines and perfumes. Today, bedframes and other furniture made of rare Hawaiian sandalwood are priceless collector's items.

The trade with China sparked the economy of Hawai'i, turning it from a barter-based system in which a fisherman would trade his catch for *taro* to a mercantile world that dealt in hard cash.

The strong central government that Kamehameha the Great established through military might was funded with duties, customs and port fees levied on returning traders, but the decision by Kamehameha and other *ali'i* to order their retainers on all the islands to collect the perfumed wood as a tithe undermined Hawaiian society, setting in motion a wave of change that was as horrible as it was rapid. Believing that the *mana* of the gods was now also measured by possession of western goods, the royalty filled warehouses with brocade cloth and other trade items from China purchased with thousands of piculs of sandalwood.

Irreparable damage was done to the virgin forests and native plants of the Hawaiian Islands by the indiscriminate felling of sandalwood trees. The closely knit *ohana* system of food-gathering in rural villages also suffered as men were pulled from their *taro* patches and fishing canoes and forced to hike into the chilly uplands to gather the valuable timber. Many died in Kaua'i's damp Kōke'e forest, and many villages experienced a tremendous disruption as their social structure and fragile ecology was upset forever.

Meanwhile, in South China, returning Chinese adventurers painted a romantic picture of the Hawaiian

Islands and its abundance of sandalwood. Soon, in the Chinese mind, Hawai'i became the mythical Tan Hueng Shan, or the Sandalwood Mountains, a name still in use.

As in any seaport of the early 1800's, daring sailors were easily recruited for voyages to brave new worlds, and this rosy picture of the islands, as well as the increasing trade between the South China ports and Hawai'i, slowly began to draw a few of the Cantonese as entrepreneurs to its faraway shores. The "China Man," with his long, black queue of hair, large round hat, Asian-cut clothing, quiet ways and rice-based cuisine, became a common figure in the ports of Honolulu and Lahaina. Defying an imperial edict from faraway Peking, these early arrivals included would-be merchants who were among the Chinese who started general stores and restaurants from Bali to Brazil. They became the forerunners of colonies of overseas Chinese, or *wah kiu*, rebellious fortune seekers who struck out to distant points, trading their secure spot in the Middle Kingdom for a free and independent business elsewhere.

Daily life in Hawai'i today is flavored with the language of these early adventurers. To communicate with outsiders, the *Pakes* (or "father's older brother," as the Hawaiians called the Chinese immigrants) developed their own strain of English, called pidgin. The word is a corruption of "business," and pidgin English was originally used by the Chinese merchants to communicate in their polyglot dealings throughout the Pacific. Subsequently spiced with Japanese, Filipino and Portuguese expressions, pidgin English has become the "local" language.

A nameless, early Chinese immigrant is credited with the first try at manufacturing sugar from native Hawaiian cane. Though this attempt in 1802 on Lana'i failed, future Chinese settlers would bring the technology and know-how that would eventually put the Hawaiian sugar business on the map.

Driving past the tall, black lava rock chimney on the edge of Kōloa town that marks the site of Hawai'i's first successful sugar mill, I recall the days of schooners and Yankee merchants struggling to make a go of an infant industry. To the Chinese, the mill is but another milestone in a history of sugar cultivation that is centuries old in South China. The methods of milling and refining the tall green plant that Ladd & Co. tirelessly sought at Kōloa had been perfected centuries earlier by the *tong see*, or sugar masters, of South China. Introducing to Kōloa the closely-guarded secrets of this trade was Atai, a Chinese merchant who operated the Hung-tai Co. with a partner in Honolulu in the 1830's. Working with William French, a Yankee manager representing Ladd & Co., Atai used his connections in Kwantung to procure the tools needed for a Chinese sugar mill.

This cooperation proved beneficial to the Honolulu businessman who needed the Chinese techniques to develop the struggling industry and to the Chinese, who sought help in building their fortunes.

During this era, the thousand or so immigrants to Hawai'i found open acceptance from the Hawaiians. Many had some education and valuable skills. Those who intermarried with Hawaiian women were welcomed, and the industry of those who became merchants and sugar works gained them respect and social acceptance in the free-wheeling developing ports and sugar towns of the islands.

As time moved on, the ownership of Koloa Plantation passed to other men but the technical innovations perfected at Kōloa set the industry in the right direction. Within two decades, mills and plantations employing mostly Hawaiian field workers could be found from the Hāmākua Coast on the Big Island to the Hanalei Valley on Kauaʻi's northern shore. But with the Hawaiian population rapidly declining, and after it became apparent the Hawaiian men would be better *luna*, or field overseers, than laborers, growers turned to China and Southeast Asia to fill the desperate need for more workers.

The Royal Hawaiian Agricultural Society was chartered in 1850 to seek such overseas workers. The first large group of Chinese contract laborers came in 1852, when 200 men arrived from Hong Kong aboard the ship *Thetis*. The placement of this boatload of plantation workers in mills throughout the islands was a key turning point in the history of Hawaiʻi, the first major step in forming the multiracial society Hawaiʻi is today.

By 1866 there were 1,305 Chinese immigrants in Hawaiʻi. Unlike early arrivals, who had more latitude and perhaps a higher ranking in the distinct class system then prevalent in Hawaiʻi, the later group found a hard life of toil in the hot plantation fields. Their attachment to China and the Asian nation's traditions and way of life also set them apart, as many came to work for only a few years, saving their hard-earned pay to buy a home or field in China.

Looking back at the roots of many of today's successful physicians, bankers, landowners, educators and artists of Hawaiʻi descended from the first generation of Chinese immigrants, you will most likely find an incredibly hardworking ancestor. Besides toiling in the red earth of the cane fields, these honored forefathers also set up small businesses that they worked day and night, saving for the education of the eldest son and the future, and providing for large, growing families.

One of the most vivid and lasting symbols in Hawaiʻi

of the impoverished Chinese immigrant slaving to keep himself alive while saving his dollars toward his fortune is that of the *manapua* man. With a wooden yoke slung across his shoulders supporting buckets of warm and doughy half-balls of thick, white dumplings graced on top with a red Chinese character and stuffed with spiced pork fillings, the *manapua* man was the forerunner of today's lunch wagons and fast-food franchises.

Other immigrants took in laundry, opened restaurants, set up import businesses or took to the road as wandering peddlers. G.N. Wilcox, who made a fortune and gave away another through his Grove Farm plantation, recalled such traveling Chinese merchants of the 1860's.

"Since there was but the one store, they would get what they could carry, or take some little cart, and peddle their goods from place to place. When night came, they would put up at the best place they could find. You know the Hawaiians are very hospitable. The Chinaman would pick out the biggest house he could find and simply go there, and put up for the night . . . It was the peddlers who later started other stores on the island on sites leased from Hawaiians."

In addition to struggling to make a dollar, the immigrant workers also faced a growing animosity that peaked in the post-Civil War era, partly as a reaction to the "coolie trade" after a war aimed at freeing slaves, partly as a reaction during a job shortage in post-'49er-days California, and partly out of ignorance of the Chinese culture and a fear that Oriental civilization would supplant the western Polynesian society then in control.

This fear became law in the 1880's. Though some leaders in Hawai'i saw the Chinese as a benefit, as a race that would intermarry and bolster the rapidly dwindling number of Hawaiians and fill the labor force, the rulers of the Hawaiian kingdom initiated steps to control immigration, enforcing a federal law. The U.S. Chinese Exclusion Act of 1882 forcibly stopped the supply of Chinese immigrants, and plantations turned to recruiting their workers in Japan, the Philippines, Korea, Puerto Rico, Portugal, Russia, Germany, Scandinavia, and the South Seas Islands. This was another crucial turning point in the history of Hawaiʻi. Had China remained the main source of labor, the face of Hawaiʻi would be vastly different today, perhaps a land with a capital and people resembling Hong Kong.

As the waves of new workers began arriving in the declining years of the Hawaiian kingdom, some Chinese merchants and planters were moving up the ladder of society. Perhaps the most prominent Chinese of this era on Kauaʻi were the "rice kings" of Waimea and Kapaʻa.

Hee Fat and Wong Aloiau of Kapaʻa and Leong Pah On of Waimea lived in impressive palatial homes, married Hawaiian women, became friends of the Hawaiian royalty and accumulated fortunes and extensive landholdings by growing and trading rice, helping to make the industry second only to sugar for several decades. The successful merchant-growers were among the many Chinese rice farmers drawn to Kauaʻi by its rich soil, climate and abundant water supply. Their fortunes grew as the market for rice broadened in Hawaiʻi and the West Coast states in the days before railroads brought goods across the American continent. *Taro* patches were converted to rice paddies, water buffalo were imported from Asia, and hundreds of Chinese workers were recruited from South China to irrigate and work the paddies.

The Chinese laborers of this era have left lasting contributions to Kauaʻi. In the early 1900's, crews of Chinese coolies dug miles of water tunnels and strung power lines from deep in Wainiha Valley on the north shore to a power plant at Eleele; the result is a hydroelectric system that still serves Kaua'i.

Rapidly fading now, however, are the remnants of plantation houses turned into communal meeting halls with doorways surrounded by red planks decorated with greetings and proverbs in gold-leaf characters, and the temples simply decorated on the exterior but filled with ornate altars and red, burning candles lit to Taoist gods. Gone are the haphazardly thrown-together work camps, where gambling, drinking and opium smoking were vices to drain the hard-earned wages and decimate the small savings of workers hoping to return to their hometowns in China with a substantial grubstake.

A few of the meeting halls and temples, like Hop Hing in Lāwa'i (a temple linked to Kōloa's first Chinese settlers), are being carefully preserved today by the Kauai Museum, the Bishop Museum and Chinese societies throughout the state. But the power and influence the sites once held for a sizeable portion of the islands' population is forever gone.

Particularly influential in the Chinese plantation communities was the Hoong Moon or Three Dots Society, an ancient secret political and ritualistic society of China transplanted to the islands. Also known as triads, or gangs, the society was formed in the latter part of the seventeenth century, after invading Manchus established the Ching dynasty. After the failure of the Taiping Rebellion, which occurred between 1850 and 1864, many triad members escaped to Hawai'i. The presence of these rebels in overseas Chinese colonies in Hawai'i made the Manchu rulers indifferent to the plight of the migrants and made it necessary for the *wah kiu* to organize for protection.

Because the societies brought together the various

Chinese subcultures, they also created a new kind of world for the once strictly segregated groups. The societies were very active, offering religious services, fellowship and advice for fulfilling the requirements of, and advancing in, the western world of Hawai'i. Those who joined the brotherhood made secret oaths, had secret signs, and deep obligations to fellow members.

There were eight Hoong Moon societies on Kauai, including a chapter along the banks of the Hanalei River named Hung Sin Tong, where martial arts and physical culture were practiced. Many outsiders were wary of the organizations and, following a "serious riot" in 1884 when "a number of Chinamen known to be connected with certain secret societies threatened to take the life of the District justice and Deputy Sheriff of Hanalei," King Kalākaua signed an act "to prevent unlawful secret associations." Based on the Dangerous Societies Suppression Ordinance which the British had adopted in Malaya in 1869, the law forced reforms and licensing upon the societies.

The north shore of Kaua'i was also the locale of a series of controversial raids on opium smokers who labored at the Kilauea Plantation. During the Christmas holidays of 1889, police apprehended two Chinese laborers at the Kīlauea barracks for possession of the round black balls of imported opium. As they left, Chinese workers attacked, throwing rocks and bottles and badly injured one of the policemen. After the incident, Kīlauea was labeled as the center of opium traffic on Kaua'i by Sheriff Samuel Wilcox, and a Chinese man was shot in a subsequent raid.

Opium smoking was a touchy issue with the Chinese. Manufactured in Asia, the drug was easily smuggled into port, and it was a welcome relief for men who faced endless days of hard work, were thousands of miles away from their homeland, and had few Chinese women available (except for mail-order brides brought from China in arranged marriages). Legalizing opium became an explosive issue during Kalākaua's reign after the government offered an import monopoly for its sale in the Kingdom. A local Chinese purchased the rights for $30,000, but a sly agent of Kalākaua resold the license for an untidy profit of $125,000.

The twentieth century proved a quieter time for Hawai'i's Chinese, as the second and third generations assimilated into the mainstream of island life. Today the Chinese in Hawai'i are as American as any racial group in the islands, and they continue to hold prominent positions as wise movers and shakers, controlling land tracts and corporations that have their roots in the toil of a single persevering ancestor who sailed to the Sandalwood Mountains to make his and his family's fortune.

As I drive past the aging sugar mills, picturesque isolated cemeteries, and abandoned camps that still mark the early days of the Chinese on Kaua'i, I now see a myriad of events both in my life and the life of the island that are seemingly engraved with the bright-red ink character of a Chinese chop mark; a figure engraved with the twists and turns of a line of ancestors stretching forward from the early dawn of Chinese culture to the islands of today that symbolizes a people with a history deeply rooted in the red soil of Kaua'i, and in the blood and life of the islands.

◈　◈　◈

XXI. KAUA'I SOJOURN
A 19th-Century Travel Writer's Idyllic Visit

Isabella Bird is noted as the first woman to extensively tour the world and write about her travels. The English writer was widely read in the Victorian era and was the first woman named to the Royal Geographical Society. Today Bird's works are still considered valuable sources of information, as well as pleasurable reading. She arrived on Kauai in 1873, a veteran, middle-aged writer.

In The Hawaiian Archipelago: Six Months Among the Palm Groves, Coral Reefs, and Volcanoes of the Sandwich Islands, *Bird describes Kaua'i in the days when the sugar cane plantations at Kōloa, Līhu'e, Kīlauea and the west side had become Kaua'i's dominant economic and social force. The missionary stations Bird visited were in their maturity. Inter-island travel was aboard steamers like the*

Kilauea, *which Bird rode across the wide and trade wind-tossed Kauai Channel.*

She spent an idyllic week at the valleys of Kōloa in the area of today's National Tropical Botanical Gardens. Kōloa, the site of Hawai'i's first commercial sugar cane plantation and an early missionary station, is still a lovely, small town on the island's south shore, much like the Kōloa that Bird visited over 100 years ago.

Bird's description of Hanalei on the north shore would be apt today, as the romantic district remains one of the most spectacularly beautiful locations in the Hawaiian Islands.

The Hawaiian Archipelago: Six Months Among the Palm Groves, Coral Reefs, and Volcanoes of the Sandwich Islands *was first published in 1875. A number of editions have been issued, some with period photographs.*

I AM SPENDING a few days on some quaint old mission premises, and the "guest house," where I am lodged, is an adobe house, with walls two feet thick, and a very thick grass roof comes down six feet all round to shade the windows. It is itself shaded by date palms and algarobas, and is surrounded by hibiscus, oleanders, and the datura arborea, which at night fill the air with sweetness. I am the only guest, and the solitude of the guest house in which I am writing is most refreshing to tired nerves. There is not a sound but the rustling of trees.

The first event to record is that the trade winds have set in, and though they may yet yield once or twice to the Kona, they will soon be firmly established for nine months. They are not soft airs as I supposed, but riotous, rollicking breezes, which keep up a constant clamour, blowing the trees about, slamming doors, taking liberties with papers, making themselves heard and felt everywhere, flecking the blue Pacific with foam, lowering the mercury three degrees, bringing new health and vigour with them, wholesome, cheery, frolicsome north-easters. They brought me here from Oahu in eighteen hours, for which I thank them heartily.

You will think me a Sybarite for howling about those eighteen hours of running to leeward, when the residents of Kauai, if they have to go to Honolulu in the intervals between the quarterly trips of the Kilauea, have to spend from three to nine days in beating to windward. These inter-island voyages of extreme detention, rolling on a lazy swell in tropical heat, or beating for days against the strong trades without shelter from the sun, and without anything that could be called accommodation, were among the inevitable hardships to which the missionaries' wives and children were exposed in every migration for nearly forty years.

When I reached the wharf at Honolulu the sight of the Jenny, the small sixty-ton schooner by which I was to travel, nearly made me give up this pleasant plan, so small she looked, and so cumbered with natives and their accompaniments of mats, dogs, and calabashes of *poi*. But she is clean, and as sweet as a boat can be which carries through the tropics cattle, hides, sugar, and molasses. She is very low in the water, her deck is the real "fisherman's walk, two steps and overboard" and on this occasion was occupied solely by natives. The Attorney General and Mrs. Judd were to have been my fellow voyagers, but my disappointment at their non-appearance was considerably mitigated by the fact that there was not stowage room for more than one white passenger! Mrs. Dexter pitied me heartily, for it made her quite ill to look down the cabin hatch; but I convinced her that no inconveniences are legitimate subjects for sympathy which are endured in the pursuit of pleasure. There was just room on deck for me to sit on a box, and the obliging, gentlemanly master, who, with his son and myself, were the only whites on board, sat on the taffrail. The Jenny spread her white duck sails, glided gracefully away from the wharf, and bounded through the coral reef; the red sunlight faded, the stars came out, the Honolulu light went down in the distance, and in two hours the little craft was out of sight of land on the broad, crisp Pacific. It was so chilly, that after admiring as long as I could, I dived into the cabin, a mere den, with a table, and a berth on each side, in one of which I lay down, and the other was alternately occupied by the captain and his son. But limited as I thought it, boards have been placed across on some occasions, find eleven whites have been packed into a space six feet by eight! The heat and suffocation were nearly intolerable, the black flies swarming, the mosquitoes countless and vicious, the fleas agile beyond anything, and the cockroaches gigantic. Some of the finer cargo was in the cabin, and large rats, only too visible by the light of a swinging lamp, were assailing it, and one with a portentous tail ran over my berth more than once, producing a stampede among the cockroaches each time. I have seldom spent a more miserable night, though there was the extreme satisfaction of knowing that every inch of canvas was drawing. Towards morning the short jerking motion of a ship close hauled, made me know that we were standing in for the land, and at daylight we anchored in Koloa Roads. The view is a pleasant one. The rains have been abundant, and the land, which here rises rather gradually from the sea, is dotted with houses, abounds in signs of cultivation, and then spreads up into a rolling country between precipitous ranges of mountains. The hills looked something like those of Oahu, but their wonderful greenness denotes a cooler climate and more copious rains, also their slopes and valleys are densely wooded, and Kauai obviously has its characteristic features, one of which must certainly be a superabundance of that most unsightly cactus, the prickly pear, to which the motto nemo *me impune lacessit* most literally applies.

I had not time to tell you before that this trip to Kauai was hastily arranged for me by several of my Honolulu friends, some of whom gave me letters of introduction, while others wrote forewarning their friends of my arrival. I am often reminded of Hazel's question, "Is thy servant a dog that he should do this thing ?" There is no inn or boarding house on the island, and I had hitherto believed that I could not be concussed into following the usual custom whereby a traveller throws himself on the hospitality of the residents. Yet, under the influence of Honolulu persuasions, I am doing this very thing, but with an amount of mauvaise honte and trepidation, which I will not voluntarily undergo again. My first introduction was to Mrs. Smith, wife of a secular member of the Mission, and it requested her to find means of forwarding me a distance of twenty-three miles. Her son was at the landing with a buggy, a most unpleasant index of the existence of carriage roads, and brought me here; and Mrs. Smith most courteously met me at the door. When I presented my letter I felt like a thief detected in a first offence, but I was at once made welcome, and my kind hosts insist on my remaining with them for some days. Their house is a pretty old-fashioned looking tropical dwelling, much shaded by exotics, and the parlour is homelike with new books. There are two sons and two daughters at home, all, as well as their parents, interesting themselves assiduously in the welfare of the natives. Six bright looking native girls are receiving an industrial training in the house. Yesterday being Sunday, the young people taught a Sunday school twice, besides attending the native church, an act of respect to Divine service in Hawaiian which always has an influence on the native attendance.

We have had some beautiful rides in the neighbourhood. It is wild, lonely, picturesque coast, and the Pacific moans along it, casting itself on it in heavy surges, with a singularly dreary sound. There are some very fine specimens of the phenomena called "blow-holes" on the shore, not like the "spouting cave" at Iona, however. We spent a long time in watching the action of one, though not the finest. At half tide this "spouting horn" throws up a column of water over sixty feet in height from a very small orifice, and the effect of the compressed air rushing through a crevice near it, sometimes with groans and shrieks, and at others with a hollow roar like the warning fog-horn on a coast, is magnificent, when, as to-day, there is a heavy swell on the coast.

Kauai is much out of the island world, owing to the infrequent visits of the Kilauea, but really it is only twelve hours by steam from the capital. Strangers visit it seldom, as it has no active volcano like Hawaii, or colossal crater like Maui, or anything sensational of any kind. It is called the "Garden Island," and has no great wastes of black lava and red ash like its neighbours. It is queerly shaped, almost circular, with a diameter of from twenty-eight to thirty miles, and its area is about 500 square miles. Waialeale, its highest mountain, is 4,800 feet high, but little is known of it, for it is swampy and dangerous, and a part of it is a forest-covered and little explored tableland, terminating on the sea in a range of perpendicular precipices 2,000 feet in depth, so steep it is said, that a wild cat could not get round them. Owing to these, and the virtual inaccessibility of a large region behind them, no one can travel round the island by land, and small as it is, very little seems to be known of portions of its area.

Kauai has apparently two centres of formation, and its mountains are thickly dotted with craters. The age and density of the vegetation within and without those in this Koloa district, indicate a very long cessation from volcanic action. It is truly an oddly contrived island. An elevated rolling region, park-like, liberally ornamented with clumps of *ohia*, *lauhala*, *hau* (hibiscus) and *koa*, and intersected with gullies full of large eugenias, lies outside the mountain spurs behind Koloa. It is only the tropical trees, specially lie *lauhala* or "screw pine," the whimsical shapes of outlying ridges, which now and then lie like the leaves in a book, and the strange forms of extinct craters, which distinguish it from some of our most beautiful park scenery, such as Windsor Great Park or Belvoir. It is a soft tranquil beauty, and a tolerable road which owes little enough to art, increases the likeness to the sweet home scenery of England. In this part of the island the ground seems devoid of stones, and the grass is as fine and smooth as a race course.

The latest traces of volcanic action are found here. From the Koloa Ridge to, and into the sea, a barren uneven surface of pahoehoe extends, often bulged up in immense bubbles, some of which have partially burst, leaving caverns, one of which, near the shore, is paved with the ancient coral reef!

The valleys of Kauai are long, and widen to the sea, and their dark rich soil is often ten feet deep. On the windward side the rivers are very numerous and picturesque. Between the strong winds and the lightness of the soil, I should think that like some parts of the Highlands, "it would take a shower every day." The leeward side, quite close to the sea, is flushed and nearly barren, but there is very little of this desert region. Kauai is less legible in its formation than the other islands. Its mountains, from their impenetrable forests, dangerous breaks, and swampiness, are difficult of access, and its ridges are said to be more utterly irregular, its lavas more decomposed, and its natural sections more completely smothered under a profuse vegetation than those of any other island in the tropical Pacific. Geologists suppose, from the degradation of its ridges, and the absence of any recent volcanic products, that it is the oldest of the group, but so far as I have read, none of them venture to conjecture how many ages it has taken to convert its hard basalt into the rich soil which now sustains trees of enormous size. If this theory be correct, the volcanoes must have gone on dying out from west to east, from north to south, till only Kilauea remains, and its energies appear to be declining. The central mountain of this island is built of a heavy ferruginous basalt, but the shore ridges contain less iron, are more porous, and vary in their structure from a compact phonolite, to a ponderous basalt.

The population of Kauai is a widely scattered one of 4,900, and as it is an out of the world region the people are probably better, and less sophisticated. They are accounted rustics, or "pagans," in the classical sense, elsewhere. Horses are good and very cheap, and the natives of both sexes are most expert riders. Among their feats, are picking up small coins from the ground while going at full gallop, or while riding at the same speed wringing off the heads of unfortunate fowls, whose bodies are buried in the earth.

There are very few foreigners, and they appear on the whole a good set, and very friendly among each other. Many of them are actively interested in promoting the improvement of the natives, but it is uphill work, and ill-rewarded, at least on earth. The four sugar plantations employ a good deal of Chinese labour, and I fear that the Chinamen are stealthily tempting the Hawaiians to smoke opium...

LIHUE, KAUAI, APRIL 17

Before leaving Kauai I must tell you of a solitary expedition I have just made to the lovely valley of Hanalei. It was only a three days' "frolic," but an essentially "good time." Mr. Rice provided me with a horse and a very pleasing native guide. I did not leave till two in the afternoon, as I only intended to ride fifteen miles, and, as the custom is, ask for a night's lodging at a settler's house. However, as I drew near Mr. B.'s ranch, I felt my false courage oozing out of the tips of my fingers, and as I rode up to the door, certain obnoxious colonial words, such as "sundowners," and "bummers," occurred to me, and I felt myself a "sundowner" when the host came out and asked me to dismount. He said he was sorry his wife was away, but he would do his best for me in her absence, and took me down to a room where a very rough-looking man was tenderly nursing a baby a year old, which was badly burned or scalded, and which began to cry violently at my entrance, and required the united efforts of the two bereaved men to pacify it. I took it while they went to make some tea, and it kicked, roared, and fought until they came back. By that time I had prepared a neat little speech, saying that I was not the least tired, and would only trouble them for a glass of water; and, having covered my cowardice successfully, I went on, having been urged by the hospitable ranchman to be sure to stay for the night at his father-in-law's house, a few miles further on. I saw that the wishes of the native went in the same direction, but after this experience I assured myself that I had not the necessary nerve for this species of mendicancy, and went on as fast as the horse could gallop wherever the ground admitted of it, the scenery becoming more magnificent as the dark, frowning mountains of Hanalei loomed through the gathering twilight.

But they were fifteen miles off, and on the way we came to a broad, beautiful ravine, through which a wide, deep river glided into the breakers. I had received some warnings about this, but it was supposed that we could cross in a ferry scow, of which, however, I only found the bones. The guide and the people at the ferryman's house talked long without result, but eventually, by many signs, I contrived to get them to take me over in a crazy punt, half full of water, and the horses swam across. Before we reached the top of the ravine, the last redness of twilight had died from off the melancholy ocean, the black forms of mountains looked huge in the darkness, and the wind sighed so eerily through the creaking lauhalas, as to add much to the effect. It became so very dark that I could only just see my horse's ears, and we found ourselves occasionally in odd predicaments, such as getting into crevices, or dipping off from steep banks; and it was in dense darkness that we arrived above what appeared to be a valley with twinkling lights, lying at the foot of a precipice, and walled in on all sides but one by lofty mountains. It was rather queer, diving over the wooded pali on a narrow track, with nothing in sight but the white jacket of the native, who had already indicated that he was at the end of his resources regarding the way, but just as a river gleamed alarmingly through the gloom, a horseman on a powerful horse brushed through the wood, and on being challenged in Hawaiian replied in educated English, and very politely turned with me, and escorted me over a disagreeable ferry in a scow without rails, and to my destination, two miles beyond.

Yesterday, when I left, the morning was brilliant, and after ascending the *pali*, I stayed for some time on an eminence which commands the valley, presented by Mr. Wyllie to Lady Franklin, in compliment to her admiration of its loveliness. Hanalei has been likened by some to Paradise, and by others to the Vale of Kaschmir. Everyone who sees it raves about it. "See Hanalei and die," is the feeling of the islanders, and certainly I was not disappointed, nor should I be with Paradise itself were it even a shade less fair! It has every element of beauty, and in the bright sunshine, with the dark shadows on the mountains, the waterfalls streaking their wooded sides, the river rushing under *kukuis* and ohias, and then lingering lovingly amidst lively greenery, it looked as if the curse had never lighted there.

Its mouth, where it opens on the Pacific, is from two to three miles wide, but the boundary mountains gradually approach each other, so that five miles from the sea a narrow gorge of wonderful beauty alone remains. The crystal Hanalei flows placidly to the sea for the last three or four miles, tired by its impetuous rush from the mountains, and mirrors on its breast hundreds of acres of cane, growing on a plantation formerly belonging to Mr. Wyllie, an enterprising Ayrshire man, and one of the ablest and most disinterested foreigners who ever administered Hawaiian affairs. Westward of the valley there is a region of mountains, slashed by deep ravines. The upper ridges are densely timbered, and many of the ohias have a circumference of twenty-five feet, three feet from the ground. It was sad to turn away for ever from the loveliness of Hanalei, even though by taking another route, which involved a ride of forty miles, I passed through and in view of, most entrancing picturesqueness. Indeed, for mere loveliness, I think that part of Kauai exceeds anything that I have seen.

The atmosphere and scenery were so glorious that it was possible to think of nothing all day, but just allow oneself passively to drink in sensations of exquisite pleasure. I wish all the hard-worked people at home, who lead joyless lives in sunless alleys, could just have one such day, and enjoy it as I did, that they might know how fair God's earth is, and how fairer His Paradise must be, if even from this we cannot conceive "of the things which He hath prepared for them that love Him" I never before felt so sad for those whose lives are passed amidst unpropitious surroundings, or so thankful for my own capacity of enjoying nature.

Just as we were coming up out of a deep river, a native riding about six feet from me was caught in a quicksand. He jumped off, but the horse sank half way up its body. I wanted to stay and see it extricated, for its struggles only sank it deeper, but the natives shrugged their shoulders, and said in Hawaiian, "only a horse," and something they always say when anything happens, equivalent to "What's the odds?" It was a joyously-exciting day, and I was galloping down a grass hill at a pace which I should not have assumed had white people been with me, when a native rode up to me and said twice over, "*Maikai! Paniola*," and laughed heartily. When my native came up, he pointed to me and again said, "*paniola*;" and afterwards we were joined by two women, to whom my guide spoke of me as paniola; and on coming to the top of a hill they put their horses into a gallop, and we all rode down at a tremendous, and, as I should once have thought, a breakneck speed, when one of the women patted me on the shoulder, exclaiming, "Maikai! Maikai! Paniola." I thought they said "Spaniola," taking me for a Spaniard, but on reaching Lihue, and asking the meaning of the word, Mrs. Rice said, "Oh, lassoing cattle, and all that kind of thing." I was disposed to accept the inference as a compliment; but when I told Mrs. R. that the word had been applied to myself, she laughed very much, and said she would have toned down its meaning had she known that!

We rode through forests lighted up by crimson flowers, through mountain valleys greener than Alpine meadows, descended steep palis, and forded deep, strong rivers, pausing at the beautiful Wailua Falls, which leap in a broad sheet of foam and a heavy body of water into a dark basin, walled in by cliffs so hard that even the ferns and mosses which revel in damp, fail to find roothold in the naked rock. Both above and below, this river passes through a majestic canyon, and its neighbourhood abounds in small cones, some with crateriform cavities at the top, some broken down, and others, apparently of great age, wooded to their summits. A singular ridge, called Mauna Kalalea, runs along this part of the island, picturesque beyond anything, and, from its abruptness and peculiar formation, it deceives the eye into judging it to be as high as the gigantic domes of Hawaii. Its peaks are needle-like, or else blunt projections of columnar basalt, rising oftimes as terraces. At a beautiful village called Anahola the ridge terminates abruptly, and its highest portion is so thin that a large patch of sky can be seen through a hole which has been worn in it.

I reached Lihue by daylight, having established my reputation as a paniola by riding forty miles in 7-and-a-half hours, "very good time" for the islands. I hope to return here in August as my hospitable friends will not allow me to leave on any other condition. The kindness I have received on Kauai is quite overwhelming, and I shall remember its refined and virtuous homes as long as its loveliness and delicious climate.

XXII. HAWAIIAN PASTIMES AT NI'IHAU & NĀ PALI

TRADITIONAL HAWAIIAN GAMES & AMUSEMENTS

In this brief description of Hawaiian sports and folk culture—which is a transcript of a speech given before the American Folklore Society in New York City in the 1890's—Victorian researcher H. Carrington Bolton of Columbia University in Manhattan presents insights on unique Hawaiian traditions enjoyed on both Kaua'i and Ni'ihau.

Especially interesting are the firebrand "Hawaiian-style fireworks" thrown from plateaus along Nā Pali, as well as at Hā'ena on the north shore—legendary activities once performed for Hawaiian royalty, as well as the maka'āinana, the common people. Hawaiian fireworks were launched from flat plateaus along Nā Pali at Nu'alolo Kai and near Mount Makana on the island's isolated northwest coastline.

Bolton's look at surfing is perhaps the most accurate description made in the nineteenth century of the Hawaiian sport. This account has been overlooked in most histories of surfing and criticizes earlier writers for watching surfers at wind-blown, onshore surf spots, rather than the offshore areas where surfing is best. In the article there is a reference to a large glass plate magic lantern show of images taken by Bolton. If the whereabouts of the glass plates could be found, it would yield the earliest photograph of surfers.

Other details about fishing, Hawaiian "marbles" and other activities round out this gem.

ON THE FERTILE island of Kauai, at the northwest end of the group, one which is less visited by tourists than some others, a unique pastime was until recently carried on at rare intervals of time, that replaced the pyrotechnical displays of other nations. On the northwest coast of Kauai precipitous cliffs rise abruptly from the sea to a height of one thousand to two thousand feet (Pali), and from these giddy heights the ingenious and beautiful display of floating firebrands took place. An eye-witness (Mrs. Francis Sinclair) thus describes the scene:

> On the dark, moonless nights, upon certain points of these precipices, where a stone would drop sheer into the sea, the operator takes his stand with a supply of *papala* sticks (a light and porous indigenous wood), and, igniting one, launches it into space. The buoyancy of the wood, and the action of the wind sweeping up the face of the cliffs, cause the burning branch to float in mid-air, rising or falling according to the force of the wind, sometimes darting far seaward, an again drifting towards the land. Firebrand follows firebrand, until,

to the spectators who enjoy the scene in canoes upon the ocean hundreds of feet below, the heavens appear ablaze with great shooting stars, rising and falling, crossing and recrossing each other in a weird manner. So the display continues until the firebrands are consumed or a lull in the wind permits them to descend slowly and gracefully into the sea.

The Papala tree (Charpentiera ovaia) attains the height of about twenty feet, and grows only upon the highlands from two to three thousand feet above the sea. When in full bloom it has a very peculiar and graceful appearance, reminding one of the most delicate seaweed. The wood is very light and porous, and, being easily ignited, has been chosen by the natives for their grand and original pyrotechnics. (Mrs. Francis Sinclair, Jr., *Indigenous Flowers of the Hawaiian Islands*. London, 1885. 4 vo. Plates. Cf. Hillebrand's *Flora of the Hawaiian Islands*.)

While a guest of Mr. George S. Gay, on the little island of Niihau, I enjoyed opportunities of learning several points of folk-lore interest. This islet of the Pacific is about twenty-two miles long, varies in width from four to eight miles, and embraces, approximately, seventy thousands acres. The natives residing here now number less than one hundred, and their isolation has preserved them from the evils attendant upon civilization, especially that variety of civilization introduced by sailors at every seaport of the world. The inhabitants, however, have not been exempt from the decadence in numbers which is rapidly de-Hawaiianizing the kingdom; for, at the census of 1832, they numbered over one thousand. The circumstance that, for twenty-five years, the entire island has been owned by a single family of Scotch origin, engaged in sheep-raising, and who have had the welfare of the natives at heart, especially in limiting the supply of alcoholic liquours, has further tended to preserve them from obvious evils. A sort of patriarchal life exists on Niihau; the only white family residing there receives tribute from the natives, who supply at stated times and in their courses fish, cocoanuts, sweet potatoes, and a certain amount of labor.

Here I witnessed, by the courtesy of Mr. Gay, the sport of surf-riding, once so universally popular, and now but little seen. Six stalwart men, by previous appointment, assembled on the beach of a small cove, bearing with them their precious surf-boards, and accompanied by many women and a few children, all eager to see the strangers, and mildly interested in the sport. After standing for their photographs, the men removed all their garments, retaining only the *malo*, or loin-cloth, and walked into the sea, dragging or pushing their surf-boards as they reached deeper water.

These surf-boards, in Hawaiian "wave-slidding-boards" (*Papa-he-nalu*), are made from the wood of the viri-viri (Erythrina corallodendrum), or bread-fruit tree; they are eight or nine feet long, fifteen to twenty inches wide, rather thin, rounded at each end, and carefully smoothed. The boards are sometimes stained black, and frequently rubbed with *cocoanut* oil, and are preserved with great solicitude, sometimes wrapped in cloths. Children use smaller boards.

Plunging through the nearer surf, the natives reached the outer line of breakers, and watching their opportunity they lay flat upon the board (the more expert kneeled), and, just as a high billow was about to break over them, pushed landward in front of the combers. The waves rushed in were apparently always on the point of submerging the rider; but, unless some mishap occurred, they drove him forward with rapidity on to the beach, or into shallow water. At the time of the exhibition, the surf was very moderate, and the natives soon tired of the dull sport; but in a high surf it is, of course, exciting, and demands much skill born of experience.

As commonly described in the writings of travelers, an erroneous impression is conveyed, at least to my mind, as to the position which the rider occupies with respect to the combing wave. Some pictures, too, represent the surf-riders on the seaward slope of the wave, in positions which are incompatible with the results. I photographed the men of Niihau before they entered the water, while surf-riding, and after they came out. The second view shows plainly the positions taken, although the figures are distant and consequently small.

A few days later, on another beach, I was initiated in the mysteries of surf-riding by my host, who is himself quite expert; and while I cannot boast of much success, I at least learned the principle, and believe that practice is only needed to gain a measure of skill. For persons accustomed to bathing in the surf, the process is far less difficult than usually represented.

The Pacific Ocean bordering the Hawaiian Islands is well stocked with fish, and the natives depend on them for the nitrogenous food needed to supplement the starchy *poi*. On Niihau, they fish for squid with two strong hooks (formerly made of bone, now of English manufacture), attached to a line that is weighted in a peculiar fashion. The hooks are fastened between a spotted cowry shell (cypæa) and a hemispherical mass of granular olivine (grooved on the convex surface to secure the line). The stones are about the size and shape of a half-orange; the material is sought by the men of Niihau on the neighboring tiny island of Kaula, which is frequently visited for the purpose of collecting a supply. The Hawaiians believe that the shell and the green stone attract the squid, and is necessary to their capture; certain specimens of the stone are regarded as very choice and are highly treasured. They also have the superstition that the stones lose their charm if you cook a squid caught with the given stone, and to injure an enemy the native tries to steal a piece of a squid caught by him, and by cooking it to deprive the fishing-stone of its virtue. Squid-fishing is commonly practiced on all the islands, but the use of olivine and cypæa shell is peculiar to Niihau. The natives eat the squid both raw and cooked. It is also dried for future consumption.

A traveler in the tropics is prepared for the bountiful resources of nature that makes it possible to sustain life with a minimum of artifice and exertion, but I confess to surprise at learning that even children's marbles grow on shrubs. I saw boys playing with the hard, almost perfectly spherical seeds of the *Kakalaioa* plant. The name of the plant signifies thorny, and is singularly appropriate; it grows in rocky places in the lowlands. The seed pods, which grow on long stalks, are thickly covered with sharp spines something like a chestnut burr. They are first green, then brown, and when ripe almost black, and grow in bunches of eight to thirteen. Each pod has one or two seeds, stony hard and lead color. The seeds, when dried, are very tough, and, shaken in a bag, rattle with a metallic sound much like true marbles. The game, of course, is a foreign importation, and, so far as I could ascertain, is not protected by a high tariff.

Before leaving the interesting island of Niihau, and bidding my kind hosts *Aloha*, I visited the sonorous sand-dunes at Kaluakahua. My study of musical sand is recorded elsewhere; here I would only make brief mention of a superstition connected with it. The Hawaiians say that the sounds produced when the sand slides down the steep dunes are caused by uhane, spirits, who grumble at being disturbed. These sandhills are used by the natives for interments, as bleached and well-preserved skeletons and skulls still evidence.

I landed at Niihau by the monthly steamer, but I left the island in an open whaleboat, crossing the channel to Kauai. My companion on this voyage had secured at Kaluakahua a very fine skull, with teeth in perfect preservation, and altogether an ethnological treasure. Mr. Gay cautioned him not to let the superstitious boatmen see the skull, lest they should refuse to start on the voyage, an he concealed it in a piece of baggage. The transit from Kii to Waimea is often made in four to six hours, but on this occasion head winds and no wind, strong tides and heavy seas, combined against us, and, though the *Kanakas* rowed bravely, we spent thirteen and a half weary hours in the little boat. My companion who suffered terribly from seasickness, now regards the superstition of the Hawaiian sailors as well founded, and vows never to undertake another sea voyage with a skull in the portmanteau!

XXIII. GUIDE TO KAUA'I – 1875
SELECTION FROM HAWAI'I'S FIRST GUIDE BOOK

Henry M. Whitney, one of the first haole *children born on Kaua'i, was the son of missionary parents Samuel and Mercy Partridge Whitney. After working in the printing and publishing world of New York, he returned to Hawai'i to found the* Pacific Commercial Advertiser, *the forerunner of the* Honolulu Advertiser.

This selection offers a tour of the entire island from the viewpoint of a traveler to Hawai'i in the 1870's. Whitney traveled by steamer from Honolulu and journeyed on foot, by horse and by boat from the capital near Līhu'e north and south to the far reaches of the plantation town of Mānā, near Barking Sands.

Most Kaua'i visitors in Whitney's era were interested in migrating to the kingdom of Hawai'i and most likely were

*entrepreneurs in search of opportunity on the growing island.
The advertisements inserted throughout the guide promote
railroad links from California to New York, and even within
Australia, obviously aimed at the businessman of the day.*

*Many of the sights that intrigued this early travel writer
remain as major attractions today.*

THIS, THE NORTHERNMOST of the Hawaiian group,
with its cooling breezes, has been aptly named the "Garden
Island of Hawaii." It is nearly circular, has an area of 520
square miles, one-half of which is adapted to grazing and
agriculture. It lies between 21⁰ 47' and 22⁰ 46' north
latitude, while its eastern point is in longitude 159⁰ 18'
and its western extremity reaches 159⁰ 55' west.

This island is unrivaled for its agreeable climate and
with its charming valley, broad plains, picturesque cliffs,
views, waterfalls and lofty mountains, it offers attractions
to the traveler unexcelled by any other in the group. By
the monthly trip of the inter-island steamer a fine
opportunity is offered for a short visit and a circuit of the
island, while regular schooners run weekly between
Honolulu and its various ports.

The roads and bridges on the island of Kauai are said
to be the best in the group. It is quite possible to drive in
a light vehicle from Hanalei to Mana point, a distance of
65 miles.

NAWILIWILI BAY

This beautiful little cove affords an anchorage for
vessels of less than 500 tons burden. The outer bar has
three fathoms of water, and the anchorage is open to a
heavy swell when the south-east winds blow, rendering it
at such times unsafe; but Niumalu at the mouth of the
river is a safe shelter for small craft in all seasons. This

place is the residence of the Governor and other officers of the island.

Leaving the steamer, going inland, the mountains and valleys will be found covered with forests, excepting where fires and the woodman's ax have denuded the land. The high shore plain which forms here, extending with varying width around the southern, eastern and northern sides of the island, is a region of grass and shrubbery, shaded with occasional groves of *pandanus* and *kukui* trees. On this windward side of Kauai, the mountain tops are covered with rain clouds, and the declivities are threaded with white cascades streaming down almost vertically in uninterrupted lines, one, two, and even three thousand feet.

LIHUE

Two miles inland from the bay, is the site of one of the pioneer sugar plantations, which is worthy of note, for its extent and its success, but particularly for its system of irrigation, by means of a canal which brings the mountain water over a distance of ten miles to every cane field. The estate is the property of a Joint Stock Company, of which Mr. Paul Isenberg is the resident manager and part owner. It comprises about ten thousand acres, running from the shore to the mountains and including extensive tracts of level plains, several sugar estates. It is considered one of the best conducted and most profitable plantations in the group, as it is one of the oldest.

Between Lihue and Koloa is a precipitous basaltic range of hills, where the ancient chiefs battled for supremacy, and where one bold warrior, the last of his defeated clan, made a frightful leap from a beetling crag into the river and thus made his escape.

Leaving Lihue, and proceeding northward towards Hanalei, two roads present almost equal claims to the rider. The one along the sea is by way of Honomaulu river to the mouth of the Wailua river, where a shallow harbor separates it from the ocean. Here the surf often breaks heavily, shifting the sands and thus fording becomes dangerous. The other road, which is perhaps the pleasanter, lies inland over a plain to Wailua river above.

THE FALLS

The road here descends from the high plain to a low marshy flat near the sea, with here and there banks of sand, and dense groves of hau trees. A ferry of fifty yards takes horse and rider over for five cents. Wailua river, seven miles from Lihue, is the deepest on the islands, being twenty fathoms not far from its mouth. No one should fail to ascend this stream in a canoe, as its rich, wild palisades and tropical scenery are worth seeing. The falls are magnificent after a heavy rain. Approaching them from above, without warning, an abyss of 180 feet opens its wonders to the eye. Black and emerald rocks, beautiful ferns, fleecy foam and silver gleamings among leafy trees combine with the roar and mist in unrivaled beauty and grandeur. The breadth of the fall is fifty feet, and at low water it pours its larger sheet on one side; the other is so thin as to make each drop seem to fall by itself. But when the winter rains set in, the banks are full, and crossing above is impossible; then the roar of rushing water is incessant and the sight is sublime. Two cascades are higher up the river, one 70 and the other 100 feet.

Not far from the falls, on the brink of a small crater, may be seen the remains of a large mansion, embowered in exotic trees and shrubbery, formerly the headquarters of an extensive cattle ranch and dairy.

The village of Wailua by the sea, once large and populous, was the home of the famous Queen Kapule, better known as Deborah, the favorite wife of Kaumualii, the last king of Kauai.

MAUNA WAIALEALE

This is the central peak of Kauai, and its ridges overtop all others. Its sides are precipitous, well clad in green, and interspersed with cascades and waterfalls. The scenery of this and other mountains, less high but piercing the plain below with sharp, green spurs or peaks, broken, tottering and craggy, variegate the scene to the distant ocean's horizon.

The excursion to its summit is considered a most difficult feat, but to those who can bear the necessary fatigue and exposure, it will repay the effort. It can only be made on foot, and with a guide, and will occupy at least three days; one night being generally spent at or near the top. The trip will furnish to the botanist, or the conchologist in search of land-shells, a rare opportunity to gratify his curiosity and pursue his scientific researches.

FROM WAILUA TO HANALEI

On leaving the falls, evidence of a dense population passed away, occur on every side in dried *taro* patches, abandoned water ways and houses marked only by their rude foundations. An ancient battle ground may be found a few miles north of Wailua.

At Kealia, nine miles northward from the falls, is the ranch of Mr. E. Krull, and roaming over the broad pastures, may be seen thousands of sleek cattle, which are raised chiefly for their hides and tallow.

At Kilauea, eight miles further on, is the residence of Mr. Chas. Titcomb, whose extensive farm is one of the finest localities for raising sugar cane, coffee or ramie, to be found on the islands.

Kalihiwai valley, six miles from Hanalei, has beautiful banks, and the river is remarkable for numerous cascades. Between this valley and Hanalei, the rolling upland is covered with a *lauhala* forest, reaching to the old silk works of Mr. Charles Titcomb, which were located near the river. Some of these upland tracts, where water can be brought on to them from the neighboring streams, furnish the best of cane land, and will eventually be cultivated with sugar cane or tobacco.

HANALEI

This name covers not only a river and bay, but a district raised some hundred feet above the sea, comprising 20,000 acres of fine arable lands, well watered, especially in its eastern portion which has at least twenty streams. Sugar cane grows spontaneously and the leaves of the multicaulis attain the enormous size of fifteen inches in length by twelve in breadth.

Hanalei harbor is on the north side of the island, affording good anchorage, except in northwest winds which blow usually in the winter months. And even in strong gales, small vessels with good ground tackle can lie safely under the lee of the reef, opposite the mouth of the river. The view from the anchorage has been pronounced by travelers as one of the finest in the world. Hanalei river is lined with luxuriant foliage, and a boat ride on its smooth bosom, in a bright moonlight, rivals the Arabian Nights enchantment. Its gardens contain the olive, pomegranate, orange and grape, and among roses and shrubbery, the magnificent magnolia grandiflora scatters the exquisite fragrance of its snowy blossoms.

Princeville Plantation

Is located on the banks of this beautiful river, and has the reputation of having the best sugar mill and plant in the group. Certain it is that a large fortune was expended by its former proprietor, Mr. R.C. Wyllie, in developing the productive capacity of this valley. Since his death, in 1865, the estate has passed into other hands, and is now managed by Capt. John G. Ross, who is also part owner. With a fine mill and extensive tracts of the richest bottom as well as upland, this estate must become, when the system of irrigation is introduced, one of the most productive and valuable on our islands.

Waioli Valley

The scenery in this vicinity is romantically tropical. The soil is fertile, and produces taro, sugar cane, coffee, and indigo, with fruits and vegetables in great variety. This stream, rushing down a rocky chasm, assumes every fantastic shape possible, and a traveler describes it as a picture "more exquisite than any we have seen on the islands."

Wonderful Caves

Two caves, Waiamoo and Waiakanaloa, six miles west of Hanalei, deserve the attention of the explorer. They are divided into compartments, are filled with water and must be explored with lanterns, torches and a canoe. The natives say a gigantic *moo* (dragon) guards one of the chambers. The Hawaiian Spectator says of one: "Its entrance is gothic, from 20 to 30 feet high and as wide. The entrance to the second apartment, directly in the rear is also gothic, and one-half as large as the outer opening. The first chamber is about 150 feet long, 100 wide and 60 high; the whole forming a beautiful arch." The depth of the water at the mouth of the second cave is forty-two feet. There are said to be rooms beyond, under the mountain, waiting for the fearless explorer. The water is cold, clear and sweet, having no apparent ingress or egress, or connection with the sea.

NA PALI

Along the north-western coast of Kauai, for twenty miles, stands a bold bluff of unrivaled majesty. The ocean does not shoal from blue to green until right on the breakers and the wild surge, without a barren reef, dashes on precipitous walls of primitive rock. No cliff falls below 800 feet in elevation, and the average is above 1200. Numerous streams pour over the face of the mountain, during the wet season, and become mist before they reach the ocean.

The Kilauea on her circuit trips, steams within 400 yards of these palisades, which are interrupted only by an ancient retreat of the chiefs at Milolii, with its fortified fish ponds and impregnable valley accessible from the land only by a pole ladder.

THE BARKING SANDS OF MANA

Are prominent among the curiosities of Kauai. The sand possesses the property of ringing or barking, and it may be produced by striking the banks; by sliding down, or dragging a heavy body over them. This property of sound is fixed and can be produced in samples taken to a foreign country. Moisture deadens its resonance.

WAIMEA

Is the name of a district, village and river, distinguished in the ancient traditions of Kauai, and also famous as the place where Captain Cook, the discover of the group, first anchored in 1778, and made the acquaintance of the natives, who called his vessel a *moku* or island. The harbor, an open roadstead, affording good anchorage, sheltered from the trade wind, is in latitude $21^0 57'$, north, longitude $159^0 42'$, west. Waimea village, now only a wreck of a once populous capital, is situated on the west bank of the river. On the opposite side are the remains of the stone fort built by the Russians, in 1815, for King Kaumualii. The final conflict in 1824, that confirmed the title of the Kamehamehas and established their authority on Kauai, was fought over the walls of this fort.

THE VALLEY AND FALLS OF HANAPEPE

Situated midway between Waimea and Koloa, seven miles from each, are remarkable among the scenery of the Hawaiian Islands. The banks are precipitous; from hundreds to thousands of feet high, the brink comes unheralded on the startled observer, who finds it impossible to descend, except by a few passes. Near the sea the valley widens, and the barrier walls decrease in height, exhibiting masses of red columnar lava. Here, close by the ocean, under the cocoanut trees, by the mouth of the stream that runs down the valley, are the dwellings of the natives, whose patches of taro and bananas line the banks above. So much untilled land and other indications of a former numerous population, assure us that the estimates of Cook and Vancouver, who placed the population in 1780 at 400,000, were not far from correct.

Hanapepe valley, like most others on this island, extends inland almost to its centre. As it recedes from the shore, the mountains stretch upward, the valley walls growing higher. Rocks become cliffs, changing their form and appearance at every turn. Now a darkened narrow gorge through which the river rushes violently, now a miniature valley with just room for a tiny village, and the cultivated plots of the inhabitants; now a stone viaduct, a flume through which one may look upward as through a ventilator in a mountain tunnel.

Some five or six miles inland, the level of the valley begins rapidly to rise, creating some beautiful cascades in the stream, before the Hanapepe Fall appears in view. Jarves says, "As we approach, it is again lost to sight, until, after turning a sharp angle in the glen, it appears, and the visitor finds himself a few rods from the fall on a narrow ledge of rocks. In that direction nature's flat proclaims 'thus shalt thou come and no farther.' A perpendicular wall between three and four hundred feet in height, and forming so complete a circle that no outlet except that which the stream makes is seen; and it is only by following up its bed through dense thickets that this spot can be reached. The circle is small and the rocks above partly project over the outlet, so that it appears like a tunnel, and the sun can reach its bottom only when vertical. Nothing can be seen except a few scattering shrubs which border the top. Fleecy clouds drive rapidly past before the strong gusts of these mountain regions. The air here is exceedingly cold and chilly, and the rocks wet and slippery with spray. If the visitor is heated by this excursion, it would be dangerous for him to approach the fall before he is cooled, as the perspiration is liable to be suddenly checked. Opposite and far above him is the waterfall; there, about ten feet in width and several in depth, but ranging in volume according to the rains, springing from between two narrow and overhanging masses of basaltic columns, it leaps thirty feet, strikes a ledge of rocks, and gradually spreading and lessening in thickness, falls many more feet and strikes another ledge; from whence, falling again an equal distance into a deep and circumscribed gulf below, or whitens with its foam the whole surface of the rock from the height above."

Another writer says of this fall, "Coming out of a romantic and picturesque gorge, formed in the loftiest peaks in the central range, it leaps through its mountain gateway of basaltic pillars from precipice to precipice, nearly four hundred feet, into the bright elysian valley below. From the clear sheet of pure, rushing, leaping water above, it gradually expands in spray, whitening into foam as it descends, till it falls a never-ceasing shower into the cool basin below. We thought of various cascades and waterfalls of world-wide celebrity, but none can equal Hanapepe in the beauty, grandeur and magnificence of its surrounding scenery." The height of this waterfall is 326 feet.

WAHIAWA

Two miles East from Hanapepe are the stream and valley of Wahiawa. The scenery beyond, toward Koloa, is very fine, for the woods reach down in points resembling an English park. The hills are green, grassy, wave-like and rounded, and the mountain is watered by the streams of Waikaka, Waiheo and Lawai, each adorning its own sweet valley. A half mile above the road at "Brideswood," four miles from Koloa, may be seen the residence of Hon. D. McBryde, judge of the circuit court of this island. The site is lovely, in a grove of *kukui* and *koa* trees and surrounded with broad, rolling pastures, covered with cattle.

THE VILLAGE OF KOLOA

In fifteen miles to the northeast of Waimea, and ten miles south from Lihue. It has no harbor, but an open roadstead. The trade wind blows along and a little off shore. The anchorage is close in shore, in four or six fathoms, under the shelter of a bluff. The town is two miles from the landing, and is noted for its sugar plantation, the oldest in the group, formerly owned by Dr. R.W. Wood, and now by Messrs. Wright and Isenberg.

The Koloa district gradually rises from the sea and reaches a range of high hills, which separate it from the extensive plain of Lihue on the north. There is a fine carriage road to Lihue, passing through a gorge in the mountain ridge, and travelers will always find the ride through "the gap" a pleasant one. They can embark on the steamer either at Koloa or Lihue, though the latter place is preferable.

THE SPOUTING HORN

Is one of the natural curiosities of Koloa. It is a lofty jet of spray, which in a heavy sea is fully a hundred feet high. The waves rush through an opening in the lava rock, near the landing place, making an intermittent fountain usually fifty feet high. This is accompanied with a sound sometimes audible a mile distant.

NIIHAU

Justice demands a passing notice of this fine little island, the westernmost inhabited island of the group—once populous, and now the property of Mr. Francis Sinclair. It is used exclusively as a sheep ranch, which numbers 75,000 head. It is immediately opposite or west from Waimea, twenty miles distant, always in sight, but not easily accessible. It was formerly noted for the "Niihau mats," woven from a fine grass, which grows only on it, and which resembles the Guayaquil grass, of which the Panama hats are made. Some of these mats were woven in colors, and others had mottoes. They have become extremely rare, and like genuine "Panama hats" are very highly prized. This island was also noted formerly for the beauty of its land and sea shells, but the latter are now seldom collected by shell divers on Niihau, or indeed on any of our islands. Land shells are found on the mountains throughout the group, and some fine collections of them have been made by naturalists.

Advertising Notices in Whitney's Guide

Cabin passage from Honolulu to Kauai, $5 to $8. Steamer Kilauea leaves Honolulu every Monday for ports on Maui and Hawaii, excepting one week in the month, when she makes a trip to Kauai.

American and English gold and silver coins form the principal currency in this Kingdom. Spanish silver coins, and French silver five franc or dollar pieces, and Chilean and Peruvian dollar pieces are also current. Silver certificates, representing specie on deposit in the government treasury, are also current.

XXIV. KOOLAU THE LEPER
A TRAGIC LOVE STORY

Jack London and his wife, Charmain, sailed into Pearl Harbor in the spring of 1907 aboard their yacht The Snark. They were accompanied on the long sail that began in Oakland, California by Herbert Stolz, the son of Waimea deputy sheriff Louis Stolz. The elder Stolz was shot and killed in Kalalau Valley by the legendary Waimea paniolo *Kaluaikoolau*, the man London's story Koolau the Leper *is based on. Herbert Stolz apparently told the story to London during their voyage.*

Koolau the Leper *first appeared in 1909 in the magazine* Pacific Monthly, *and became London's best known story of Hawai'i after the publication of* The House of Pride, *a collection of his Hawai'i stories.*

London visited Kaua'i in May 1915 as a guest of a congressional party touring the island. He enjoyed a luau *put*

on by Nāwiliwili businessman Jack Coney and boarded with
the family of the Rev. John Lydgate. He drove from Līhuʻe to
Hanalei to board a steamer back to Honolulu. His driver
was Walter Sanborn of Hanalei, and the two men discussed
details of the Koʻolau story.

London biographers overlooked his Kauai visit in official
chronologies of the famous American author's life. During
my research on The Kauaʻi Movie Book *I discovered an article*
about London visiting Kauaʻi. Subsequent research dug up
more information on his short stay. Through an inquiry on
the Internet, I located Jack London Society president Jeanne
Reesman. Reesman and Earle Labor subsequently traveled to
Kauaʻi to add the chapter to London's story.

BECAUSE WE ARE sick they take away our liberty.
We have obeyed the law. We have done no wrong. And
yet they would put us in prison. Molokai is a prison. That
you know. Niuli, there, his sister was sent to Molokai seven
years ago. He has not seen her since. Nor will he ever see
her. She must stay there until she dies. This is not her will.
It is not Niuli's will. It is the will of the white men who
rule the land. And who are these white men?

"We know. We have it from our fathers and our fathers'
fathers. They came like lambs, speaking softly. Well might
they speak softly, for we were many and strong, and all
the islands were ours. As I say, they spoke softly. They
were of two kinds. The one kind asked our permission,
our gracious permission, to preach to us the word of God.
The other kind asked our permission, our gracious
permission, to trade with us. That was the beginning.
Today all the islands are theirs, all the land, all the cattle—
everything is theirs. They that preached the word of God
and they that preached the word of Rum have foregathered

and become great chiefs. They live like kings in houses of many rooms, with multitudes of servants to care for them. They who had nothing have everything, and if you, or I, or any Kanaka be hungry, they sneer and say, 'Well, why don't you work? There are the plantations.' "

Koolau paused. He raised one hand, and with gnarled and twisted fingers lifted up the blazing wreath of hibiscus that crowned his black hair. The moonlight bathed the scene in silver. It was a night of peace, though those who sat about him and listened had all the seeming of battle-wrecks. Their faces were leonine. Here a space yawned in a face where should have been a nose, and there an arm stump showed where a hand had rotted off. They were men and women beyond the pale, the thirty of them, for upon them had been placed the mark of the beast.

They sat, flower-garlanded, in the perfumed, luminous night, and their lips made uncouth noises and their throats rasped approval of Koolau's speech. They were creatures who once had been men and women. But they were men and women no longer. They were monsters— in face and form grotesque caricatures of everything human. They were hideously maimed and distorted, and had the seeming of creatures that had been racked in millenniums of hell. Their hands, when they possessed them, were like harpy-claws. Their faces were the misfits and slips, crushed and bruised by some mad god at play in the machinery of life. Here and there were features which the mad god had smeared half away, and one woman wept scalding tears from twin pits of horror, where her eyes once had been. Some were in pain and groaned from their chests. Others coughed, making sounds like the tearing of tissue. Two were idiots, more like huge apes marred in the making, until even an ape were an angel. They mowed and gibbered in the moonlight, under crowns of drooping, golden blossoms. One, whose bloated earlobe flapped like a fan upon his shoulder, caught up a gorgeous flower of orange and scarlet and with it decorated the monstrous ear that flip-flapped with his ever movement.

And over these things Koolau was king. And this was his kingdom—a flower-throttled gorge, with beetling cliffs and crags, from which floated the blattings of wild goats. On three sides the grim walls rose, festooned in fantastic draperies of tropic vegetation and pierced by cave entrances—the rocky lairs of Koolau's subjects. On the fourth side the earth fell away into a tremendous abyss, and, far below, could be seen the summits of lesser peaks and crags, at whose bases foamed and rumbled the Pacific surge. In fine weather a boat could land on the rocky beach that marked the entrance of Kalalau Valley, but the weather must be very fine. And a cool-headed mountaineer might climb from the beach to the head of Kalalau Valley, to this pocket among the peaks where Koolau ruled; but such a mountaineer must be very cool of head, and he must know the wild-goat trails as well. The marvel was that the mass of human wreckage that constituted Koolau's people should have been able to drag its helpless misery over the giddy goat trails to this inaccessible spot.

"Brothers," Koolau began.

But one of the mowing, apelike travesties emitted a wild shriek of madness, and Koolau waited while the shrill cachinnation was tossed back and forth among the rocky walls and echoed distantly through the pulseless night.

"Brothers, is it not strange? Ours was the land, and behold, the land is not ours. What did these preachers of the word of God and the word of Rum give us for the land? Have you received one dollar, as much as one dollar, any one of you, for the land? Yet it is theirs, and in return they tell us we can go to work on the land, their land, and that what we produce by our toil shall be theirs. Yet in the old days we did not have to work. Also when we are sick, they take away our freedom."

"Who brought the sickness, Koolau?" demanded Kiloliana, a lean and wiry man with a face so like a laughing faun's that one might expect to see the cloven hoofs under him. They were cloven, it was true, but the cleavages were great ulcers and livid putrefactions. Yet this was Kiloliana, the most daring climber of them all, the man who knew every goat trail and who had led Koolau and his wretched followers into the recesses of Kalalau.

"Ay, well questioned," Koolau answered. "Because we would not work the miles of sugar cane where once our horses pastured, they brought the Chinese slaves from overseas. And with them came the Chinese sickness—that which we suffer from and because of which they would imprison us on Molokai. We were born on Kauai. We have been to the other islands, some here and some there, to Oahu, to Maui, to Hawaii, to Honolulu. Yet always did we come back to Kauai. Why did we come back? There must be a reason. Because we love Kauai. We were born here. Here we have lived. And here shall we die—unless—unless—there be weak hearts amongst us. Such we do not want. They are fit for Molokai. And if there be such, let them not remain. Tomorrow the soldiers land on the shore. Let the weak hearts go down to them. They will be sent swiftly to Molokai. As for us, we shall stay and fight. But know that we will not die. We have rifles. You know the narrow trails where men must creep, one by one. I, alone, Koolau, who was once a cowboy on Niihau, can hold the trail against a thousand men. Here is Kapahei, who was once a judge over men and a man with honor, but who is now a hunted rat, like you and me. Hear him. He is wise."

Kapahei arose. Once he had been a judge. He had gone to college at Punahou. He had sat at meat with lords and chiefs and the high representatives of alien powers who protected the interests of traders and missionaries. Such had been Kapahei. But now, as Koolau had said, he was a hunted rat, a creature outside the law, sunk so deep in the mire of human horror that he was above the law as well as beneath it. His face was featureless, save for gaping orifices and for the lidless eyes that burned under hairless brows.

"Let us not make trouble," he began. "We ask to be left alone. But if they do not leave us alone, then is the trouble theirs, and the penalty. My fingers are gone, as you see." He held up his stumps of hands that all might see. "Yet have I the joint of one thumb left, and it can pull a trigger as firmly as did its lost neighbor in the old days. We love Kauai. Let us live here, or die here, but do not let us go to the prison of Molokai. The sickness is not ours. We have not sinned. The men who preached the word of God and the word of Rum brought the sickness with the coolie slaves who work the stolen land. I have been a judge. I know the law and the justice, an I say to you it is unjust to steal a man's land, to make that man sick with the Chinese sickness, and then to put that man in prison for life."

"Life is short, and the days are filled with pain," said Koolau. "Let us drink and dance and be happy as we can."

From one of the rocky lairs calabashes were produced and passed around. The calabashes were filled with the fierce distillation of the root of the ti plant; and as the liquid fire coursed through them and mounted to their brains, they forgot that they had once been men and women, for they were men and women once more. The woman who wept scalding tears from open eye-pits was indeed a woman apulse with life as she plucked the strings

of an ukulele and lifted her voice in a barbaric love-call
such as might have come from the dark forest depths of
the primeval world. The air tingled with her cry, softly
imperious and seductive. Upon a mat, timing his rhythm
to the woman's song, Kiloliana danced. It was
unmistakable. Love danced in all his movements, and,
next, dancing with him on the mat, was a woman whose
heavy hips and generous breast gave the lie to her disease-
corroded face. It was a dance of the living dead, for in
their disintegrating bodies life still loved and longed. Ever
the woman whose sightless eyes ran scalding tears chanted
her love-cry, ever the dancers danced of love in the warm
night, and ever the calabashes went around till in all their
brains were maggots crawling of memory and desire. And
with the woman on the mat danced a slender maid whose
face was beautiful and unmarred, but whose twisted arms
that rose and fell marked the disease's ravage. And the two
idiots, gibbering and mouthing strange noises, danced
apart, grotesque, fantastic, travestying love as they
themselves had been travestied by life.

But the woman's love-cry broke midway, the
calabashes were lowered, and the dancers ceased, as all
gazed into the abyss above the sea, where a rocket flared
like a wan phantom through the moonlit air.

"It is the soldiers," said Koolau. "Tomorrow there will
be fighting. It is well to sleep and be prepared."

The lepers obeyed, crawling away to their lairs in the
cliff, until only Koolau remained, sitting motionless in
the moonlight, his rifle across his knees, as he gazed far
down to the boats landing on the beach.

The far head of Kalalau Valley had been well chosen
as a refuge. Except Kiloliana, who knew back trails up the
precipitous walls, no man would win to the gorge save by
advancing across a knife-edged ridge. This passage was a

hundred yards in length. At best, it was a scant twelve inches wide. On either side yawned the abyss. A slip, and to right or left the man would fall to his death. But once across he would find himself in an earthly paradise. A sea of vegetation laved the landscape, pouring its green billows from wall to wall, dripping from the cliff lips in great vine masses, and flinging a spray of ferns and air plants into the multitudinous crevices. During the many months of Koolau's rule, he and his followers had fought with this vegetable sea. The choking jungle, with its riot of blossoms, had been driven back from the bananas, oranges, and mangoes that grew wild. In little clearings grew the wild arrowroot; on stone terraces, filled with soil scrapings, were the taro patches and the melons; and in every open space where the sunshine penetrated were papaya trees burdened with their golden fruit.

Koolau had been driven to this refuge from the lower valley by the beach. And if he were driven from it in turn, he knew of gorges among the jumbled peaks of the inner fastnesses where he could lead his subjects and live. And now he lay with his rifle beside him, peering down through a tangled screen of foliage at the soldiers on the beach. He noted that they had large guns with them, from which the sunshine flashed as from mirrors. The knife-edged passage lay directly before him. Crawling upward along the trail that led to it he could see tiny specks of men. He knew they were not the soldiers, but the police. When they failed, then the soldiers would enter the game.

He affectionately rubbed a twisted hand along his rifle barrel and made sure that the sights were clean. He had learned to shoot as a wild-cattle hunter on Niihau, and on that island his skill as a marksman was unforgotten. As the toiling specks of men grew nearer and larger, he estimated the range, judged the deflection of the wind that swept at right angles across the line of fire, and calculated the chances of overshooting marks that were so far below his level. But he did not shoot. Not until they reached the beginning of the passage did he make his presence known. He did not disclose himself, but spoke from the thicket.

"What do you want?" he demanded.

"We want Koolau, the leper," answered the man who led the native police, himself a blue-eyed American.

"You must go back," Koolau said.

He knew the man, a deputy sheriff, for it was by him that he had been harried out of Niihau, across Kauai, to Kalalau Valley, and out of the valley to the gorge.

"Who are you?" the sheriff asked.

"I am Koolau, the leper," was the reply.

"Then come out. We want you. Dead or alive, there is a thousand dollars on your head. You cannot escape."

Koolau laughed aloud in the thicket.

"Come out" the sheriff commanded, and was answered by silence.

He conferred with the police, and Koolau saw that they were preparing to rush him.

"Koolau," the sheriff called. "Koolau, I am coming across to get you."

"Then look first and well about you at the sun and sea and sky, for it will be the last time you behold them."

"That's all right, Koolau," the sheriff said soothingly. "I know you're a dead shot. But you won't shoot me. I have never done you any wrong."

Koolau grunted in the thicket.

"I say, you know, I've never done you any wrong, have I?" the sheriff persisted.

"You do me wrong when you try to put me in prison," was the reply. "And you do me wrong when you try for the thousand dollars on my head. If you will live, stay where you are."

"I've got to come across and get you. I'm sorry. But it is my duty."

"You will die before you get across."

The sheriff was no coward. Yet was he undecided. He gazed into the gulf on either side, and ran his eyes along the knife-edge he must travel. Then he made up his mind.

"Koolau," he called.

But the thicket remained silent.

"Koolau, don't shoot. I am coming."

The sheriff turned, gave some orders to the police, then started. on his perilous way. He advanced slowly. It was like walking a tight rope. He had nothing to lean upon but the air. The lava rock crumbled under his feet, and on either side the dislodged fragments pitched downward through the depths. The sun blazed upon him, and his face was wet with sweat. Still he advanced, until the halfway point was reached.

"Stop!" Koolau commanded from the thicket. "One more step and I shoot."

The sheriff halted, swaying for balance as he stood poised above the void. His face was pale, but his eyes were determined. He licked his dry lips before he spoke.

"Koolau, you won't shoot me. I know you won't."

He started once more. The bullet whirled him half about. On his face was an expression of querulous surprise as he reeled to the fall. He tried to save himself by throwing his body across the knife-edge; but at that moment he knew death. The next moment the knife-edge was vacant. Then came the rush, five policemen, in single file, with superb steadiness, running along the knife-edge. At the same instant the rest of the posse opened fire on the thicket. It was madness. Five times Koolau pulled the trigger, so rapidly that his shots constituted a rattle. Changing his position and crouching low under the bullets that were biting and singing through the bushes, he peered out. Four of the police had followed the sheriff. The fifth lay across the knife-edge, still alive. On the farther side, no longer firing, were the surviving police. On the naked rock there was no hope for them. Before they could clamber down Koolau could have picked off the last men. But he did not fire and, after a conference, one of them took off a white undershirt and waved it as a flag. Followed by another, he advanced along the knife-edge to their wounded comrade. Koolau gave no sign, but watched them slowly withdraw and become specks as they descended into the lower valley.

Two hours later, from another thicket, Koolau watched a body of police trying to make the ascent from the opposite side of the valley. He saw the wild goats flee before them as they climbed higher and higher, until he doubted his judgment and sent for Kiloliana, who crawled in beside him.

"No, there is no way," said Kiloliana.

"The goats?" Koolau questioned.

"They come over from the next valley, but they cannot pass to this. There is no way. Those men are not wiser than goats. They may fall to their deaths. Let us watch."

Side by side they lay among the morning-glories, with the yellow blossoms of the hau dropping upon them from overhead, watching the motes of men toil upward, till the thing happened, and three of them, slipping, rolling, sliding, dashed over a cliff lip and fell sheer half a thousand feet.

Kiloliana chuckled.

"We will be bothered no more," he said.

"They have war guns," Koolau made answer. "The soldiers have not yet spoken."

In the drowsy afternoon, most of the lepers lay in their rock dens asleep. Koolau, his rifle on his knees, fresh-cleaned and ready, dozed in the entrance to his own den. The maid with the twisted arm lay below in the thicket and kept watch on the knife-edge passage. Suddenly Koolau was startled wide awake by the sound of an explosion on the beach. The next instant the atmosphere was incredibly rent asunder. The terrible sound frightened him. It was as if all the gods had caught the envelope of the sky in their hands and were ripping it apart as a woman rips apart a sheet of cotton cloth. But it was such an immense ripping, growing swiftly nearer. Koolau glanced up apprehensively, as if expecting to see the thing. Then high up on the cliff overhead the shell burst in a fountain of black smoke. The rock was shattered, the fragments falling to the foot of the cliff.

Koolau passed his hand across his sweaty brow. He was terribly shaken. He had no experience with shellfire, and this was more dreadful than anything he had imagined.

"One," said Kapahei, suddenly bethinking himself to keep count.

A second and a third shell flew screaming over the top of the wall, bursting beyond view. Kapahei methodically kept the count. The lepers crowded into the open space before the caves. At first they were frightened, but as the shells continued their flight overhead the leper folk became reassured and began to admire the spectacle. The two idiots shrieked with delight, prancing wild antics as each air-tormenting shell went by. Koolau began to recover his confidence. No damage was being done. Evidently they could not aim such large missiles at such long range with the precision of a rifle.

But a change came over the situation. The shells began to fall short. One burst below in the thicket by the knife-edge. Koolau remembered the maid who lay there on watch, and ran down to see. The smoke was still rising from the bushes when he crawled in. He was astounded. The branches were splintered and broken. Where the girl had lain was a hole in the ground. The girl herself was in shattered fragments. The shell had burst right on her.

First peering out to make sure no soldiers were attempting the passage, Koolau started back on the run for the caves. All the time the shells were moaning, whining, screaming by, and the valley was rumbling and reverberating with the explosion. As he came in sight of the caves, he saw the two idiots cavorting about, clutching each other's hands with their stumps of fingers. Even as he ran, Koolau saw a spout of black smoke rise from the ground, near to the idiots. They were flung apart bodily by the explosion. One lay motionless, but the other was dragging himself by his hands toward the cave. His legs trailed out helplessly behind him, while the blood was pouring from his body. He seemed bathed in blood, and as he crawled he cried like a little dog. The rest of the lepers, with the exception of Kapahei, had fled into the caves.

"Seventeen," said Kapahei. "Eighteen," he added.

This last shell had fairly entered into one of the caves. The explosion caused all the caves to empty. But from the particular cave no one emerged. Koolau crept in through the pungent, acrid smoke. Four bodies, frightfully mangled, lay about. One of them was the sightless woman whose tears till now had never ceased.

Outside, Koolau found his people in a panic and already beginning to climb the goat trail that led out of the gorge and on among the jumbled heights and chasms. The wounded idiot, whining feebly and dragging himself along on the ground by his hands, was trying to follow.

But at the first pitch of the wall his helplessness overcame him and he fell back.

"It would be better to kill him," said Koolau to Kapahei, who still sat in the same place.

"Twenty-two," Kapahei answered. "Yes, it would be a wise thing to kill him. Twenty-three—twenty-four."

The idiot whined sharply when he saw the rifle leveled at him. Koolau hesitated, then lowered the gun.

"It is a hard thing to do," he said.

"You are a fool, twenty-six, twenty-seven," said Kapahei. "Let me show you."

He arose and, with a heavy fragment of rock in his hand, approached the wounded thing. As he lifted his arm to strike, a shell burst full upon him, relieving him of the necessity of the act and at the same time putting an end to his count.

Koolau was alone in the gorge. He watched the last of his people drag their crippled bodies over the brow of the height and disappear. Then he turned and went down to the thicket where the maid had been killed. The shellfire still continued, but he remained; for far below he could see the soldiers climbing up. A shell burst twenty feet away. Flattening himself into the earth, he heard the rush of the fragments above his body. A shower of hau blossoms rained upon him. He lifted his head to peer down the trail, and sighed. He was very much afraid. Bullets from rifles would not have worried him, but this shell fire was abominable. Each time a shell shrieked by he shivered and crouched; but each time he lifted his head again to watch the trail.

At last the shells ceased. This, he reasoned, was because the soldiers were drawing near. They crept along the trail in single file, and he tried to count them until he lost track. At any rate, there were a hundred or so of them—all come after Koolau the leper. He felt a fleeting prod of pride. With war guns and rifles, police and soldiers, they came for him, and he was only one man, a crippled wreck of a man at that. They offered a thousand dollars for him, dead or alive. In all his life he had never possessed that much money. The thought was a bitter one. Kapahei had been right. He, Koolau, had done no wrong. Because the haoles wanted labor with which to work the stolen land, they had brought in the Chinese coolies, and with them had come the sickness. And now, because he had caught the sickness, he was worth a thousand dollars—but not to himself. It was his worthless carcass, rotten with disease or dead from a bursting shell, that was worth all that money.

When the soldiers reached the knife-edged passage, he was prompted to warn them. But his gaze fell upon the body of the murdered maid, and he kept silent. When six had ventured on the knife-edge, he opened fire. Nor did he cease when the knife-edge was bare. He emptied his magazine, reloaded, and emptied it again. He kept on shooting. All his wrongs were blazing in his brain, and he was in a fury of vengeance. All down the goat trail the soldiers were firing, and though they lay flat and sought to shelter themselves in the shallow inequalities of the surface, they were exposed marks to him. Bullets whistled and thudded about him, and an occasional ricochet sang sharply through the air. One bullet ploughed a crease through his scalp, and a second burned across his shoulder blade without breaking the skin.

It was a massacre, in which one man did the killing. The soldiers began to retreat, helping along their wounded. As Koolau picked them off he became aware of the smell of burnt meat. He glanced about him at first, and then discovered that it was his own hands. The heat of the rifle was doing it. The leprosy had destroyed most of the nerves in his hands. Though his flesh burned and he smelled it, there was no sensation.

He lay in the thicket, smiling, until he remembered the war guns. Without doubt they would open up on him again, and this time upon the very thicket from which he had inflicted the damage. Scarcely had he changed his position to a nook behind a small shoulder of the wall where he had noted that no shells fell, then the bombardment recommenced. He counted the shells. Sixty more were thrown into the gorge before the war guns ceased. The tiny area was pitted with their explosions until it seemed impossible that any creature could have survived. So the soldiers thought, for, under the burning afternoon sun, they climbed the goat trail again. And again the knife-edged passage was disputed, and again they fell back to the beach.

For two days longer Koolau held the passage, though the soldiers contented themselves with flinging shells into his retreat. Then Pahau, a leper boy, came to the top of the wall at the back of the gorge and shouted down to him that Kiloliana, hunting goats that they might eat, had been killed by a fall, and that the women were frightened and knew not what to do. Koolau called the boy down and left him with a spare gun with which to guard the passage.

Koolau found his people disheartened. The majority of them were too helpless to forage food for themselves under such forbidding circumstances, and all were starving. He selected two women and a man who were not too far gone with the disease, and sent them back to the gorge to bring up food and mats. The rest he cheered and consoled until even the weakest took a hand in building rough shelters for themselves.

But those he had dispatched for food did not return, and he started back for the gorge. As he came out on the brow of the wall, half a dozen rifles cracked. A bullet tore through the fleshy part of his shoulder, and his cheek was cut by a sliver of rock where a second bullet smashed against the cliff. In the moment that this happened, and he leaped back, he saw that the gorge was alive with soldiers. His own people had betrayed him. The shellfire had been too terrible, and they had preferred the prison of Molokai.

Koolau dropped back and unslung one of his heavy cartridge belts. Lying among the rocks, he allowed the head and shoulders of the first soldier to rise clearly into view before pulling the trigger. Twice this happened, and then, after some delay, in place of a head and shoulders a white flag was thrust above the edge of the wall.

"What do you want?" he demanded.

"I want you, if you are Koolau the leper," came the answer.

Koolau forgot where he was, forgot everything, as he lay and marvelled at the strange persistence of these haoles who would have their will though the sky fell in. Aye, they would have their will over all men and all things, even though they died in getting it. He could not but admire them, too, what of that will in them that was stronger than life and that bent all things to their bidding. He was convinced of the hopelessness of his struggle. There was no gainsaying that terrible will of the haoles. Though he killed a thousand, yet would they rise like the sands of the sea and come upon him, ever more and more. They never knew when they were beaten. That was their fault and their virtue. It was where his own kind lacked. He could see, now, how the handful of the preachers of God and the preachers of Rum had conquered the land. It was because—

"Well, what have you got to say? Will you come with me?"

It was the voice of the invisible man under the white flag, There he was, like any haole, driving straight toward the end determined.

"Let us talk," said Koolau.

The man's head and shoulders arose, then his whole body. He was a smooth-faced, blue-eyed youngster of twenty-five, slender and natty in his captain's uniform. He advanced until halted, then seated himself a dozen feet away.

"You are a brave man," said Koolau wonderingly. "I could kill you like a fly."

"No, you couldn't," was the answer.

"Why not?"

"Because you are a man, Koolau, though a bad one. I know your story. You kill fairly."

Koolau grunted, but was secretly pleased.

"What have you done with my people?" he demanded. "The boy, the two women, and the man?"

"They gave themselves up, as I have now come for you to do."

Koolau laughed incredulously.

"I am a free man," he announced. "I have done no wrong. All I ask is to be left alone. I have lived free, and I shall die free. I will never give myself up."

"Then your people are wiser than you," answered the young captain. "Look—they are coming now."

Koolau turned and watched the remnant of his band approach. Groaning and sighing, a ghastly procession, it dragged its wretchedness past. It was given to Koolau to taste a deeper bitterness, for they hurled imprecations and insults at him as they went by; and the panting hag who brought up the rear halted and with skinny, harpy-claws extended, shaking her snarling death's head from side to side, she laid a curse upon him. One by one they dropped over the lip edge and surrendered to the hiding soldiers.

"You can go now," said Koolau to the captain. "I will never give myself up. That is my last word. Good-by."

The captain slipped over the cliff to his soldiers. The next moment and without a flag of truce, he hoisted his hat on his scabbard, and Koolau's bullet tore through it. That afternoon they shelled him out from the beach, and as he retreated into the high inaccessible pockets beyond, the soldiers followed him.

For six weeks they hunted him from pocket to pocket, over the volcanic peaks and along the goat trails. When he hid in the lantana jungle, they formed lines of beaters, and through lantana jungle and guava scrub they drove him like a rabbit. But ever he turned and doubled and eluded. There was no cornering him. When pressed too closely, his sure rifle held them back and they carried their wounded down the goat trails to the beach. There were times when they did the shooting as his brown body showed for a moment through the underbrush. Once, five of them caught him on an exposed goat trail between pockets. They emptied their rifles at him as he limped and climbed along his dizzy way. Afterward they found bloodstains and knew that he was wounded. At the end of six weeks they gave up. The soldiers and police returned to Honolulu, and Kalalau Valley was left to him for his own, though headhunters ventured after him from time to time and to their own undoing.

Two years later, and for the last time, Koolau crawled into a thicket and lay down among the ti leaves and wild ginger blossoms. Free he had lived, and free he was dying. A slight drizzle of rain began to fall, and he drew a ragged blanket about the distorted wreck of his limbs. His body was covered with an oilskin coat. Across his chest he laid his Mauser rifle, lingering affectionately for a moment to wipe the dampness from the barrel. The hand with which he wiped had no fingers left upon it with which to pull the trigger.

He closed his eyes, for, from the weakness in his body and the fuzzy turmoil in his brain, he knew that his end was near. Like a wild animal he had crept into hiding to die. Half conscious, aimless and wandering, he lived back in his life to his early manhood on Niihau. As life faded and the drip of the rain grew dim in his ears, it seemed to him that he was once more in the thick of the horse-breaking, with raw colts rearing and bucking under him, his stirrups tied together beneath, or charging madly about the breaking corral and driving the helping cowboys over the rails. The next instant, and with seeming naturalness, he found himself pursuing the wild bulls of the upland pastures, roping them and leading them down to the valleys. Again the sweat and dust of the branding pen stung his eyes and bit his nostrils.

All his lusty, whole-bodied youth was his, until the sharp pangs of impending dissolution brought him back. He lifted his monstrous hands and gazed at them in wonder. But how? Why? Why should the wholeness of that wild youth of his change to this? Then he remembered, and once again, and for a moment, he was Koolau, the leper. His eyelids fluttered wearily down and the drip of the rain ceased in his ears. A prolonged trembling set up in his body. This, too, ceased. He half lifted his head, but it fell back. Then his eyes opened, and did not close. His last thought was of his Mauser, and he pressed it against his chest, with his folded, fingerless hands.

▓ ▓ ▓

George H. Read

XXV.   THE LAST CRUISE
OF THE SAGINAW
A 1,200-MILE OPEN-BOAT RESCUE
VOYAGE FROM KURE ATOLL TO KAUA'I

*To the northwest of Kaua'i is a string of islands known
by some as the northwestern chain. In ancient Hawai'i it
was believed fishermen from Kaua'i would sail to Nihoa and
Necker, two of the closest of these islands, to live and fish for
extended periods. When favorable, strong, west winds blew,
the fishermen would sail back to Kaua'i with their cargoes of
dried fish and sea birds.*

*At the end of this chain is Kure Atoll, which consists of a
small lagoon and enclosing reef. Until recently, Kure housed
a Coast Guard LORAN Station, which helped to guide
aircraft and shipping in Hawaiian waters. The station has
been decommissioned and the atoll has been returned to the
thousands of sea birds and the colony of Hawaiian monk
seals that inhabit it.*

Nearby Midway was the target of a Japanese attack in World War II. Holding back the Japanese here in 1942 probably saved Hawai'i from a land invasion.

The Saginaw, *whose wreck is the focus of the following selection, is but one of many ships that have gone aground in these waters. A classic tale of shipwreck, the* Saginaw's *story is linked to Kaua'i through an amazing 1,200-mile, open-boat rescue voyage that ended near Hanalei.*

Author George H. Read was a survivor of the well-known shipwreck which made headlines across the country. Today the gig which made the journey to Kaua'i from Kure is on display at the U.S. Naval Academy at Annapolis, Maryland. The graves of the unfortunate seamen who drowned or died upon arrival at Kaua'i's north shore were moved from Hanalei to Honolulu years ago. Some believe Robert Louis Stevenson drew on the Saginaw *incident in his writings.*

IN SAN FRANCISCO our captain, Lieutenant-Commander Montgomery Sicard, had received orders to proceed to the Midway Islands, via Honolulu . . .

In a northwesterly direction from the Sandwich Islands there stretches for over a thousand miles a succession of coral reefs and shoals, with here and there a sandy islet thrown up by the winds and waves. They are mostly bare of vegetation beyond a stunted growth of bushes. These islets are called atolls by geographers, and their foundations are created by the mysterious *polyps* or coral insects.

These atolls abound in the Pacific Ocean, and rising but a few feet above the surface, surrounded by uncertain and uncharted currents, are the dread of navigators.

Near the centre of the North Pacific and near the western end of the chain of atolls above mentioned, are two small sand islands in the usual lagoon, with a coral reef enclosing both. They were discovered by an American captain, N. C. Brooks, of the Hawaiian bark *Gambia*, and by him reported; were subsequently visited by the United States Steamer *Lackawanna* and surveyed for charting.

No importance other than the danger to navigation was at that time attached to these mere sandbanks. Now, however, the trans-Pacific railroads, girdling the continent and making valuable so many hitherto insignificant places, have cast their influence three thousand miles across the waters to these obscure islets. The expected increase of commerce between the United States and the Orient has induced the Pacific Mail Steamship Company to look for a halfway station as a coaling-depot, and these, the Midway Islands are expected to answer the purpose when the proposed improvements are made. To do the work of deepening a now shallow channel through the reef, a contract has been awarded to an experienced submarine engineer and the Saginaw has been brought into service to transport men and material. Our captain is to superintend and to report monthly on the progress made. Thus, with the voyages out and return, coupled with the several trips between the Midways and Honolulu, we have the prospect of a year's deep-water cruising to our credit.

FEBRUARY 22, 1870

Once more separated from home and friends, with the Golden Gate dissolving astern in a California fog (than which none can be more dense) old Neptune gives us a boisterous welcome to his dominions, and the howling of wind through the rigging, with the rolling and pitching of the ship as we steam out to sea, where we meet the full force of a stiff "southeaster," remind us that we are once more his subjects.

On the fourteenth day out we hear the welcome cry of "Land Ho!" at sunrise from the masthead. It proved to be the island of Molokai.

[The crew subsequently spent the spring, summer and early fall blasting a channel at the narrow entrance to the lagoon at Midway Island the *Saginaw* made several supply trips to Honolulu during this period, *ed*.]

With the homeward-bound pennant flying from the mainmast head and with the contractor's working party on board, we sailed from the Midway Islands on Friday, October 29, at 4 P.M. for San Francisco. We had dragged high up on the beach the scow from which the divers had worked, secured the house doors, and taken a last look at the blinding sand with thankful hearts for leaving it.

As Doctor Frank, our surgeon, and myself were walking down the beach to the last boat off to the ship, there occurred an incident which I will relate here for psychological students.

He remarked, as we loitered around the landing, that he felt greatly depressed without being able to define any cause for it and that he could not rid himself of the impression that some misfortune was impending. I tried to cheer him up; told him that the "blues" were on him, when he ought to be rejoicing instead; that we had a fair wind and a smooth sea to start us on a speedy return to the old friends in San Francisco. It was in vain, however; he expressed a firm belief that we should meet with some disaster on our voyage and I dropped the subject with a "pooh pooh."

As soon as we readied the open sea, the captain ordered the ship headed to the westward and the pressure of steam to be reduced, as with topsails set we sailed along to a light easterly breeze. It was his intention, he stated, to come within sight of Ocean Island (today known as

Kure Atoll, ed.) about daylight and to verify its location by steaming around it before heading away for San Francisco.

It should be noted that it is in the direct line of a naval commander's duty, when he is in the neighborhood of such dangers to navigation, to confirm by observation their position on the charts as well as to rescue any unfortunate persons that fate may have cast away upon them. Our own subsequent situation gives proof of the wisdom of such a regulation.

Ocean Island is about fifty miles to the westward of the Midway Islands, is of similar formation, and is the last one (so far as our chart shows) in the chain of ocean dangers that I have referred to as extending more than a thousand miles to the westward from the Sandwich Islands. It was on this reef that the British ship *Gledstanes* was wrecked in 1837, and the American ship *Parker* in September, 1842, the crew of the latter vessel remaining there until May, 1843, when they were taken off...

...The evening following the departure passed quietly in our wardroom quarters and in fact all over the ship. Officers and men were more than usually fatigued after the preparations for sea both on shore and on board. There was none of the general hilarity accompanying a homeward cruise. There was also a prevailing dread of a long and tedious journey of over three thousand miles, mostly to be made under sail, and we all knew the tendency of the old Saginaw in a head wind to make "eight points to leeward," or, as a landlubber would say, to go sideways. We occupied ourselves in stowing and securing our movables, and after the bugle sounded "Out lights" at 9 p.m. the steady tramp of the lookouts and their half-hour hail of "All's well" were all that disturbed the quiet of the night.

The night was dark, but a few stars were occasionally visible between the passing clouds. The sea continued smooth and the ship on an even keel. When I turned in at ten o'clock I had the comforting thought that by the same time to-morrow night we should be heading for San Francisco. We were making about three knots an hour, which would bring Ocean Island in sight about early dawn, so that there would be plenty of time to circumnavigate the reef and get a good offing on our course before dark.

How sadly, alas! our intentions were frustrated and how fully our surgeon's premonitions were fulfilled! My pen falters at the attempt to describe the events of the next few hours. I was suddenly awakened about three o'clock in the morning by an unusual commotion on deck; the hurried tramping of feet and confusion of sounds. In the midst of it I distinguished the captain's voice sounding in sharp contrast to his usual moderate tone, ordering the taking in of the topsails and immediately after the cutting away of the topsail halliards. Until the latter order was given I imagined the approach of a rain squall, a frequent occurrence formerly, but I knew now that some greater emergency existed, and so I hastily and partly dressed myself sufficiently to go on deck.

Just before I reached the top of the wardroom ladder I felt the ship strike something and supposed we were in collision with another vessel. The shock was an easy one at first, but was followed immediately by others of increasing force, and, as my feet touched the deck, by two severe shocks that caused the ship to tremble in every timber. The long easy swell that had been lifting us gently along in the open sea was now transformed into heavy breakers as it reached and swept over the coral reef, each wave lifting and dropping with a frightful thud the quaking ship. It seemed at each fall as though her masts and smokestack would jump from their holdings and go by the board. To a landsman or even a professional seaman who has never experienced the sensation it would be impossible to convey a realizing sense of the feelings aroused by our sudden misfortune. There is a something even in the air akin to the terror of an earthquake shock— a condition unnatural and uncanny. The good ship that for years has safely sailed the seas or anchored in ports with a free keel, fulfilling in all respects the destiny marked out for her at her birth, suddenly and without warning enters upon her death-struggle with the rocks and appeals for help. There is no wonder the brave men—men having withstood the shock of battle and endured the hardships of fiercest storms—should feel their nerves shaken from their first glance at the situation. The captain had immediately followed his orders, to take in the sails that were forging us on towards the reef, by an order to back engines. Alas! the steam was too low to give more than a few turns to the wheels, and they could not overcome the momentum of the ship. In less than an hour of the fierce pounding the jagged rock broke through the hull and tore up the engine and fire room floor; water rushed in and reached the fires; the doom of our good ship was now apparent and sealed.

I hastily returned to my stateroom, secured more clothing, together with some of the ship's papers, then ascended to the hurricane deck to await developments or to stand by to do rescue work as ordered…

…The night was clear and starlit, but we could see nothing of any land. Perhaps we had struck on some uncharted reef, and while strenuously employed in getting the boats over the side opposite the sea we waited anxiously for daylight. The scene was one for a lifelong remembrance and is beyond my power adequately and calmly to describe.

There was at first some confusion, but the stern and composed attitude of the captain and his sharp, clear orders soon brought every one to his senses, and order was restored.

One of the most reassuring things to me at this time was the sight of our colored wardroom steward in double irons for some offense, sitting on a hatch of the hurricane deck, whistling "Way down upon the Suwanee River." He seemed to me far from realizing the gravity of the situation, or else to possess great courage. At any rate, it diverted my thoughts of danger into other channels. He said the key to the irons could not be found. The irons were soon severed, however, with a chisel and hammer, and he went below to aid the men with his knowledge of the stowage of the officers' provender. His confinement was never renewed, for he did good work in the rescue of food.

A few of the more frightened ones had at first, either through a misunderstanding or otherwise, rushed to our largest boat—the launch—hanging at the starboard quarter and partly lowered it before the act was noticed. A large combing sea came along and tore it from their hold, smashing it against the side of the ship and then carrying its remnants away with its tackles and all its fittings. This was a great loss, we felt, if we should have to take to the boats, for we did not know at that time where we were. The same wave also carried off one of the crew, a member of the Marine Guard, who had been on the bulwarks; and whisking him seaward, returned him miraculously around the stern of the ship to the reef, where his struggles and cries attracted the notice of others. He was hauled over the lee side, somewhat bruised and water-soaked, but, judging from his remarks, apparently not realizing his wonderful escape from death.

As the night wore on, the wind increased and also the size of the breakers. The ship, which had first struck the reef "bows on," was gradually swung around until she was at first broadside to the reef, and then further until the after part, to which we were clinging, was lifted over the jagged edge of the perpendicular wall of rock. She was finally twisted around until the bow hung directly to seaward, with the middle of the hull at the edge. Thus the ship "seesawed" from stem to stern with each coming wave for an hour or more and until the forward part broke away with a loud crash and disappeared in the deep water outside. Our anchors, that had been "let go," apparently never touched bottom until the bow went with them.

All that was left of our good ship now heeled over towards the inner side of the reef, the smokestack soon went by the board and the mainmast was made to follow it by simply cutting away the starboard or seaward shrouds. Over this mast we could pass to the reef, however, and there was comparative quiet in the waters under our lee. This helped us in passing across whatever we could save from the wreck, and in this manner went three of our boats, the captain's gig, one of the cutters, and the dinghy, without much damage also secured in this way an iron lifeboat belonging to the contractor.

As the first gray streaks of dawn showed us a small strip of terra firma in the smooth water of the lagoon and not far from the reef, many a sigh of relief was heard, and our efforts were redoubled to provide some means of prolonging existence there. At any rate, we knew now where we were and could at least imagine a possible relief and plan measures to secure it.

Although the sea had robbed us of the larger part of our provisions, in the forward hold there were still some of the most important stowed within the fragment we were clinging to, which contained the bread and clothing storerooms. With daylight our task was made easier.

A line was formed across the reef and everything rescued was passed over the side and from hand to hand to the boats in the lagoon, for transfer to the island. Thus we stood waist-deep in the water, feet and ankles lacerated and bleeding, stumbling about the sharp and uneven coral rock, until five in the afternoon, and yet our spirits, which had been low in the dark, were so encouraged by a sight of a small portion of dry land and at least a temporary escape from a watery grave that now and then a jest or a laugh would pass along the line with some article that suggested a future meal.

At five o'clock in the afternoon the order was given to abandon the wreck (which was done while hoping that it would hold together until to-morrow), and as the sun went down on the "lone barren isle," all hands were piped by the boatswain's whistle to supper.

A half-teacup of water, half a cake of hardtack, and a small piece of boiled pork constituted our evening meal, to which was added a piece of boiled mutton that had been intended for the wardroom table.

After this frugal meal all hands were mustered upon the beach to listen to a prayer of thankfulness for our deliverance and then to a few sensible and well-timed remarks from the captain enjoining discipline, good nature, and economy of food under our trying circumstances. He told us that by the Navy Regulations he was instructed, as our commanding officer, to keep up, in such sad conditions as we were thrown into, the organization and discipline of the Service so far as applicable; that he would in the event of our rescue (which we should all hope for and look forward to) be held responsible for the proper administration of law and order;

that officers and crew should fare alike on our scanty store of food, and that with care we should probably make out, with the help of seal meat and birds, a reduced ration for some little time. He would detail our several duties tomorrow. Then we were dismissed to seek "tired nature's sweet restorer" as best we could.

With fourteen hours of severe labor, tired, wet, and hungry, we were yet glad enough to sink to rest amid the bushes with but the sky for a canopy and a hummock of sand for a pillow. In my own case sleep was hard to win. For a long time I lay watching the stars and speculating upon the prospects of release from our island prison. Life seemed to reach dimly uncertain into the future, with shadow pictures intervening of famished men and bereaved families.

I could hear the waves within a few rods of our resting-places—there was no music in them now—lapping the beach in their restlessness, and now and then an angry roar from the outside reef, as though the sea was in rage over its failure to reach us. I realized that for more than a thousand miles the sea stretched away in every direction before habited shores and for treble that our native land; that our island small dot in the vast Pacific—a dot so small that few maps give it recognition. Truly it was a dismal outlook that "tired nature" finally dispelled and that sleep transformed into oblivion; for I went to sleep finally while recalling old stories of family gatherings where was always placed a vacant chair for the loved absent one should he ever return.

(From Sunday, October 30 until Thursday, November 17 the crew adjusted to life on a desert island and made preparations for a rescue boat to sail south-southeast to the main Hawaiian Islands).

Friday November 18

The weather has been fine since the breaking up of the storm of the second.

As to work, every one has had his duties portioned out to him, and there is no doubt of the captain's wisdom in providing thus an antidote to homesickness or brooding. Faces are—some of them—getting "peaked," and quite a number of the party have been ill from lack of power to digest the seal meat; but there are no complaints, we all fare alike. Medicines are not to hand, but a day or two of abstinence and quiet generally brings one around again. In the evenings, when we gather around the smoking lamp after supper, there are frequent discussions over our situation and prospects. They are, however, mostly sanguine in tone, and it is not uncommon to hear the expression "when we get home." No one seems to have given up his hope of eventual relief. It has been very noticeable, too, at such times that no matter where the conversation begins it invariably swings around, before the word is passed to "douse the glim," to those things of which we are so completely deprived—to narratives of pleasant gatherings—stories of banquets and festival occasions where toothsome delicacies were provided. It would seem as though these reminiscences were given us as a foil to melancholy, and they travel along with us into our dreams.

Upon one point we are all agreed, that we are very fortunate in being wrecked in so agreeable a climate, where heavy clothing is unnecessary. The temperature has been, aside from the storm we had soon after the landing, between seventy and seventy-five degrees during the day and around fifty degrees at night. We are very sensible of the discomforts that would be ours if tumbled upon some of the islands of the northern ocean in winter.

The moonlit nights have been grand, and calculated to foster romance in a sailor's thoughts were the surroundings appropriate. As it is, the little cheer we extract from them is in the fact that we see the same shining face that is illuminating the home of our loved ones.

Often in my corner of the tent, Mr. Foss and I pass what would be a weary hour otherwise, over a game of chess, the pieces for which he has fashioned from gooney (Albatross) bones and blocks of wood.

Mr. Main has made a wonderful nautical instrument—a sextant—from the face of the Saginaw's steam gauge, together with some broken bits of a stateroom mirror and scraps of zinc. Its minute and finely drawn scale was made upon the zinc with a cambric needle, and the completed instrument is the result of great skill and patience. Mr. Talbot has tested it and pronounces it sufficiently accurate for navigating purposes.

Another officer has made a duplicate of the official chart of this part of the Pacific, and still another has copied all the Nautical Almanac tables necessary for navigation.

I have been directed by the captain to make a selection from the best-preserved supplies in the storehouse most suitable for boat service, and calculate that Talbot will have the equivalent of thirty-five days' provender at one-half rations, although many of the articles are not in the regular ration tables.

This morning the boat was surrounded by many men and carried bodily into water that was deep enough to float her. There she was anchored and the stores carried out to her. Mr. Butterworth, standing waist deep in the water, put on the last finishing touches while she was afloat by screwing to the gunwales the rowlocks for use in calm weather.

There was expended from store-book the following articles: ten breakers (a small keg) of water, five days' rations of hard tack sealed in tin, ten days of the same in canvas bags, two dozen small tins of preserved meat, five tins (five pounds each) of dessicated potato, two tins of cooked beans, three tins of boiled wheaten grits, one ham, six tins of preserved oysters, ten pounds of dried beef, twelve tins of lima beans, about five pounds of butter, one gallon of molasses, twelve pounds of white sugar, four pounds of tea and five pounds of coffee. A small tin cooking apparatus for burning oil was also improvised and furnished…

…With the navigating instruments and the clothing of the voyagers on board, the boat was pronounced ready and we went to dinner. There was little conversation during the meal. The impending departure of our shipmates hung like a pall of gloom over us at the last and was too thought-absorbing for speech. Talbot seemed to be the most unconcerned of all, but as I watched him I felt that the brave fellow was assuming it to encourage the rest of us. I had a long friendly talk with him, last evening, during which he seemed thoroughly to estimate the risk he was to take, and entrusted to me his will to be forwarded to his parents in Kentucky in case he should not survive the journey.

All hands have been given permission to send letters by the boat, so all papers, together with a bill of exchange for two hundred pounds sterling, which by order of the captain I have given to Talbot, have been sealed air tight in a tin case. I sent the following letter to my home in Philadelphia, which I will insert here, as it partially represents the state of affairs:

> You will of course be surprised to receive a letter from this desert island, but it now has a population of ninety-three men, the Saginaw's crew. In short, we were wrecked on the coral reef surrounding it,

and the Saginaw is no more. We left Midway Islands on the evening of Friday, October 28, and the next morning at three o'clock found ourselves thumping on the reef. We stayed by the ship until daylight, when we got out three boats and all the provisions we possibly could. We also saved the safe, part of the ship's books, about one fourth of my clothing, and my watch. If you could see me now you would hardly recognize me: a pair of boots almost large enough for two feet in one, ragged trousers, an old felt hat, and no coat—I keep that for evenings when it is cool. I have my best uniform saved, having rescued it to come ashore in. We had to wade about two hundred feet on the reef, and I stood in water about one half of the day helping to pass provisions to the boats; then went ashore and spread them on the beach to dry.

We have been living on very short allowance, being thankful for a spoonful of beans, a small piece of meat twice a day, with a cup of tea or coffee in the morning. I am indeed thankful that no lives were lost, and hope to see you all in three months' time. The gig has been decked over and is to start for Honolulu, to-morrow or next day, for relief.

Ocean Island is similar in formation to Midway, but is larger and the coral reef is farther from the land.

We had for breakfast this morning some of the *brown albatross* or *goonies*, as they call them. We shall not want for meat for some time, as there is an abundance of fish seal and turtle, but the flour, rice, and hard bread will not last more than two and one half months.

I hope this will reach you before you get anxious about us, for if the gig should not be successful we may have to stay here until the middle of March. I shall send this in her to be mailed from Honolulu. Our executive officer and four men go in her, and a perilous trip it will be, for she is only twenty feet long and the distance is over a thousand miles. Look us up on the map.

Most of our sails were saved and we are comparatively comfortable in good tents. I am well but hungry. We have dug wells, but found no fresh water. However, we are getting some from a condenser fitted by our chief engineer. Altogether we have more conveniences than might be expected and are in good health generally. I should like to write to friends, but space in the boat is scarce and everybody is writing.

The hour set for the boat's departure (four o'clock) arrived and we were all mustered upon the beach.

Prayers were read by the captain, after which final farewells were said and the brave men who were to peril their lives for us waded off to the gig and climbed on board. They quickly stepped the little masts, spread the miniature sails, raised their anchor, and slowly gaining headway stood off for the western channel through the reef. With full hearts and with many in tears, we gave them three rousing cheers and a tiger, which were responded to with spirit, and we watched them until the boat faded from sight on the horizon to the northward.

As I write this by the dim light of a candle the mental excitement due from the parting with our shipmates seems still to pervade the tent and no one is thinking of turning in.

Mr. Bailey, the foreman of the contractor's party, came into the tent soon after we had gathered for the evening. He had in his band a small book and on his face a smile as he passed it around, showing each one an open page of the book; when he reached me I saw it was a pocket Bible opened at the fifty-first chapter of Isaiah, where Mr. B.'s finger rested under the words, "The isles shall wait upon me and on my arm shall they trust." He did not speak until I had read, and then said he had opened the Bible by chance, as was his habit every evening. Poor Bailey! We all feel very sorry for him. He is a fine character, well advanced in years; and having by economy accumulated considerable money, had bought himself a home, before coming out, to which he was intending to retire when this contract was completed.

By invitation from the captain I accompanied him in walking around the entire island, avoiding, however, the extreme point to the westward, where albatross were nesting. He talked but little, and I saw that his eyes often turned to the spot where the gig had disappeared from view. As we separated in front of his little tent he said with a voice full of pathos to me, "Good-night, Paymaster; God grant that we see them again."

I find that I have so far omitted to give the personnel of Talbot's crew. As stated before there were many volunteers, but the surgeon was ordered to select from a list given him four of the most vigorous and sturdy of the applicants and report their names to the captain. There was considerable rivalry among them. In fact I was accidentally a witness to a hard-fought wrestling-match between two of the crew who sought the honor of going and risking their lives. The defeated one, I was told, was to waive his claim in favor of the victor.

The following letter, which has gone in the boat from our captain to the Admiral of the Pacific fleet, gives the personnel of the boat's crew and other information.

Ocean Island, Pacific Ocean
November 16, 1870

Rear Admiral John A. Winslow
Commanding Pacific Fleet
Sir:— I have the honor to recommend that the attention of the Department be particularly called to the fine conduct of Lieutenant J. G. Talbot. The day after the wreck of the Saginaw, Lieutenant Talbot came to me and volunteered to take one of the ship's boats to Honolulu in order to bring back relief for the officers and crew of the vessel. He has been most zealous and spirited through this whole affair and of the greatest assistance to me.

His boat (by the usual route at this season) will probably have to sail and pull some fifteen hundred miles, and I think some recognition of his handsome conduct would be proper.

The names of the crew are as follows: Lieutenant J. G. Talbot; Coxswain William Halford; Quartermaster Peter Francis; Seaman John Andrews; Seaman James Muir. The last two are contractor's men and were specially enlisted by me from Mr. Townsend's party for one month. They were men of such fine qualities and endurance that I thought it proper to let them go.

The enlistment was made with the express understanding between myself and them that it did not interfere with their previous contract with Mr. Townsend.

I am very respectfully,
Your obedient servant,
Montgomery Sicard,
Lieut. Comdr.–commanding.

HALFORD'S STORY OF THE OPEN BOAT SAIL TO KAUAI

When we left Ocean Island, November 18th, we ran to the north to latitude 32', there took the westerly winds and ran east to, as Mr. Talbot supposed, the longitude of Kauai (Kowee), but it proved ultimately that we were not within a degree of that longitude. We then stood south. Five days out we lost all light and fire and had no means of making either—no dry tinder or wood, although we had flint and steel. About five or six days before making Kauai we succeeded in getting a light with a glass taken from an opera glass. We suffered much from wet, cold, and want of food. The ten days' ration of bread in a canvas bag was mostly spoiled; the two tins of cooked beans could not be eaten, causing dysentery, as did also the boiled wheat; the gallon of molasses leaked out, and the sugar, tea, and coffee were spoiled by wetting. To the dessicated potato, five five-pound tins of which were given us at the last moment before sailing, we attributed the preservation of our lives from starvation. For the last week it was all we had, mixed with a little fresh water.

We had heavy weather while running to the eastward; hove to with the sea anchor twice, the last time lost it. We then made another drag from three oars, which was also lost. Then we made still another from two oars and a square of sail by crossing them. That lasted for three turns of bad weather; but the third time it broke adrift and all was lost.

Mr. Talbot was ill with diarrhoea for seven or eight days, but got better, although he continued to suffer much from fatigue and hardship. He was somewhat cheerful the whole passage. Muir and Andrews were sick for two or three weeks. Francis was always well.

We did not make land within a week of what had we expected. The first land we saw was Kawaihua Rock, at the southern end of Niihau (Neehow) Island, on Friday morning, December 16th. We stood north by east, with the island in sight all day. During that night and Saturday stood northeast by north, and on Saturday night headed east and south southeast.

Sunday morning the wind allowed us to head southeast with the island of Kauai in sight, and Sunday night we were off the Bay of Halalea (Hanalei) on the north coast. We then hove to with head to the northwest, the wind having hauled to the westward. We laid thus until eleven p.m. It being my watch on deck I called Mr. Talbot and told him that the night was clear and I could see the entrance to Halalea Harbor. He ordered the boat to be kept away and steered for the entrance. As we came near the entrance it clouded up and became dark, so we hove to again with head to the northwest. At one a.m. I called my relief. Andrews and Francis came on deck, as did also Mr. Talbot. After I went below the boat was again kept away toward the land for a short time and again hove to. At a little past two a.m. Sunday morning she was kept away again for the third time. I remained below until I felt from the boat's motion that she was getting into shoal water. Then I awoke Muir and told him it was time we went on deck. He did not go, but I did. Just as I got to the cockpit a sea broke aboard abaft. Mr. Talbot ordered to bring the boat by the wind. I hauled aft the main sheet with Francis at the helm and the boat came up into wind. Just then another breaker broke on board and capsized the boat. Andrews and Francis were washed away and were never afterwards seen. Muir was still below, and did not get clear until the boat was righted, when he gave symptoms of insanity. Before the boat was righted by the sea Mr. Talbot was clinging to the bilge of the boat and I called him to go to the stern and there get up on the bottom. While he was attempting to do so he was washed off and sank. He was heavily clothed and much exhausted. He made no cry. I succeeded in getting on to the bottom and stripped myself of my clothes. Just then the sea came and righted the boat. It was then that Muir put his head up the cockpit, when I assisted him on deck. Soon afterward another breaker came and again upset the boat; she going over twice, the last time coming upright and headed on to the breakers. We then found her to be inside of the large breakers, and we drifted toward the shore at a place called Kalihi Kai, about five miles from Hanalei. I landed with the water breast-high and took with me a tin case of dispatches and letters. On board there was a tin box with its cover broken containing navigation books, charts, etc., also Captain Sicard's instructions to Lieutenant Talbot, with others, among which were Aluir's and Andrews's discharge papers; they having been shipped November 15th for one month. They belong to the contractors in whose employ they were previous to that time. This box also contained Francis's and my transfer papers and accounts destined for the Mare Island Navy Yard. This box with everything not lashed fell into the water when we were first upset.

I landed about three a.m., but saw no one until daybreak, when, seeing some huts, I went to them and got assistance to get the boat onto the beach. I had previously, by making five trips to the boat, succeeded in bringing ashore the long tin case first mentioned, the chronometer, opera glasses, barometer, one ship's compass, boat's binnacle compass, and had also assisted Muir to the shore. He was still insane, saying but little and that incoherently. He groaned a great deal.

I was now much exhausted and laid myself down to rest until sunrise, when I looked for Muir and found him gone from the place I left him. Soon after I found him surrounded by several natives, but he was dead and very black in the face.

During the day I got some food and clothing from the natives—one of them called Peter. After resting myself Peter and I went on horseback over to Hanalei to Sheriff Wilcox and Mr. Burt. Then we returned with the sheriff and coroner to Kalihi Kai, where an inquest was held over the bodies of Lieutenant Talbot and Muir, the former having drifted ashore just before I left Kalihi Kai for Hanalei. Mr. Talbot's forehead was bruised and blackened, apparently from having struck the boat or wreckage.

After the inquest the two bodies were taken to Hanalei, put into coffins and buried the next day in one grave at a place where a seaman belonging to the U.S.S. Lackawanna was buried in 1867. Funeral services were performed by Mr. Kenny by reading the Episcopal burial service, and the two Misses Johnson (daughters of an American missionary) singing.

Before I left Hanalei for Honolulu it was reported by a half-white who had been left to watch the shore at Kalihi Kai that Andrew's body had come ashore and had been taken care of.

Captain Dudoit, the schooner *Wainona*, offered to bring me direct to Honolulu, leaving his return freight at

Wainiea (Wainiha?) for another trip. I accepted the same through Mr. Bent, and we sailed for Honolulu on the evening of Tuesday, December 20, and arrived at Honolulu at eleven a.m., December 24, bringing with me the effects saved as aforementioned. I went, on landing, immediately to the United States Consul's office, where I saw him and told him my story.

Halford has told me of several remarkable incidents which happened during the voyage of the gig and which, although not considered essential in his official statement, would be lifelong memories to him.

Of one of these he says—and I give his own words: "We were scudding before a gale of wind under a reefed square sail. A nasty sea was running at the time. I was standing in the after hatch steering; had the reeving string of the cover that was nailed around the combings drawn tight under my armpits to keep out the sea as it washed over the boat, when I felt a shock. The boat almost capsized, but the next sea lifted her over. I looked astern and saw a great log forty or fifty feet long and four or five feet in diameter, water-logged and just awash. We had jumped clean over it. It was a case of touch and go with us."

Of another incident he says: "One night I had relieved Peter Francis at the tiller and he had crawled forward on deck. Somehow or other he got overboard; luckily we had a strong fishing-line trailing astern all the voyage, but never got as much as a bite until it caught Francis and we got him on board again. It was a bright moonlight night."

Of another happening he says: "Then, when our provisions had run out entirely, a large bird came and landed on the boat and looked at me as I stood at the tiller. The other four at this time were very weak from want of food and from dysentery; they were more dead than alive. I caught the bird, tore off the feathers, cut it up in five pieces, and we all had a good meal. It was raw, but it tasted good. About thirty-six hours after this, just at break of day, as I was sitting at the tiller, I felt something strike my cheek. It was a little flying-fish. I caught it, and soon a school of them came skipping along, several dropping on deck. I captured five or six of them and they gave us the last meal we had on the gig: for at daylight I saw land—Tahoora or Kaula Rock."

Our captain has made the following report to the Secretary of the Navy, which adds to and confirms the story of the lone survivor of the gig:

> Honolulu, Hawaiian Islands,
> January 18, 1871
>
> Sir:—I forward herewith the brief report called for by regulation of the death of Lieutenant J. G. Talbot (and also three of the crew of the United States Steamer Saginaw) at the island of Kauai (Hawaiian Group).
>
> I feel that something more is due to these devoted and gallant friends, who so nobly risked their lives to save those of their shipmates, and I beg leave to report the following facts regarding their voyage from Ocean Island and its melancholy conclusion.
>
> The boat (which had been the Saginaw's gig and was a whaleboat of very fine model) was prepared for the voyage with the greatest care. She was raised on the gunwale eight inches, decked over, and had new sails, etc.
>
> The boat left Ocean Island November 18, 1870. The route indicated by me to Lieutenant Talbot was

to steer to the northward "by the wind" until he got to the latitude of about 39 degrees north, and then to make his way to the eastward until he could "lay" the Hawaiian Islands with the northeast trade winds. He seems to have followed about that route. The boat lost her sea anchor and oars in a gale of wind and a good deal of her provision was spoiled by salt water. The navigation instruments, too, were of but little use, on account of the lively motions of the boat. When she was supposed to be in the longitude of Kauai she was really about one and one half degrees to the westward; thus, instead of the island of Kauai she finally sighted the rock Kauhulaua, (the southwestern point of land in the group) and beat up from thence to the island of Kauai. She was hove off the entrance of Hanalei Bay during part of the night of Monday, December 19th, and in attempting to run into the Bay about 9.30 a.m. she got suddenly into the breakers (which here made a considerable distance from the shore) and capsized.

I enclose herewith a copy of the deposition of William Halford, coxswain, the only survivor of this gallant crew; his narrative being the one from which all accounts are taken. I have not seen him, personally, as he left here before my arrival.

Peter Francis, quartermaster, and John Andrews, coxswain, were washed overboard at once and disappeared. Lieutenant Talbot was washed off the boat, and when she capsized he clung to the bottom and tried to climb up on it, going to the stern for that purpose; the boat gave a plunge and Halford thinks that the boat's gunwale or stern must have struck Mr. Talbot in the forehead as he let go his hold and went down.

James Muir was below when the boat struck the breakers, and does not appear to have come out of her until she had rolled over once. He must have suffered some injury in the boat, as he appears to have been out of his mind and his face turned black immediately after his death. As will be seen by Halford's statement, Muir reached shore, but died of exhaustion on the way to the native huts.

The body of John Andrews did not come on shore until about December 20th. All clothes had been stripped from it. The body of Peter Francis has never been recovered.

The bodies are buried side by side at Hanalei (Kauai). The service was read over them in a proper manner. Suitable gravestones will be erected over them by subscription of the officers and crew of the Saginaw.

As soon as we had gotten on Ocean Island after the Saginaw's wreck, Lieutenant Talbot volunteered to take this boat to Honolulu, and the rest volunteered as soon as it was known that men might perhaps be wanted for such service.

Mr. Talbot was a very zealous and spirited officer. I had observed his excellent qualities from the time of his joining the Saginaw (September 23, 1870) in Honolulu. During the wreck and afterwards he rendered me the greatest assistance and, service by his fine bearing, his cheerfulness, and devotion to duty. His boat was evidently commanded with the greatest intelligence, fortitude, and gallantry and with the most admirable devotion. May the Service always be able to find such men in the time of need.

The men were fine specimens of seamen—cool and brave, with great endurance and excellent physical strength. They were, undoubtedly, those best qualified in the whole party on Ocean Island to perform such a service. Both Lieutenant Talbot and his men had very firm confidence in their boat and looked forward with cheerfulness to the voyage. Such men should be the pride of the Navy, and the news of their death cast a deep gloom over the otherwise cheerful feelings with which the *Kilauea* was welcomed at Ocean Island.

I do not know that I sufficiently express my deep sense of their devotion and gallantry; words seem to fail me in that respect.

Previous to the sailing of the boat from Ocean Island I had enlisted John Andrews and James Muir as seamen for one month. Since I have ascertained their fate I have ordered them to be rated as petty officers (in ratings allowed to most of the "fourth rates"), as I have thought that all the crew of that boat should have stood on equal footing as regards the amount they might be entitled to in case of disaster, as they all incurred the same risk.

Andrews and Muir belonged to the party of temporarily transferred to the U.S. Steamer *Saranac* for discharge or detail as their period of enlistment may require. The gig came with us and will be temporarily stored until it is decided as to her future. We have started a subscription for a suitable memorial to the gig's heroes, and the other ships of the squadron have generously offered their help. The most approved plan seems to be a marble tablet on the walls of the chapel at the Naval Academy, and the captain has made a sketch of one as it would appear there.

(Note. November 1, 1871. The tablet as designed has been completed and delivered at the Naval Academy. The following picture shows its appropriate character, and I deem it a fitting conclusion to my story. The gig is also to go to the Naval Academy to be deposited in the Museum.)

❖ ❖ ❖

XXVI. MILOLI'I AND NU'OLOLO
INTERVIEW OF KAUMEHEIWA
IN THE GARDEN ISLAND NEWSPAPER

*Miloli'i and Nu'alolo are two very isolated valleys on
the west end of the Nā Pali coast. Miloli'i is an arid valley,
used today as a camping stopover for some Nā Pali travelers.
Nu'alolo is actually two valleys: Nu'alolo Kai and Nu'alolo
Aina. A hanging valley, Nu'alolo in the days of old Hawai'i
was easily defended from invaders who could only access the
inhabited plateau by climbing a narrow trail. Incredibly
scenic, Nu'alolo is famed in Hawaiian legend.*

*The Garden Island has been Kaua'i's newspaper of record
since 1902 and is the chief source of information for major
events on the island. This interview with a Hawaiian man
who spent his youth in the valleys of the wondrous Nā Pali
coast appeared in the Tuesday, October 16, 1917 edition of
the newspaper. Recorded by the Rev. J. M. Lydgate, the Līhu'e*

minister for whom the County of Kaua'i's Lydgate Park, near
the south bank of the mouth of the Wailua River, is named,
this rare account is but one of many perpetuated by the local
historian who was a founder of the Kaua'i Historical Society.

Kaumeheiwa's story is a fascinating window to a way of
life that ended when the last Hawaiian families moved out
of Nā Pali in the early twentieth century for the modern
comforts of the villages along Kaua'i's north shore and west
side. The use of Nu'ololo, the archaic spelling of what is known
today as Nu'alolo, is the spelling that Lydgate apparently
employed.

An unpublished transcript of an account of life in Kalalau
Valley in an interview of John Hanohano Pā recorded by
Tiare Emory in the 1940's is located in the reference library
of the Bishop Museum.

I WAS BORN at Kalalau, June 1869. My father was
Mokunui who was konohiki (chief) of Kalalau, Nuololo
and Milolii. He was also the school teacher at Kalalau for
years.

When I was a small boy we moved to Milolii for my
mother's health. Her name was Puhaihai. She lost her mind
at Kalalau—she wasn't violently crazy, but mildly so. There
was a fine *kahuna* at that time at Milolii, so she was taken
there with us children to be treated by him. Did he cure
her? Well, I don't know. Nowadays, they say kahunas are
a fraud—but I know anyhow she got better. Yes, it took
some time—9 or 10 months I think, and she liked it so
well there that we just stayed on for some eight years or
so.

MILOLII

In those days Milolii was quite a village with about
two dozen people I suppose living right there on the beach

close together. You can see still right where the houses were. We lived on the Waimea side of the stream, up on that height. We had a big house and a small one. How about school? Oh, no, there wasn't any school at Milolii. I had to go to Mana. We went Monday morning early and came home Friday afternoon by canoe, me and two others. Of course if it was rough we stayed over. There was one of the boys, Ae-ae, who had no use for school and when it came time to go he couldn't be found. He would steal up the valley and hide till the canoe was gone.

Afterwards he went to Lihue and got a job on the plantation where he finally got to be steam plow man and got mighty good pay in spite of being as ignorant as a goat! While I, who went to school faithfully and am educated, have to work on the roads. It is strange how things go!

Milolii was quite a different place in those days. There were *taro* patches all up here on the side hill and on all the *palis* there was sugar cane growing, the choice varieties that we don't see these days—*ulaula, opukea,* and *lahi*: and bananas—*maia, haa* and *loaha.* And there was the chief's taro patch and *loi koele* (irrigated land section) which had to be kept up in good shape. And whenever the *moi* (saltwater food fish) came not to Milolii, a big supply of *poi* and dried fish and bananas and sugar cane sufficed.

Milolii was a great place in those days for growing *calabash gourds* down on the beach in the winter months, and they were monsters, some of them three feet in diameter. They were stored away in caves. They were too bulky to put in the houses—great stores of them, all sizes, big and little. Then they were sold out gradually to the neighboring districts. The big one brought about $4.00 apiece.

Some of them were beautifully paneled—all decorated—you know what that is. How was it done? Oh, no, not by drawings on the outside but by putting in a decoration of *alahu* leaves and letting that soak through for a long time. These *pawehi* (beautiful) ones cost more than $5.00 up.

Fishing being the main thing, of course every man had to have a canoe. These canoes were made mostly from *kukui* (candlenut tree). You could get good sized ones of kukui, but only small, one man ones, of *koa*. The big koa ones came from Hawaii and they cost a lot of money.

No, there was no church at Milolii. We went to Mana to church sometimes, but we weren't very strong on going to church.

The people lived at Milolii till sometime in the seventies, I think when there was an unusually big freshet that cut out the water heads and ruined the ditches: and by that time there were only old people and they weren't equal to renewing them, so they moved away. The house timbers standing there must be 50 years old or more. They were old when I was a boy.

NUOLOLO

There are two Nuololos—N. Luna and N. Lalo. N. Luna was up in the valley where the people raised their taro and N. Lalo was down here where they fished. They lived at both places. The taro lands up the valley are fine, broad and fertile, not like those at Milolii. The only way of getting from one place to another was by way of the *pali* trail and ladder. This ladder was 30 or 40 ft. long—well made with side pieces about 6 inches in diameter, and with rungs carefully let in. The whole thing was lashed to the pali. It leaned out to sea so that it was mighty scary for anyone to go up who wasn't used to doing it. But for those who were used to doing it, it was just like going along the road. And when it came to the narrow place, even the thin man drew in his breath;—these people would do it as easy as could be. And they would bring down heavy loads on their heads, and then at that scary place they would transfer the load to the other knee and balance on the other foot.

The last man who lived at Nuololo was a hermit named Hina Kuhi. He was the most unsocial of men. He would run and hide if he saw anyone coming. He lived in a cave all by himself for 3 years after all the rest had gone. Finally one day he was roasting a bit of goat meat under the cliff, there where the ruins of the houses are at the *makai* end. He was leaning over the fire when a great stone fell from the cliff and broke his back and smashed him up so that he couldn't move, and he lay there suffering and helpless for 3 days until fortunately his brother happened to come over from Mana. But he couldn't do anything for him but stay with him till the end.

Nuololo is the most famous place in Hawaiian story for hau (lowland tree wood) fireworks. That peak right over our head. Puu Maile, is the place where they set them off. How did they get up there? Oh, they went up from the side of N. Luna. The agile ones would go up in 3 hours. It is 1,500 feet high, and exceedingly precipitous. They went always in the day time, with their load of fire faggots and waited there until the wind died down and then they launched them off. Yes they came down at night, each man had a torch and you could trace them as they came. Each man got $10.00 for the trip. The faggots were *hau* or *papala* (light, flammable wood found in north Kauai). Papala was the best. The fire streamed out at the rear like the tail of the comet. You know what papala is do you? Yes, it is a soft spongy wood, and has to be dried for about a year.

On five different occasions royal parties have celebrated fire works occasions here. Queen Emma once. Liliuokalani twice and Lunalilo once.

◈　◈　◈

Chris Cook

XXVII.   PRINCE JONAH KŪHIŌ KALANIANA'OLE
THE PEOPLE'S PRINCE

Prince Jonah Kūhiō Kalaniana'ole, popularly known in Hawai'i as the "People's Prince," was born at a simple Kaua'i fishing village near Kōloa on the island's south shore. Today Prince Kūhiō Park marks the site where an annual holiday celebration commemorates his birth.

Called the "Last of the Ali'i" by some, Kūhiō's public career and life began at the closing years of the Hawaiian kingdom, and ended at the beginning of modern, 20th-century Hawai'i. During the overthrow of the Hawaiian kingdom, Kūhiō supported the monarchy, but later reconciled himself to assisting the Hawaiian people within the framework of the territorial government.

As Hawai'i's first appointed delegate to the U.S. Congress, Kūhiō wisely supported and fought in Washington and

Honolulu for the creation of Hawaiian Homelands legislation.
His name is frequently referred to in today's quest by the
Hawaiian people for the creation of a sovereign nation of
their own.

ALI'I JONAH KŪHIŌ Kalaniana'ole, Ke Alii
Maka'āinana–The Prince of the People, firmly declared
himself "Not Guilty!" to a court convened to try him of
charges tied to an attempted overthrow of the Hawaiian
Republic in 1895.

Just days before, the sturdily-built, mustached, 23-
year-old Hawaiian prince had roamed the midnight streets
of Honolulu with his compatriot John Wise. There was
revolution in the midnight air and isolated gunfire in the
streets of Honolulu as the pair desperately searched for
the rebel forces. Their plans involved a cache of smuggled
arms, the might of several dozen fellow royalists and the
approval of the dethroned Queen Lili'uokalani, Hawai'i's
last monarch. The fate of the overthrown Hawaiian
kingdom hung in the balance.

The statuesque Hawaiian would probably have been
Hawai'i's king if the revolt had succeeded and the
monarchy had endured into the twentieth century. Instead,
he found himself laboring as a mason in a cell in Iwilei
Prison outside of Honolulu.

Kūhiō's anger over the overthrow of the monarchy by
a mostly *haole* armed citizens group smoldered during the
months of his imprisonment. His bitterness welled up
following his release, and in 1896 he set sail on a cruise
around the world to see if his fate, and his happiness, lay
on distant shores. With his wife Elizabeth, Kūhiō visited
Paris and toured the Continent, hunted big game on an
African safari, and sided with the British in the Boer War
in South Africa.

The time away from his troubles in Hawaiʻi and his exposure to new worlds brought peace to Kūhiō's spirit, though his flesh railed out against the racial prejudices ingrained in the turn-of-the-century western world. He used boxing and martial arts skills acquired as a youth against a German noble who insisted he leave an inn because of his skin color. Indignantly, Kūhiō quickly strode over to the count's table and "beefed" him as only a strong Hawaiian could. Kūhiō and his party continued their gathering unbothered.

Kūhiō returned to Hawaiʻi a changed man, sophisticated to the world of the mainland and beyond, and ready to take on his natural role as a leader in the newly declared Territory of Hawaiʻi.

However, he would continue to embrace his heritage as an *aliʻi* of Hawaiʻi, never forgetting his allegiance to the Hawaiian people as his thinking became progressive, and he moved quickly to take steps to move his homeland and his people into the twentieth century.

The roots of this heritage went deep into Kūhiō's past. Born in a simple thatched Hawaiian dwelling on March 26, 1871 at Hoai Bay—the site of the ancient fishing village Kukuiʻula, where high chiefs of Kauaʻi once gathered along the black lava rock and white sand shoreline just west of Waikomo Stream near Kōloa on Kauaʻi's south shore—Kūhiō, from birth, led the life of an *aliʻi*. He was the third child of high *aliʻi* David Kahalepouli Piikoi and his royal wife Kekaulike Kinoʻike, and a direct descendant of Prince Keʻeaumoku, the grandfather of Kamehameha the Great.

Educated at St. Albans School and Punahou in Honolulu, he was a stocky child with sparkling eyes and rich brown skin, known for an ever-present smile. Pierre Jones, the French teacher at St. Albans, nicknamed him

"Cupid." The moniker stuck throughout his boyhood, and remained a fond nickname throughout his life.

In 1880 his father passed away and his mother was appointed governess of the island of Hawaiʻi. However, Kūhiō remained in Honolulu, attending Punahou school rather than joining his mother. A storybook life also began for the young prince when Queen Kapiʻolani, wife of the reigning monarch King Kalālakua, became legal guardian of the boys, and they became official members of the royal household.

Later, on Feb. 12, 1883, in special ceremonies Kūhiō knelt before the King in the throne room at ʻIolani Palace and "Cupid" became a prince, along with his brothers Edward and David. The lads joined the court of the Merrie Monarch and often took part in royal ceremonies. The merry King reciprocated by avidly following the sporting activities of "Cupid" and his brothers.

Kūhiō was a standout football player at Punahou and practiced *lua*, the ancient art of Hawaiian wrestling. He rowed for and helped found the Leilani Boat Club and was feared for his skillful and powerful boxing style.

After his mother Kekaulike passed away in 1884, Kūhiō was sent to St. Matthews Military Academy in San Mateo, California. There he immersed himself in his studies, as well as sports, and during summer breaks became friendly with his cousin, Princess Kaʻiulani, the fragile part-Scottish Hawaiian beauty whom Robert Louis Stevenson captured forever in verse when he described her childhood beauty. Kaʻiulani lived at the graceful, yet lively, estate of ʻAinahau in Waikīkī with her Scottish father and her Hawaiian *aliʻi* mother.

As he neared college age, Kūhiō was enrolled in a unique educational program sponsored by King Kalākaua and paid for with funds allocated by the

Hawaiian legislature for about 20 young Hawaiians to study overseas.

Kalākaua believed that England was the most suitable country to send his successors and opted for Kūhiō to study law at King's College, Oxford, and the teenaged Prince may also have studied agriculture at the Royal Agricultural College. He and his brother David often visited their cousin Ka'iulani, who was also being educated in Great Britain. Though the young Scottish-Hawaiian beauty favored David, who was known as Koa, over his younger brother, she retained a close friendship with her cousin and co-heir to the Hawaiian throne until her untimely death at the age of 23.

Princess Ka'iulani was the only surviving child in her generation of the Kalākaua dynasty. To insure an heir, Prince Jonah and his brothers, Prince David Kawānanakoa and Prince Edward Keali'iahonui, were drawn into his line of succession by Kalākaua.

Kūhiō's foreign education continued after his brother Edward passed away after contracting typhoid fever at school in California. Kalākaua sent him to Japan in 1888, and for nearly a year he enjoyed a total immersion in the Japanese culture as a welcome guest of the Japanese government. Besides an education in the ways of the nation that was supplying many of his kingdom's sugar plantation workers, the Merrie Monarch also hoped "Cupid" would wed a Japanese princess to strengthen the King's position in the Pacific Basin.

However, Kūhiō chose not to take a Japanese bride and instead returned to embark on his life's work. The King had great plans for "Cupid" and his surviving brother David, and wanted the thickly-built sons of the *ali'i* to one day attain positions in the high offices of the Hawaiian government, and in time possibly to become the King of Hawai'i.

Prince Kūhiō's first steps toward this goal was taking a position in the Ministry of the Interior and Customs of the Hawaiian kingdom.

However, fate interrupted his plans when in 1891 Kalākaua died at the Palace Hotel in San Francisco during a mainland excursion. Following an elaborate funeral and burial service at the Royal Mausoleum, Lili'uokalani was proclaimed Hawai'i's Queen by the constitutional government of the Hawaiian kingdom. The Queen proclaimed Ka'iulani her heir-apparent.

Kūhiō became active in Lili'uokalani's court, and the dowager queen placed David and "Cupid" in her line of succession, securing again the brothers' place in the royal Hawaiian court.

To Kūhiō's dismay, the Hawaiian kingdom began a rapid fall during the first two years of Lili'uokalani's reign. And, after she declared her intent to rewrite the Kingdom's constitution, a band of white revolutionaries overthrew the Kingdom's government in 1893 to form the Republic of Hawai'i.

Seven years later, following his return from Africa, Kūhiō made an unexpected move when he organized the Republican Party in Hawai'i. His brother David had become a Democrat and Kūhiō was unexpectedly asked to become a Republican, a member of the party that overthrew the Queen.

Kūhiō told doubters that he saw an advantage in an alliance with the mostly *haole* Republicans and that he hoped to aid his fellow native Hawaiians through the somewhat radical move. Initially the relationship between the Hawaiian chief and the Republican party bosses was uneasy, but in 1902 he defeated Robert Wilcox, the former rebel and leader of the Home Rule Party, and his path to four terms as Hawai'i's Delegate to Congress was paved.

In Kūhiō's first election he campaigned for home rule on each island and for more government jobs for Hawaiians in the rural districts. After winning, he initiated legislation that formed the four county governments that still exist in Hawai'i.

For the next two decades the voters favored Kūhiō as their spokesman to Congress and figurehead in Washington. During this time he became well known and well liked in the nation's capital. Socially he was known as a good host and a good guest, as well as a congenial drinking partner and card player. Politically he gathered a wide circle of supporters, including President Teddy Roosevelt, whom he accidentally met one day while sitting in a park near the White House.

His voice in Washington, even though as a territory Hawai'i's vote went uncounted in deciding legislation, became powerful, and he played a key role in the passing of bills that greatly strengthened Hawai'i's economy and set the course of the future 50th State's destiny. In fact, he introduced the first-ever statehood bill in the House of Representatives in 1919.

Kūhiō also foresaw the important role tourism would play in Hawai'i's future and believed that the best way to aid Hawai'i in Washington was by bringing Washington to Hawai'i. In 1907 Kūhiō selected a group of prominent congressional legislators who served on important committees that dealt with Hawai'i, and convinced the Territorial Legislature to invite them to visit. One senator and 25 congressmen, with their families, arrived in May aboard the U.S.S. *Buford.* The touring group's three-week visit to O'ahu, Kaua'i, Maui and Hawai'i was a great success. The delegation met hundreds of island people, saw firsthand the majestic beauty of the islands, and the economic and military potential of Hawai'i. They returned to Washington as friends of Hawai'i.

While politically maneuvering his way through Washington, Kūhiō never forgot the Hawaiians who still considered him an *ali'i* and protector. He said in 1920, "If conditions remain as they are today, it will only be a matter of a short space of time when this race of people, my people, renowned for their physique, their courage, their sense of justice, their straight-forwardness, and their hospitality, will be a matter of history."

The same year a census showed that only 23,723 Hawaiians remained, and that many were destitute. Kūhiō hoped to return many of the Hawaiians to the *'āina* by settling them on farmlands. In July 1921 Congress established the Hawaiian Homes Commission Act, which would allow the lease of government lands for 99 years at low rates to those "of not less than one-half Hawaiian blood."

The first settlement was on the island of Moloka'i and was named the Kalaniana'ole Settlement, in honor of Kūhiō. Today, following many ups and downs in the program, Hawaiian homesteading is on the rise and a very visible reminder throughout the islands of Kūhiō's long lasting influence.

' Kūhiō's other accomplishments for the Hawaiian people included the founding on May 13, 1903 of the Order of Kamehameha to perpetuate the memory and deeds of the "Napoleon of Hawai'i," and in 1918 he organized one of Hawai'i's most significant groups, the Hawaiian Civic Club, which to this day continues to preserve the traditions of the Hawaiian people and perpetuate their language, music, arts and folklore.

His other accomplishments as a politician include encouraging the development of Pearl Harbor as a major naval base, the introduction of the National Park Service to Hawai'i, and an active role in the passage of the 19th Amendment, which gave the vote to women for the first time.

Even on his deathbed at Waikīkī on January 7, 1922, Kūhiō remained loyal to the Hawaiian people. He whispered a command to his attendants to tell the Hawaiian people: "Stick together and try to agree to the best of your ability to meet the most important problem— the rehabilitation of our race."

In respect to Delegate Kūhiō, the House in Washington adjourned upon his passing. Eight days later the last elaborate royal funeral Hawai'i would ever see honored Kuhio, who was laid to rest with the *ali'i* of the Hawaiian kingdom in the Royal Mausoleum in cool Nu'uanu Valley above bustling Honolulu.

Over the last six decades, Kūhiō's deeds, as well as his life as a Hawaiian prince and as a public servant, have remained fresh in the memory of Hawai'i's people and at the landmarks named in his honor. Perhaps the best known is Kūhiō Beach at Waikīkī, which was formerly the site of his grand Waikīkī home, where he displayed cherished mementos of the Kalākaua era.

The birthday of Prince Cupid is also a legal holiday in Hawai'i, celebrated in late March each year. Known throughout the state as Kūhiō Day, the holiday is marked by the Hawaiian societies he helped found when they gather at Kūhiō Park in Kōloa cloaked in their feathered capes and black *holokū*. The park was established in 1924, when the Kaumuali'i Chapter of the Order of Kamehameha raised $150,000 from the public for a memorial park in memory of Kūhiō. The five-acre site was purchased from the McBryde Sugar Co. Ltd. for one dollar and on June 19, 1928 a plaque commemorating

Prince Cupid was unveiled. Over 10,000 attended the *luau* and ceremonies marking the occasion, and the steamer *Mauna Kea* brought 343 passengers from other islands, including the Royal Hawaiian Band. The day's festivities included a song contest, wrestling matches, a colorful pageant, and Hawaiian chanting and singing.

Today this monument still clearly marks the spot of Kūhiō's birth, and Kūhiō is lovingly remembered as the *aliʻi* who, while bringing Hawaiʻi into the twentieth century, never forgot the needs of his people.

Aliʻi, congressman, humanitarian, loyal husband, son of Kauaʻi and citizen prince, Prince Kūhiō bridged the final days of the Hawaiian monarchy and the first decades of Hawaiʻi's modern era. Along the way he guided the Hawaiian people, and the destiny of the Hawaiian Islands, during a time of revolution and lasting change.

❖   ❖   ❖

Clifford Gessler

XXVIII. WAIʻALEʻALE & BEYOND
A Tour of the "Wettest Spot On Earth"

Clifford Gessler came to Hawaiʻi from the University of Wisconsin in 1924 and until 1934 was literary editor of the Honolulu Star-Bulletin. *His books about the Pacific include* The Dangerous Island, Road My Body Goes, The Reasonable Life, Some Aspects of Polynesian Life, *and* Hawaii Isles of Enchantment, *published in 1937 and from which this chapter is taken.* Hawaii Isles of Enchantment *is considered one of Gessler's best pieces.*

While focusing on the mystery and natural wonders of Waiʻaleʻale, the "Wettest Spot on Earth" with an annual rainfall of over 400 inches, Gessler continues with a nostalgic look at an island and people he obviously loved.

The 1930's were an era of change on Kauaʻi. Still rather isolated even from Honolulu, the island was on the verge of being greatly opened up to the outside world through the arrival of American soldiers and Marines during World War II. With an economy based on sugar cane and local needs, Kaua'i wasn't as hard hit by the Depression as the mainland United States.

KAUAI FROM THE sea, is green and rose: the bright volcanic earth showing through the rich vegetation which has caused its inhabitants to claim for it the name given to an unidentified island somewhere in these seas by an early Spanish navigator: the *Garden Island*.

At nearer view, it is a maze of worn peaks, striped canyons, and gulches cutting long low fields rippling with cane, and tree-dotted upland pastures sloping to the misty mass the great central mountain, Waialeale, long thought to the wettest place on earth. On a slippery trail, high on the spongy dome, stands a government rain-gauge, which by official measurement proclaims it second in rainfall only to one spot in the known world.

Yet the whole island does not share without labor the gift of the rain god. Kauai sugar planters, like those of other islands, have built vast irrigation works, as their predecessors the Hawaiians and the still earlier *menehune* did on a smaller scale, before them. And a few miles from that boggy mountaintop the Barking Sands lie all but rainless beneath the sun.

Few even of island residents have trodden the upper forests of Waialeale. That great wet roof, only a few miles from motor roads and electric power and the sugar fields that live by its waters, remains virtually unexplored–a legendary place, populated, according to report, by wild swine, equally fierce wild cattle, and survivors of bright birds from whose feathers Hawaiians of old made helmets and mantles for their chiefs.

There, too, is the reputed haunt of the last of the menehune, fabulous dwarfish race said by Hawaiians to have occupied once all the islands. The coasts are dotted with stone fishponds, inland valleys with ditches and trails attributed to their architectural skill.

Science, disentangling the maze of myth, has concluded tentatively that the menehune actually existed, though not as small in size or equipped with such supernatural powers as the legends assert. It identifies them, like the Little People of Ireland and the elves and goblins of the European continent, with an early group of settlers-the first wave of Polynesian migration, overwhelmed by the twelfth century invasion from the south. Their simpler social organization, lower grade of culture, and slighter physique have been exaggerated by legend to make the myth of the dwarfs.

Kauai seems to have been their last stronghold. From mountain retreats they ventured forth by night and at times were induced to build stone-works for the conquerors. The tale is that they worked only at night and if the project was not finished before dawn, left it forever uncompleted.

The last menehune probably perished, or was absorbed into the invading people, long ago, but popular report tells of strange dwarfish beings on these mountain trails, who vanish mysteriously when one seeks a nearer view. A Honolulu scientist tells of a night in one of the precipitous, rarely entered valleys that plunge from Waialeale toward the wild northwestern coast. Seeking "land shells," snail-like creatures that cling to leaves and logs and rocks, he had become separated from his companions and was spending the night in a cave. He was awakened by a sound as of hammering on stone. Looking out, he saw a light flickering on the trail. Thinking his companions were seeking him, he called out. The light vanished and a listening silence flowed into the somber valley under the dark looming cliffs.

In the morning, he found new stones laid in an evident attempt to repair the trail. When he overtook his party at the end of the day, they told him they had not been near the place.

"Bootleggers," he explained to himself with a scientist's hardheadedness, "repairing the trail by night to haul contraband *okolehao* down the mountain from a hidden still."

But the old Hawaiian to whom he told the story smiled a knowing smile. "The menehune work only at night," he said.

There is, too, the story of a Honolulu business man, hunting wild goats in another of those lost valleys, who awoke at night, in his camp, to hear voices speaking in an archaic Polynesian dialect-though he and his companions, in all their trip through that valley, saw no sign of present habitation nor any human face.

A trail leads, however, up the precipitous ridges into a great spongy plateau near the summit, the Alakai Swamp. Somewhere among those thickly overgrown, miry trails and fog-veiled pools is the sacred lake whither Hawaiians made the long and hazardous journey on foot to present offerings even, it is said, up to the early twentieth century.

Dr. William Alanson Bryan, who spent three weeks on the mountain and four days in the swamp, said afterward that his return to civilization from that watery jungle "has always seemed little short of the miraculous." He and his companions were never out of dense fog during the expedition.

"The thin turf which covered the quagmire," he wrote, "would tremble for yards in all directions at every step and too often would give way, plunging us hip-deep in mire."

Such is Waialeale, where an inch and a third of rain falls daily, three and a quarter feet a month, forty feet a year!

The lowlands of Kauai, like those of most of the other islands, are sealike with cane. Some lands on this rich isle have borne crops of sugar year after year without replanting, for more years than I should venture to quote. Between the fields the road, traversed at apparently reckless speed by hardy planters and laborers, winds over red earth that was the basis for one of the late Bishop Restarick's favorite stories. A Kauai man, he used to say, toured around the world. In San Francisco, on his way home, he entered a Turkish bath where the rubber immediately identified him as from Kauai, by the color of the dirt.

Along that road we crossed the mouths of canyons; Waimea, the most celebrated; Olokele and Hanapepe, less accessible but as wild and beautiful. We turned up between red-banked ditches in which water apparently flowed uphill, to look down from a rocky point into the tremendous chasm of Waimea. Great conical ridges stood like pillars, their sides tinted in blending or contrasting or delicately shaded hues; the winding distances were misty lavender; a bright ribbon of stream coiled half a mile below. Shadows of clouds painted light and dark the various reds and yellows of the cliffs. For twenty-five miles that canyon stretched before us, a vast hall sculptured by the gods. Above its battlements soared long-tailed boson birds, floating on air currents against the blue vault of the sky.

Lower down, the Waimea River flowed between bright green rice fields and groves of palms. In the cliffs behind them, we knew, lay bones of ancient chiefs. Somewhere among those rock tombs, they say, remains an unfound treasure, the green feather mantle of Kauai kings. There were many red and not a few yellow feather robes but, the tale whispers, only one of green. Its value might surpass that of the "million dollar *mamo*" of Kamehameha the Great in the Bishop Museum.

History stared back at us from the cliff where an arrow chiseled into the rock preserves the memory of Captain Cook's landing, and from the lichened stones of the fort built by the Russians in 1816. The thick, sloping stone walls still stood in a rough parallelogram; in an inner court a pyramid where the flags of the Czar and of Kamehameha had flown.

I knew well the drowsy country towns of Waimea and Kekaha, with their shabby Chinese stores and saimin restaurants, in the summer when the world was waiting for Dick Grace, Hollywood "crash" flyer, to take off from the Barking Sands for an early "trans-Pacific" flight which ended in a *kiawe* tree on the uneven pasture honored by the name of a flying field.

The village of Mana, dozing in the sunshine a few miles away, was our headquarters, having the only telephone in miles. I would sit on the steps of the Japanese store, watching miles of cane rippling in the breeze and the Philippine woman across the way, on the veranda of her cottage, smoking a short pipe as she suckled a plump brown baby. In mid-afternoon the men would come in from the fields, short, sturdy Ilocanos in blue dungarees and checkered *palakas*, to buy cheap tobacco or those jars of preserved fish that are their delight. It was a peaceful scene, that village of neat brown cottages among the fields, with its one dusty street in which, through most of the day, the only thing moving was a slow mongrel dog. Sky smiled at earth and earth smiled back as the cane distilled rich juice from earth and sun.

We slept, when a night take-off seemed imminent, upon or rather in the sands themselves, burrowing into them to escape clouds of mosquitoes. The "barking" of the sands, which in our experience was only a faint puppylike squeak, failed to keep the flying nuisances away.

The sands when very dry, however, produce, in response to stirring, a sound somewhat suggesting the barking of a dog. The early traveler Bates described it, when his horse trampled over the dunes, as "of distant thunder or the starting of heavy machinery." It was loud enough to startle the horse.

The dunes are perhaps a hundred feet high, a desolate stretch of country, yet with a wild charm, pricked with small shrubs and the beginnings of kiawe trees. It was a sun-baked land by day, miles from a drink of water, more miles from food. We would sit in the small shade of the car while the aviator, day after day, urged his heavily loaded plane down the bumpy field, only to blow out his tires in the heated air. At last, after weeks of these attempts, the tiny plane soared. We saw it from the road, circling over the lighthouse at Kilauea, then come faltering back, its tail shaking on a cracked longiron, to fold into a tree at the edge of the field, whence the flyer and his puppy mascot emerged unscratched.

A little way beyond the sands none can pass, for the black cliffs of Napali rise sheer from the sea, cut by valleys accessible only from narrow beaches reached by boat, or hazardous trails out of the maze of ridges about Waialeale.

The southeast half of the island, however, is a pleasant country, rich with growing things. I watched the peacocks spread lordly tails in the formal Japanese gardens of Kukuiolono Park, and swam in the tall swells that ride into Lawai cove between lava rocks, curling upon a beach beneath lofty palms. Near by, the Spouting Horn, a salt-water geyser similar to the Oahu Blowhole, waved its plume of spray high in the salty air. And in the little harbor of Kukuiula the, blue-hulled sampans lay, or chugged out to long voyages under the coppery brilliance of the sun. Picturesque villages clustered under the broad umbrellas of ancient trees. Inland, waterfalls tumbled veil-like over precipices; among them Waipahee, known irreverently to tourists as the Sliding Bathtub, where visitors and natives alike slithered down a natural chute over water-smoothed rock to a deep pool. Around these streams the *ohia-ai* bore juicy, deep-red, apple like fruit; wild *taro* uncurled tender leaves; *guavas* ripened on sturdy shrubs. On rolling plains and mountain slopes, ranch cattle roamed among gnarled upland pandanus trees. Farther inland, the cloud-clothed bulk of Waialeale brooded somberly over all.

Beyond Anahola, where a perforation high in a rocky ridge marks where the spear of an ancient warrior pierced the mountain, the country is less luscious. There were pineapples, however, on the uplands and cane along the shores, as I drove in summer mornings past the Oriental rice straw huts that are pointed out to unsuspecting strangers as "Hawaiian grass houses," and past the great grove of candlenut trees whose light-green, star-shaped leaves once shaded gatherings of missionaries and of chiefs. At Kalihiwai, fishermen were drawing a net around a school of akule in the bay, to leave them thus imprisoned in their own element for days while supplies were drawn off gradually as the market demanded.

I spent easeful weeks in a cabin of *ohia* logs by a quiet bay off the main road. In that secluded region Hawaiians dwelt, as of old, beside the sea, each with his patch of taro behind his house and the food-giving reef for his front yard. There they would wade, glass-bottom box in hand, at low tide, darting spears at fish clustering below or hunting the lair of the octopus: thrusting a short spear where stones drawn into a hole betrayed his hiding place;

drawing out the shaft with tentacles writhing about it; smoothing them down with a broad hand and leaning forward to bite the creature's central nerve ganglion, disabling the prey and freeing the hands for another catch. At night they would stretch nets across narrow channels through the reef and drive fish into them by splashing with hands and feet and beating the water with branches. Everything from odd, stubby Hawaiian lobsters to staring-eyed young hammerhead sharks would come out of the net when it was drawn up on the sand. They would pound fish in a sack and sink it a little way offshore to attract live fish; then cast lines to catch beautiful savory *ulua* and *papio*.

It is another country, under the water: the strange, dim, unearthly country of the reef. Vermilion-red sea-urchins slowly wave slender spikes in the warm tide; stupid, ugly sea-slugs lie sunning themselves in the shallows; strange painted fishes glide and plane through coral caverns: fishes that disdain a hook and can be captured only with the spear. Once, peering over the edge of one of those chasms where fresh water has kept a dear channel through the coral, I saw a dozen baby sharks playing in the transparent water, far below.

Across the shallow bay, horsemen rode in the evening, hoofs splashing softly, cowboys from Princeville ranch, homeward bound, singing of Hanalei.

As their song proclaimed, "Hanalei, beautiful in the great rain!" Rice-green Hanalei, its broad river rolling between paddied fields and misty green and lavender mountains, and the sea rolling in to meet the stream. Beyond the quiet town at its mouth the valley slopes gently upward to the spurs of Waialeale. Long-horned *carabao* plow muddy fields, and men and women in broad straw hats or sometimes in quaint rain-coats of rice straw like animated haystacks, wade in irregularly banked pools, planting pre-grown young rice. The green of it rising above the water is marvelously fresh and bright, a lasting delight to the eyes. When the milky juice solidifies and swells the tiny husks, long rows of motley rags flutter on cords manipulated from ramshackle watch towers; tin cans rattle and shot-guns roar from high platforms, scaring away rice-birds that raid the crop.

There was a silk farm in early days along the river. An uncharitable visitor attributed its failure to the stern New England piety of the missionaries. Silkworms must be tended daily; they keep no Sabbaths. But the Christian native help, according to report, refused righteously to work on the Lord's Day, and the worms, and with them the industry, became martyrs to the faith.

I should like to explore sometime more deeply the caverns near the Haena shore. Out of a jungle of *pandanus* and guava one enters the fern-wreathed entrance of the Dry Cave, where a fugitive chief once hid, to sally forth like a ghost from a tomb and slay his enemies after they had thought him dead. Motor-cars now profane that dim sanctuary, where crude pictures carved in the rock perhaps record the waiting days of that Hawaiian King Alfred.

Years ago no Hawaiian would enter the first of the two wet caves, sometimes called the Water of Terror. It was believed to be the home of a dragon which had once swallowed an entire party of adventurers. The terror has been forgotten now, and Hawaiian musicians enter without fear to sing against an answering choir of echoes above the cold, clear water that lies deep on the cavern floor.

A little way beyond, a Gothic arch opens upon the Water of Kanaloa. Ferns grow deep within the cave; bodies of swimmers shine strangely green in refracted light. A hundred yards within, another chamber lies darkly beyond a second Gothic portal rising from deep water. It is said the cave goes on, room after vaulted room, deep under the mountain, but I know none who has ventured there to see.

There is no road beyond the caves, where the land lifts jaggedly into the tangled wilderness of the Napali coast. But a little of this wild country has been tamed. From the other side of the island we drove up a narrow road climbing out of the sugar fields to the summer camps in the cool upland of Kokee. Kokee does not resemble at all the popular notion of a Hawaiian landscape. It might be a bit of any wooded mountain country. Its meadows lie checkered with sun and shade; air comes clean and cool and bracing; we seemed far, there, from the busy world. Birds from America, Europe, and the Orient, with which birdlovers have stocked the forest, flew in at open doorways to take crumbs and grain from our hands.

Beyond Kokee swirl trout streams, and hunters sometimes venture over headlong trails or seaward by boat to lost valleys that tumble precipitously to the sea. Along these ridges to Kalalau fled Koolau the leper to defy, from goatlike retreats, the armed expeditions sent from Honolulu. Jack London told that story long ago. But I heard a different story on Kauai. It is whispered there that Koolau was no leper, but victim of a plot—denounced as a leper that a rival might, when Koolau should be banished to Molokai, seize his property and his wife.

A Hawaiian "ladder"—a log with transverse pieces attached—drops down a sheer cliff to a ledge leading into a cave whence another "ladder" slants over a precipice into a still more remote valley. Such is the entrance to the country of the unconquerable. Here lived a tribe apart, admitting no allegiance to the kings of Kauai or to

Kamehameha himself. Against armaments of their time the valley was impregnable. A few guards could defend the approach against thousands; withdraw the ladders, and there was no way in by land.

The entrance by sea, at the valley mouth, was and is as precarious. A rope was lowered from an overhanging cliff into a sea cave, accessible only in calm weather. The cliff bulges; one had to grasp the rope on the run and swing out, clambering or being drawn dangerously up the rock. Hence, perhaps, the line of a Hawaiian bard: "Nualolo, swinging in the wind..."

Civilization conquered where armies could not. The valley stands empty now, tenanted only by wild swine, wild goats and birds, and the quaint, beautiful, land mollusks whose delicately tinted, striated shells collectors prize. For the white man brought trade and industry and the lure of towns. The wild hillmen little by little forsook their lonely fastnesses and trickled down to the populous coast. The terraces of their fields, the crumbling walls of their watercourses remain; a few house platforms overgrown with jungle. The wind cries in the tree-tops of the lost valley; the long grasses rustle. And at night the rare explorer hears ghostly voices from hollow caverns in the stern cliffs.

From Mana and Kekaha we used to look across the channel to a red, gray, and brown island like the crest of a sea-monster, knowing it for a forbidden land. The island barony of Niihau is the most kapu place in a country where that four-letter word for "No Trespassing" is an all too familiar sight. Its isolation is enforced by a stern, if paternal, ownership. The story may be sketched briefly here as I heard it on Kauai.

The story goes back to Scotland, in 1840, when Captain Francis Sinclair and his wife left a farm near

Stirling Castle to seek wider fortunes in New Zealand. There the quest had only begun. After Captain Sinclair was drowned, the widow and her family, with flocks and herds and piano embarked on the clipper Bessie, owned by her son-in-law. Tahiti failed to please them; British Columbia kept them only a few months, before they put to sea again for California. Blown out of her course, the Bessie made port at Honolulu, and in 1864 the Sinclairs bought the island of Niihau from the ever-needy monarchy for $10,000.

Descriptions of Niihau are mainly from hearsay, for few but the owners, the Australian foreman, and the thirty-odd native families who live there have set foot on its rocky shores. Even government officials have been unable to obtain permission to land.

One version attributes this *tabu* to desire to keep the natives uncontaminated. A less friendly one suggests that it proceeds from canny maintenance of uncontrolled exploitation. The probable truth is that it is just lairdly exclusiveness.

Kauai residents describe Niihau as a place without movies, liquor, or tobacco; without radio, post-office, or school above early grades—and also without police or jail. For infraction of the patriarchal—or matriarchal—law, deportation is the penalty. Since all transportation is by family boat, none may leave without permission. It is said if any do leave, they are not permitted to return. Everybody goes to church; when members of the continuing branch of the family are on the island, services last practically all day.

It is a peaceful, if somewhat dull life the Hawaiians of Niihau live: herding sheep and cattle over the dry pastures, weaving rushes into mats made nowhere else, making wreaths of shells and of peacock feathers to be marketed by the lairds.

Beyond Niihau the islands grow smaller: Lehua, an islanded Diamond Head; Kaula, bleak rock towering from boisterous seas, each of these two with its lighthouse, erected with difficulty and danger. Maui Kaito, aged crippled newsboy whose bent figure was for many years a familiar sight hobbling through the streets of Honolulu, chanting in his native language by way of crying his wares, or clanging a metal rattle, swam with a line to effect landing for the construction, when no other would attempt the feat.

Beyond, still more islands lie, a thousand miles and more to the lagoon ring of Kure—bits of coral or of lava rock, each with its own story.

XXIX. WORLD WAR II
ON KAUAI & NIIHAU
HONOR, DUTY & CHANGE

*The years of World War II—1941 through 1945—
brought great change to Kaua'i. Many of the island's quiet
rural towns were inundated with GIs from the mainland
United States, some of whom married local girls or moved
back to Kaua'i once their war service was completed.*

*Kaua'i's Japanese-Americans and Filipino-Americans
also reached new levels of achievement through serving their
country both on-island and overseas. This resulted in sweeping
political change following the war.*

*During the writing of this story I became friendly with
a number of WWII vets and local residents who lived on
Kaua'i during the war. All had interesting stories. Alan Fayé
provided enough great stories to fill a book. However, the
most memorable acquaintance made during my interviews*

*was Col. Duke Curran (ret. U.S. Army). Duke spent years
and a considerable amount of his own money in organizing
and staging a 50th reunion of New York's famed "Fighting
69th," one of the first units to reach the island after Pearl
Harbor. The night of the biggest celebration of the reunion
was exceptionally humid. I had received word from the county
Civil Defense office that Hurricane Iniki was bearing down,
sucking up warm air from the equator. I took Duke and
former state senator Billy Fernandes aside and told them about
the hurricane. Too late to turn back now, the party went on
and the next morning the Fighting 69th vets, many in their
seventies, had another battle to fight, helping the island recover
from Iniki. I briefly saw Duke immediately following the
hurricane and congratulated him on throwing a reunion no
one would ever forget.*

YOUNG ALAN FAYÉ Jr. rose early at his family's
Waimea beachfront home on the morning of December
7, 1941. The sun had already risen out of the Pacific and
lit towering Mount Wai'ale'ale, as it had done for eons.

It was an apparently peaceful day off from the
plantation fields and mills, a day following a pattern pretty
much in place since the mid-1800's.

The rickety Interisland Airways amphibian seaplane
was scheduled in from Honolulu at 8 a.m. and Alan and
his family had driven out in their '34 Ford woody to Burns
Field at Port Allen to see his father off to the big city on the
only flight of the day. With Fayé senior were other plantation
managers traveling to the annual meeting of Hawaiian sugar
planters scheduled for the next day. Instead, the 9-year-old
boy found himself immersed in a world war.

"The plane didn't arrive and after a while Ambrose
Smith, my uncle's chauffeur, turned the radio on in Uncle
Lindsay's car and called, 'Hey, you guys, come, listen.'

"Webley Edwards was on the air and was saying, 'This practice sure looks real! There are planes buzzing all around and even the black smoke in the distance looks real.'

"Just then a bomb blasted a building next to the KGMB radio station and there was a moment of silence... followed by, 'Hey, this is no maneuvers, this is the real McCoy!'

"Minutes later the Kauai National Guard arrived in a pickup truck armed to the teeth, ready to hold off the impending invasion. Each Guardsman had a WWI-vintage Springfield rifle and a clip that held five rounds of ammo!"

Later that day the war first touched down on Kaua'i when one of 25 U.S. Navy planes that managed to get airborne during the Pearl Harbor attack made an emergency refueling stop at Burns Field, then Kaua'i's only paved airstrip. The pilot took off and immediately oil drums were rolled out to close down the runway. At Barking Sands military airstrip near Mānā, junk cars were towed from Waimea Garage to clutter the runway, shutting down the field.

The island reacted first with incredulity that the war was actually on, but Kaua'i's people quickly sprang into action. Charlie Fern, the editor of *The Garden Island* newspaper and operator of Kaua'i's radio station KTOH rallied the 1,000-man provisional police. Formed early in 1941 with men from every town and village on Kaua'i in anticipation of war and armed with privately-owned rifles, handguns and not a few Ben Franklin Store air guns, the men by nightfall took control of every power plant, waterworks, bridge and all intersections along Kūhiō and Kaumuali'i Highway. Word spread quickly among the 35,000 Kauaians of the rural, two-traffic light island and, by noon, the ambulance corps was mobilized, and many Kaua'i women, trained as nurses' aides by the Red Cross, went to hospitals to prepare to accept casualties.

Radio news bulletins broadcast from Līhu'e on KTOH continued during the day (thanks to an oversight by military authorities who immediately shut down all other radio stations in Hawai'i), confirming that Pearl Harbor had indeed been sneak-attacked by Japanese bombers, and that Hawai'i civilians and over 2,000 U.S. sailors and soldiers were dead; 19 warships had been sunk. One broadcast was followed strangely enough by "It's So Peaceful in the Country," a popular tune of the day. On O'ahu word spread that Kaua'i had been invaded by the Japanese.

That evening, Fayé (who would become an honorary preadolescent sergeant in the 33rd Army infantry during the war, and go on to become a NASA pilot following college), recalls the reality of war sinking in after he helped secure the family dairy and plantation lands. "We had the old RCA radio on and we were running around outside with flashlights covered with sheets of blue cellophane, wondering if there would be an invasion. We were preparing to go into the mountains as guerrilla fighters."

Hawai'i war commentator Gwenfred Allen, looking back in the years following the war, captured the moment when he wrote, "The Sunday bombs did more than start a war, they changed a way of life."

Life on Kaua'i was much simpler then. Only a handful of tourists visited the island each week, arriving on steamers at Nāwiliwili or by seaplane at Hanapēpē, staying at the Līhu'e Hotel or the Waimea Hotel for between $1.50 and $7.50 a night. A shopping trip to Līhu'e for west-siders or Hanalei folks was an occasion and a long drive from the north shore over a winding, old bumpy road that hugged the coast following ancient trails and wagon paths. Sugar cane plantations from Kīlauea to Mānā were in full swing, providing pay checks for most families on the island. Second to king cane was pineapple, with the cannery at Kapa'a the east side's major employer. Entertainment centered around churches and Buddhist temples, the plantation theaters that grew up near each mill, and hunting and fishing in the wild interior or offshore in sampans.

After the excitement of the Pearl Harbor attack and the Battle of Ni'ihau—which editor Fern called "a situation so colorful, so fantastic, that Robert Louis Stevenson, even if he had invented it, would have hesitated to try to make his readers believe it"—the island quietly and quickly did what it could to prepare for an invasion. Young school children worked gardens, highschoolers joined them and also strung barbed wire along beaches; Japanese-Americans, many of whom were excluded from the defense work, formed groups like the Sons of Mokihana to give blood, clear *kiawe* and other important, but mundane, work; Filipino plantation workers were formed into military units, drilled hard to be battle ready, and became eager to join the regular army; plantations provided heavy equipment, electricity, and grew hundreds of acres of sweet potatoes, cabbage and other foodstuffs to ensure a food supply for the island.

Each evening at dusk, University of Hawai'i professor Stanley D. Porteus recalled, a veil of mystery fell on the island.

"Venus setting over the mountains could be a parachute flare, the reflection of stars submarine lights at sea. And if the foe lurked offshore, what about the women and children in unguarded homes? These were the disturbing thoughts of the watchers, in a blackout so complete that even the consolatory cigarette could not be lit. The men of Kauai were left to themselves. I do not know what happened to all the women but one at least lay out under the stars on Koloa Beach, her rifle and a box of shells beside her, determined to pick off any boatload of the enemy that came ashore."

Three weeks after Pearl Harbor the island stirred again when at 1:30 a.m. on December 30 a Japanese submarine sitting about four miles offshore lobbed about 15 three-inch shells at targets in Nāwiliwili and lit up Kalapakī Bay with bright flares. Damage was minor, just a small cane fire and shrapnel holes in the second story of a home overlooking the bay. Termed a "punch in the nose" by many, the incident would be Kaua'i's first and the last Japanese attack of the war.

On Easter Sunday of 1942 the first mainland troops ever to be stationed on Kaua'i arrived on a rainy day that turned the dirt roads of the island into slippery obstacles. Spread around the island by trucks driven sometimes by female members of Kaua'i's Women's Motor Corps, the troops of the 27th Division under General Anderson were fresh from New York, Pittsburgh and other big cities, and found Kaua'i as exotic as the South Pacific. Local pidgin, and place names, were a mysterious foreign language for the mainland boys, but the locals were as mystified by some of the troops' tongues. Ray H. Smith, the 9-year-old son of Koloa Union Church minister Howard A. Smith and his wife, Gertrude, both former missionaries to China, found the accent of friendly Brooklyn troops who tipped him royally for fetching them cans of pineapple juice, "the strangest pidgin I ever heard."

At the head of the 27th was the famous "Fightin' 69th" Regiment, members of New York's highly-decorated, mostly Irish 165th Infantry. Confederate General Robert E. Lee gave the regiment its nickname during the Civil War in acknowledgment of its men's bravery. Among its most famed veterans were Col. "Wild Bill" Donovan, who became head of the OSS during WWII, the redoubtable chaplain Father Francis Duffy, and the noted American poet Joyce Kilmer of New Brunswick, New Jersey, killed on the banks of the Ourcq in France during WWI.

Retired Army Colonel Duke Curran, now a resident of Kapa'a, Kaua'i, living just a few miles from Kapa'a High School where he was billeted upon arrival in 1942, was one of the men of the Fightin' 69th who landed here. He continues a 50-year friendship with the Lizama family of Kapa'a and recalls meeting Joe, Ben and Vincent Lizama on his first day at the Kapa'a base, as well as his first look at Kaua'i—"The island was beautiful, the first tropical island many of us ever saw. But the beauty was overshadowed by our job, to protect the island against a Japanese attack."

Curran, with more than a trace of the streets of New York in his voice, and a tattoo of a Kaua'i girl of the forties on his forearm, was one of the first mainland troops on Kaua'i and labored for eight months building up island defenses. He remembers, "They must have strung 10,000 rolls of barbed wire and dug machine gun and mortar positions. They also ran armed motor and radio patrols. Our soldiers worked with the police, fire departments, the telephone company and manned switchboards at station KTOH in Lihue. The officers and NCO's trained the newly formed Kauai Volunteers. They stayed for eight months and fortified the entire island from Kekaha to Haena."

The troops set up camps on the west side and east side, including one that stood where island golfers now play the links of the Wailua Golf Course. Along with local help the 27th constructed 150 concrete pill boxes.

Ed Hess, a retiree from Pittsburgh and one of the first men of the 27th to land, reminisced about his first month on Kaua'i: "We worked very hard fortifying the island. Long days. When we arrived, word was to watch out for spies among the local people, but we found them to be very hospitable and trustworthy."

Hess also remembered Sunday *luau* with west-side Hawaiian families, and company officers returning with cigars for the enlisted men from parties thrown by the Robinson family.

Curran and Hess left Kaua'i for training at Schofield Barracks in central O'ahu once the island's defenses were complete. Curran remembers, "After Kauai, the famous Fightin' Irish Regiment fought in the Pacific area and suffered 473 killed in action and over 2,000 wounded."

Feeling more secure with thousands of regular army troops pouring in, daily life became a routine shaped by martial law with tight rationing of gas and other goods, food shortages and a territory-wide blackout each evening. However, news of Japanese victories in Asia and the west Pacific, underscored by unofficial word that a sizable Japanese attack force had sailed, possibly to invade Hawai'i, created a mood of uncertainty.

While the civilian population was kept mostly in the dark about what was unfolding, military authorities feared an amphibious invasion might come ashore at beaches offering strategic openings into and across the heart of the low-lying sections of the island. Maybe at the unprotected beaches at Wailua, or at Barking Sands. The highlands of Kōke'e were decided upon as the site of last retreat, a place where guerrilla warfare might hold off Japanese invaders indefinitely, and later the main military radar and wireless operations were moved there for protection.

Charlie Fern, also Kaua'i's first aviator, began to chronicle the war through updates of island events and insightful editorials that in retrospect seemed to aim at keeping a cohesive spirit going among the various racial groups on the island.

Once the war started everyone was fingerprinted and issued registration cards, along with gas masks and special cloth "bunny masks" complete with little rabbit ears for toddlers and infants. U.S. currency was recalled and replaced with special $1, $5, $10 and $20 greenbacks overprinted with "U.S. currency, Hawaiian series" to safeguard the U.S. dollar in world markets in case Hawaiʻi was captured by the Japanese and the islands' banks looted. Civilian patrols began to scan the air and sea for signs of attack, and more than a few false alerts of "mysterious lights" and spottings of Japanese submarines were reported along the beaches during the blackouts that were held every night.

Promising to fight alongside the mainland troops to the last, a home guard, the Kauai Volunteers, was formed prior to their arrival with Paul Townsley, a Lihue Plantation official and Kauai Electric executive, as commanding officer. Three battalions were sworn in: one from Kekaha to Hanapēpē, one from Kalāheo to Līhuʻe, and one from Kapaʻa to Kīlauea. All the volunteers were over 18 and of non-Oriental ancestry, with many Filipinos enthusiastically joining, glad to do something that might help their countrymen who were then desperately holding off Japanese invaders at Bataan and other combat fronts in their homeland.

On March 9, 1942 over 2,400 men enrolled. The volunteers supplied their own uniform of a dark blue shirt, khaki pants, a flat helmet and khaki jacket. Their insignia was a distinctive chevron with a white capital K sitting inside a dark blue capital V sewn on the left shoulder of their jackets. Night drills and four hours' training each

Sunday, plus practice with real rifles, pistols and machine guns soon honed their military skills.

The volunteers worked regular jobs—mostly on plantations, where wage controls lasted most of the war and unionization efforts were set aside for the duration— during the week, and fell in on Sundays for training. Special forces included military police and a mounted detachment of mostly Hawaiian and Portuguese *paniolo* formed by Captain Alan Fayé, Sr. to patrol *mauka* ranchlands and to act as forward scouts and spies in case of invasion. Many volunteers made do with Kau'ai-style weapons, including a regulation Filipino-style *bolo* cane knife sharpened down to a razor-blade edge.

The island's women also had adventures during the war serving in organizations like the WARD—Women's Air Raid Defense. Catherine Hoe of Lāwa'i, the wife of Raymond Hoe, then Catherine Lovell of Moloa'a, was allowed by her parents, Edward C. and Lydia Lovell, to move to Līhu'e and serve in the WARD under the watchful eye of Judge Rice's wife, Flora B. Rice, and a Mrs. Taylor and Mrs. Crawford. Catherine, then a 17-year-old incoming senior at Kauai High School, worked as what she calls a "shuffleboard pilot" plotting the strategic position on a large tabletop map of the Army Air Corp's 78th fighter squadron flying out of Barking Sands field.

Flora Rice opened Hale Nani, the Rice family estate that then stretched from today's Līhu'e branch of the Bank of Hawai'i down Rice Street to near where Rice Shopping Center now sits. Catherine and other young Kaua'i women worked 24-hour shifts, received tutoring from their Kaua'i High instructors at Hale Nani, and sometimes donned helmets and gas masks during middle-of-the-night air raid drills beneath the Kaua'i County Building.

Perhaps Catherine Hoe's favorite wartime story involved her close WARD friend Frances Texeira of Puhi and herself. "One day we were invited to take a ride in a B-24 bomber, taking off from Barking Sands. It was like an early helicopter tour of the island."

Unlike most of Kaua'i's young men and women, Japanese-American men anxious to serve had to wait until 1943 for their chance. Though the largest single ethnic group then on Kaua'i, questions about the loyalty to America of the *issei* and *nisei* Japanese-Americans lingered.

The Japanese-Americans on Kaua'i also felt the threat of being interned like California Japanese-Americans in lonely, isolated camps mostly in cold Rocky Mountain locations far from the coast. Thankfully only 1 percent of Kaua'i's Japanese people were taken into custody, those being mostly Japanese alien residents with associations with the Japanese consulate.

In May 1942 the Kauai Morale Committee was born and, under the leadership of Charles Ishii, attracted 1,600 Japanese-American families. The group purchased over $800,000 in war bonds, formed the Kiawe Corps to clear the thorny wood from exposed coastal areas, plus volunteered and generously donated funds to the Red Cross, USO and Welfare funds.

Beginning in March of '43 over 760 of Kaua'i's military-age Japanese-American men filed for induction. Most went to the European theater, a few to the Pacific battlefields and islands to serve as language translators and in intelligence operations. All told, of the 1,300 Kaua'i men who went off to war, 48 died in service, mostly as members of the famous AJA 442nd Regimental Combat team in the Italian campaign, the most decorated WWII outfit in all the U.S. Armed Forces. Kaua'i boys saw action in virtually all theaters of the war, from Bataan to Europe, as members of all the services and the Merchant Marine.

Larry Sakoda of Waimea had been drafted in November of 1941 while working at the Pearl Harbor shipyard. "I was offered a deferment at the time, but I said no, I will go."

He later fought in Italy, and reminisces, "There were plenty of Kauai soldiers over there, the men I was with were mostly from the neighbor islands. When I came back to Kauai I landed at Barking Sands, then I had to catch a car to come home, back to Waimea. I caught a ride in half-ton truck and they dropped me off on the road. The first one to see me was our dog; he stared at me for couple of seconds, then recognized me. My mother was at home, and my father was working. It was very emotional. The island was pretty much the same when I came home, but after you see other places you get restless; I started to go to Lihue more often."

Sakoda, who began taking photographs as a part-time assistant before the war in Waimea, saw an opportunity after he left the service and used his GI Bill benefits to attend photography school on the campus of Yale University in Connecticut. He returned to Kaua'i and opened a photography studio in Waimea, joining the Senda family, the Fujimotos and other Japanese-American photographers who have become renowned during this century for their photography work on the island.

Today the surviving AJA vets remain demure about the war, humbly acknowledging that they forever proved that Hawai'i's Japanese-Americans were as American as anyone else, and proud of the accomplishment of their post-war business successes, and of taking control of much of the power behind the Democratic overthrow of the Republican "Big Five" machine in the early 1950's, and of the national political prominence achieved by one of their own, wounded WWII army veteran United States Senator Daniel Inouye.

In Tomi Kaizawa Knaefler's book *Our House Divided*, WWII Army counter intelligence officer Ralph Yempuku describes well the positive change the war brought for Hawai'i's Japanese-Americans: "When the Nisei took the bull by the horns and fought to prove themselves, a lot of them got killed. But they didn't die in vain. They enabled the Nisei to advance politically, socially, and economically. The change for the Nisei has been dramatic. Today, my two sons and other AJA kids don't face any of that business of not feeling 100 percent trusted as the Nisei felt before, especially in the early part of the war. This is why I feel the Nisei boys who died didn't die in vain. They made a helluva lot possible for coming generations."

Meanwhile, the threat of a Japanese attack on the Hawaiian chain, beginning with Midway and the tiny atolls far to the northwest and then on to Kaua'i, was a daily fear. While the 27th labored to fortify Kaua'i, the attack came in early June. For three tense days, civilian and military defense groups were put on "all-out," 24-hour-a-day watches, ready to take up well-rehearsed inland evacuation plans for the island's women and children. Then, unknown to the island, on June 3 Japanese aircraft attacked the American naval base on Midway, a small atoll with a deep harbor and airstrip near the international dateline just 1,200 miles northwest of Kaua'i.

Like many Kaua'i school children, Alan Fayé and his Kekaha School classmates were confined to makeshift air raid shelters that day. He remembers feeling both scared and excited while spending 12 hours in a slit trench dug outside his school.

Unconfirmed stories circulated on Kaua'i that carrier planes with bullet holes in their fuselages had refueled at Barking Sands during the battle. A wave of exultation swept all Hawai'i on June 5 when word came of a smashing victory by the American forces. Over 20 Japanese ships, including four aircraft carriers, 275 aircraft and 4,800 men, were lost by the Japanese. Had victory gone the other way, it was likely Kaua'i would have been invaded before summer, mostly to capture its airfields for use as a base for attacks against the sizable U.S. military force on O'ahu.

The Midway win was termed crucial, but not decisive, by the military. But the threat of a Japanese invasion remained ominous and fortification work continued unabated. A small detachment of men, including troops from Kaua'i, was sent to establish a communications post on forbidden Ni'ihau. By August nearly 15,000 troops shipped from the mainland swelled the island's population count as California's 40th Division joined the New Yorkers. Most of the 27th and 40th division forces departed in October for combat training at Schofield Barracks in preparation for the island-jumping battles in the western South Pacific, and were replaced by men of the 33rd division from Chicago and the Midwest.

By mid-'43, with the war fronts now far from Kaua'i's shores, tensions eased and a regular schedule of Kauai Volunteer drills, war bond fundraising drives and live USO entertainment became the norm. Defense precautions were also returned to the Office of Civilian Defense. With concrete bunkers in place and barbed wire strung along all exposed beaches, the mission of the military bases was switched to "training divisions for combat operations." Realistic South Pacific grass huts, bamboo bridges and jungle defenses used by the Japanese in the South Pacific were set up by the U.S. Marines in Nā Pali, behind Moloa'a and Hanalei and near Wailua Homesteads to give over 15,000 troops a taste of what to expect when they hit the beach in the Solomons, Guadalcanal and other treacherous Japanese strongholds. Amphibious landings with cover by speedy PT boats, said to be used more for fishing expeditions than fishing downed pilots out of the drink, were also staged.

Kaua'i's last large influx of troops was the draftees of the 98th division who arrived in April '44. A sign that perhaps the war was winding down came in August '44, when the training centers were shut down. From then to V-J Day in the fall of 1945 only a token garrison guarded Kaua'i. All told, more than 40,000 mainland soldiers passed through.

The servicemen generally found a surplus of *aloha* spirit during their time on Kaua'i. Many were taken on tours of the island's scenic and historic spots; local homes were open to the mostly young men, many of whom were away from their own homes for the first time.

Entertainment for the troops abounded at more than a half-dozen USO clubs, with acts like home-grown Hawaiian musicians and *hula* dancers performing at Hanalei, Kapa'a, Līhu'e, Nāwiliwili, Kalāheo, Kōloa, Hanapēpē and Waimea. The troops and local thespians joined forces to put on plays to raise funds for war bond drives and the USO. But the most memorable entertainers were celebrity visitors like Bob Hope, big-mouthed comedian Joe E. Brown, dracula-caped Bela Lugosi, classical violinist Yehudi Menuhin, and an all-star 7th Air Force baseball team, including Joe DiMaggio.

Kaua'i's people also enjoyed the excitement the war brought. Blakeslee Conant, the son of Hanalei ranch manager Fred Conant, who oversaw Kauai Volunteers at Hanalei, looked back on his childhood days during WWII at Hanalei during a talk several years before his recent untimely passing. He remembered going down the coast to Nā Pali in Navy PT boats that would easily rival any of today's Nā Pali cruisers, and of Joe DiMaggio's all-star team and their trip to the north shore with stops at Hā'ena's caves.

The local people generally got along well with the troops. Veterans stationed on Kaua'i agreed that most of the troops considered it a stroke of luck to be stationed on outer islands. And while there was some friction when mainland servicemen dated local girls, and from the Kaua'i Police Department who nabbed many speeding Army drivers, problems were minimal.

Kaua'i's schools also received new mainland teachers to replace those who went off to war, or to defense jobs on O'ahu. Many of the teachers stayed after the war, bringing a fresh wave of *haole* residents. The students attended schools on irregular schedules; many classes were dismissed one day a week to work on plantation truck farms or in cane fields.

The generation coming of age on Kaua'i at the opening of the war entered a world of new opportunities unavailable, probably unthinkable, to their parents and grandparents. New friends, marriage and places far from home lured many away for good.

The coming of war also forced changes that were long in coming. To the dislike of the union, sugar-cane harvesting was mechanized, and wages frozen. However, at the same time, the need for workers on the plantations was essential and, when the wage freezes were lifted and the boys returned from war with word of how things were done elsewhere, the labor unions made impressive gains.

The days of plantation paternalism were over, small businesses flourished with a number of restaurants, and shops opened to service the military. The pickup of the economy also shifted the commercial center of island from the west side to Līhu'e, where the port of Nawiliwili and Līhu'e airport were now the gateways to Kaua'i.

The war made intermarriage more common, seeding the "golden" polyglot race of today's Hawai'i when servicemen married local girls on Kaua'i, and through local troops bringing war brides home from the mainland and Europe.

Memories of the war years were stirred up during a 50th anniversary celebration of the arrival of the first mainland U.S. troops of World War II. Over 100 veterans who arrived on Kaua'i between 1942 and 1945 held a reunion at the Coco Palms Resort. "The reunion was our first and last," Duke Curran, its organizer, said without regret during the gathering. "We did our job, now we're back for the last call; most of the men say they are glad to see the island this time, as they spent much of their time in '42 digging fortifications."

The Kaua'i Museum has also mounted a major exhibit, titled simply enough "World War II On Kauai." The display of photos, uniforms and dozens of items of memorabilia is strikingly different than the museum's fine collections of ancient Hawai'i or other distant eras of Kaua'i's history, for this time many of the participants are still alive and know the story well. Though not as striking as the Viet Nam wall, the exhibit is a touchstone of sorts for Kaua'i's WWII vets. More than one has shed tears looking over aging photos of their young buddies who died in the mountains of Italy, or in the woods of France to protect their faraway Kaua'i home when life was simpler, perhaps more gracious, and their lives were changed forever in one day by a monumental clash of east and west.

THE NIʻIHAU INCIDENT

Crash landing on a patch of sandy Niʻihau ranch land, its pilot lost and searching for an aircraft carrier pitching and rolling somewhere in the wide Pacific waters northwest of Kauaʻi, the shiny Japanese fighter bomber accidentally cast the isolated island into World War II and national prominence.

Dazed, the pilot stepped out on the wings of the plane and stumbled down to earth, exhausted, but elated, after dropping his payload on the U.S. fleet at Pearl Harbor. Immediately Hawila Kaleohano, a Niihauan who lived near the crash scene, disarmed the enemy pilot and took his identification papers. Kaleohano and his neighbors put the pilot under guard and decided to wait to take further action until the next day, when the weekly sampan from Kauaʻi was due to arrive. However, the sailing was canceled in the aftermath of the devastating bombing on Oʻahu for fear of new waves of attackers.

By the following afternoon the crafty pilot began plotting to escape. He dispatched one of his guards, a Japanese alien named Shintani, with a bribe of 200¥ for Kaleohano, seeking to have his papers returned. Kaleohano angrily refused the bribe and warned Shintani he was heading for big trouble. Shintani backed off and went into hiding. Failing with one tactic, the pilot then persuaded burly Kauaian Yoshio Harada, another guard, to get him firearms. Frightened, and confused, by the barking orders of the pilot, Harada complied. Harada stripped two machine guns off the downed fighter and mounted them in Puʻuwai, the tiny capital of Niʻihau. The plan failed when two Niihauans stole the gun's ammunition.

A reign of terror followed as Harada and the freed pilot burned down Kaleohano's house and torched the plane. The following day they took hostage Benehakaka (Bernard) Kanahele and his wife, Ella. Kanahele was sent to find Kaleohano, but returned empty-handed, for the pilot's nemesis had sailed in a whale boat to Kaua'i to get help. The angry pilot then enraged Kanahele when he threatened to kill him and his wife, but made the mistake of turning his back on the thickly-built Niihauan. Kanahele jumped him, and in the scuffle a pistol discharged, wounding Kanahele.

"Then I got mad," Kanahele later recalled, describing how he lifted the Japanese pilot up and bashed his brains out against a rock wall while his wife attacked Harada. Harada broke away long enough to shoot himself.

Lt. Jack Mizuha of the Kauai Volunteers arrived the next day, exactly one week after Pearl Harbor, with 17 enlisted men and three civilians, but found the "Battle of Ni'ihau" had already been won.

The story ran in the next day's *Garden Island* newspaper and within four days made national news. Later in the war a full-length article and photo spread appeared in the then very popular *Saturday Evening Post*. Kanahele and Kaleohano received American Legion heroism awards before the end of the year, and each a Medal of Merit from the U.S. Army at war's close.

Kanahele's expression "Then I got mad!" instantly became the first World War II lingo to enter Hawai'i's daily conversations after the story was splashed across the front pages of the Honolulu papers. A Tin Pan Alley tunesmith also immortalized the Ni'ihau heroes with a forties big-band number titled "They Couldn't Take Niihau Nohow."

▧ ▧ ▧

XXX.   KAUA'I SAVES SINATRA, TWICE

The rescue of Frank Sinatra in rough waves off Wailua is well known on Kaua'i. What's little known is the spark the island's people gave to Sinatra when he was in the doldrums in 1952.

Going through old issues of The Garden Island *while researching* The Kaua'i Movie Book, *I discovered that Sinatra sang at the Kaua'i County Fair back then. More in-depth study brought me to a pictorial biography put together by his daughter Nancy. She describes the concert under a canvas tent near where the Outrigger Kauai is today as her father's "Comeback Concert." His first-hand account in her book is touching and captures the simple, but profound,* aloha *of the island's people.*

I wrote a version of this story for The Garden Island *in the days after Sinatra's death in 1998.*

SINGER AND ACTOR Frank Sinatra is being remembered this weekend on Kaua'i. Sinatra passed away Thursday in Los Angeles.

The actor knew the island well for he turned his life around here in 1952, and almost lost it at Wailua in 1964.

His loyal fans here are mourning the passing of "The Voice."

"We're all talking to each other today," said long-time Kaua'i resident and Sinatra fan Lillian Daily of 'Anini on Friday. "One of our friends is planning a Frank Sinatra dinner party tonight. I think I have every thing he ever recorded, he was a very special person in our lives."

Daily traveled from her hometown in Roselle, New Jersey to the Paramount Theater in Manhattan in the bobbysocks era of the 1940s to hear Sinatra during his early ascent to fame.

But her most memorable Sinatra concert took place in April, 1952 under a leaky County Fair tent at a spot near the Wailua golf course.

"It was unforgettable," said Daily, who came to Kaua'i in the late 1940s when her husband launched Love's bread operation here. "Sinatra was at a low ebb in his life. He was offered a job as a soloist at the Kaua'i County Fair...can you believe that!"

"It was where the second nine holes of the golf course is today," she remembered. "It was a rainy Sunday afternoon and he did his regularly scheduled show, avoiding all these leaks. When that was *pau,* he walked to the edge of the stage and sat down and looked out at the audience and said 'What do you want to hear?.' and what ever anybody called out he sang... he sang his heart out."

Sinatra's daughter Nancy Sinatra, writing in her book *Frank Sinatra—An American Legend*, calls the Kaua'i County Fair appearance her dad's big "Comeback Concert."

The singer's buddy in Hawai'i, the late Buck Buchwach, then a reporter with the *Honolulu Advertiser*, recalled how Sinatra reacted to the concert.

"Frank told me, 'I wondered if the show really did have to go on. Then I peeked out at the audience. There were a few hundred, tops. They weren't wearing fancy clothes or expensive jewelry. They wore *aloha* shirts, jeans, *mu'umu'u* and such. Homey. And their warmth and friendliness smacked me in the face. And when two brown-skinned young girls gave me a couple of handmade *lei* and little kisses, I almost broke down.'"

Buchwach said after singing for the county fair audience—accompanied only by a pianist—Sinatra had tears in his eyes and said that the night marked the first night on his way back to the top.

"From that moment, everything seemed to go right for him," Buchwach wrote.

Well, maybe not everything, according to Mike Ashman of Princeville who was then a KTOH radio announcer who interviewed the singer on the air and got to know Sinatra during his first visit.

"Sinatra had agreed to come to Poipu and play volleyball on Sunday morning and he never showed up," Ashman said. "He was staying at the Kaua'i Inn, at the end of Rice Street, and Ava Gardner had flown in."

Sinatra and Gardner married in Pennsylvania the previous November, but her career soon eclipsed his after the singer's record sales cooled off. Their stormy marriage lasted only a few years.

"I drove to Lihue and he was in the dining room with Ava Gardner having a very serious conversation," Ashman said. "He saw me and gave me a negative wave and I left. Shortly after that they broke up, and the break up was apparently in discussion then. She left Kauaʻi and went back to Honolulu."

That November Gardner, along with the singer's friendship with movie mogul Harry Cohn, helped Sinatra get the role of Maggio, his Oscar-winning role in the Oʻahu-made film *From Here to Eternity*, a role that for good turned his career around and led to his major stardom.

On a return visit in 1964 Sinatra came within minutes of drowning in the surf off Wailua Beach. He was here to direct and star in the film *None But the Brave* and chose an isolated beach north of Moloaʻa as the principle location.

Toward the end of the filming Sinatra spent a Sunday afternoon relaxing at a beach front home once located near where the Lae Nani condominiums are today. The home became known as "The Frank Sinatra House" and was later trailered up to Wailua Homesteads. Joining him were long-time pal Jilly Rizzo, producer Howard W. Koch and his wife Ruth Koch, and some of the cast.

In an interview for *The Kauaʻi Movie Book* Koch described the day to me. He said despite his warning not to go in the ocean his wife decided to take a swim and Sinatra, noticing that the surf was up, said he would join her to protect her from the undertow. They were wading just offshore when the inside wash from a big set of waves swept them away. The next wave drew Koch toward shore, but dragged Sinatra about 200 yards out.

While a young actor tried to get Sinatra in, the others ran for help. Eventually assistance came from county supervisor Louis Gonsalves and Harold Jim, then an assistant manager at the Coco Palms, and from the Kaua'i Fire Department.

"Sinatra was in the water for about 20 minutes, in another five minutes he would have been gone," Fire Lieutenant George Keawe told *The Garden Island*. "His face was starting to turn blue."

Sinatra finally made it to the beach and he was carried into the beach house on a stretcher. After a checkup a doctor found he was okay, but exhausted. His daughter remembers that she made him eggs and peppers and the two watched TV until he fell asleep. But producer Koch recalls that he and others who watched helplessly on the beach started drinking and didn't stop "until we didn't know where we were."

Koch took over the director's chair the next day, but Sinatra was soon back in action to complete the American-Japanese production.

❖　❖　❖

Chris Cook

XXXI. NĀWILIWILI
KAUAʻI'S LEGENDARY PORT TOWN

Nāwiliwili, named for the stand of wiliwili *trees that once overlooked the scenic bay and town, is a place rich in legend and history. Many Kauaʻi legends, especially those of the* menehune, *have a Nāwiliwili locale.*

Today the port town is where the island's processed sugar cane goes out and where its oil, visitors and imports arrive.

The luxury hotel along the beach at Kalapakī and the South Pacific-like dock, where inter-island barges and cruise ships tie up, add a special flavor to Nāwiliwili's unique place on Kauaʻi. The hotel site has an interesting history—having begun as a beach home for missionary families, it became a post-war resort hotel named the Kauai Surf. Developer Christopher Hemmeter transformed the aging hotel in the mid-eighties into the Westin Kauai, an opulent "mega-resort."

This story was used by the hotel publicist to give travel writers a taste of the flavor of Nāwiliwili. The hotel is now the Kauai Marriott Resort and Beach Club.

My first introduction to Nāwiliwili was as an arriving passenger on the inter-island hydrofoil boats that once raced across the Kaua'i Channel. Coming from Honolulu on a two-hour ride across the wide channel, losing sight of land for a time, was a perfect transition into the peaceful pace of life found on Kaua'i.

NĀWILIWILI'S SPIRIT OF place is as solid as the lava beds underlying the sandy loam and clay of its soil. Kaua'i's port of call since the early twentieth century, the once sleepy beach and river town is now undergoing a renaissance of sorts.

Once a heavily populated settlement of the ancient Kaua'i princedom of Puna—which embraced a sweep of land stretching from Kōloa to Anahola—Nāwiliwili and its past is steeped in Hawaiian mythology and as ingrained within the heart of Kaua'i's history as any district of the island.

Nāwiliwili is also the gateway to Kaua'i for visitors, residents and commerce. Cruise ships and passenger jets cross paths here and a steady stream of barges, stacked high with rows of container boxes, load and unload their cargoes of foodstuffs and supplies, making the protected harbor the island's commercial hub and lifeline.

I can easily recall my first glimpse of Nāwiliwili. On a stormy autumn night, the lights of the harbor came into view as I flew over Mount Hā'upu, the silent sentinel that watches over its harbor. I fastened on the harbor lights for security as the airplane pitched back and forth in high winds.

But another passage to Kaua'i made several years later lingers in my memory as a pleasant dream. I arrived aboard a hydrofoil owned by a short-lived inter-island transport company. After an idyllic two-hour channel crossing, the hydrofoil skimmed into the glassy harbor, turning to starboard with the ease of a water-skier as it passed the massive outside breakwater, and slid sleekly into its berth along the waterfront, near the former Coast Guard station dock. Alighting onto the wharf close by Club Jetty, the restaurant-cum-nightclub, I was enthralled by the rich sunbeams breaking through the clouds hovering over Mt. Wai'ale'ale, upland and to the west. The waterfront was quiet. Except for a few beat-up taxis idling in anticipation of fares and the long blasts from a Young Brothers' tug as it chugged out, towing a barge bedecked with vehicles and open containers, the harbor was still. A few couples staying at the Kauai Surf strolled along crescent-shaped Kalapakī Beach, while local kids surfed slow, rolling waves.

For a while I was lost in a reverie and began imagining what Boat Day at Nāwiliwili might have been like forty, or even a hundred, years before. I could see the crowd of passengers covered in *lei* while their laughing friends threw brightly-colored paper streamers. A brass band played lively melodies and a lovely, grass-skirted *wahine* danced the *hula* to a tune strummed on an old *ukulele*. Smiling vendors hawked fresh pineapples and orchids. I could see old Model-A Fords, snazzy open touring cars and even horsedrawn carriages waiting with expectant greeters as the malihinis and returning *kama'aina* alighted from inter-island and transpacific ships in the days before air travel, when globe-trotting was a leisurely affair and the only way to get here from the Mainland was aboard a luxurious Matson oceanliner.

Another blast from the departing tugboat's whistle snapped me suddenly back to the present. I found a pay phone and called friends living deep in the highlands behind Wailua to pick me up. As I waited, scribbling notes in a ragged journal begun months before in Fiji, I was aware of being watched. I looked up to see a stocky Hawaiian, with graying hair and beard and two armfuls of tattoos, open the door of his early-sixties Chevy taxi, stretch his thick calves and widespread "*luau* feet" out onto the pavement and eye me with interest.

After a few minutes, he spoke in a deep, resonant voice, uniquely Hawaiian, and asked matter-of-factly, "Need a ride, *haole* boy?"

I looked around, still lost in my thoughts, and noticed I was the only passenger remaining on the dock. Walking over to the long, white taxi, my eyes caught sight of two ancient-looking, deep-orange-brown calabashes sitting on the back seat. Each was pocked by dovetailed wooden repair patches that appeared to have been installed more than a century before by a skilled woodworker.

"Well, thanks, but I've got some friends coming down to get me," I answered.

"The boat, she early," he replied. "Maybe you like try one quick tour to Menehune Fishpond?"

"Sure, why not?" I said, folding up my notebook and stowing my small pack on the wide, clear-vinyl-covered front seat.

"Joe," he said, thrusting out a large, calloused, deep-brown hand with a petroglyph-like tattoo in the fold of skin between his right thumb and index finger.

I shook his hand and off we went, the engine purring as only an old GM V-8 can. We soon stopped at an overlook on the edge of the cane fields above Nāwiliwili, near the campus of Kaua'i High School. The view encompassed a sweeping arc from Ninini Lighthouse at the north side of the bay, across the wide mouth of the harbor, and up steeply to where the peaks of the Hoary

Head Mountains perched jaggedly above Kīpū Kai to the south. As Joe and I stepped out of the old Chevy for a better look, the official tour began.

"Right after Pearl Harbor, December '41, I was a guard out here. We come out New Year's Eve morning and found shells. Just before midnight, night before, a Japanese sub fired maybe 15 rounds at Nawiliwili. Only attack on Kauai during the war. Most were duds. One, she hit a gasoline tank over 'dere, but the buggah' only denied it. Subs also shot at Hilo and Kahului that night."

He was silent for a while and the steady bubbling of irrigation water in a ditch behind us underscored the moment. I felt Joe was only scratching the surface of his knowledge of Nāwiliwili, as if he were warming up for something deeper, something truly Hawaiian, about the place. He lit up a filterless Pall Mall, took a deep drag and slowly savored the smoke before continuing.

"Way before 'dat, in the days of my grandfather's grandfather, Kuhiau *heiau* sat right here. The largest and most powerful *heiau* on Kauai. Plenty *mana*. Stone walls, 'bout four acres square with a grove of *koa* trees and a *wiliwili* tree in front. Red *lei* was made from the *wiliwili* seed; the seeds used to be all over hea'. My grandfather told me the people of Niumalu and Nawiliwili could sometimes see flashing lights—*akualelehene*—in certain seasons.

"Every stone gone now. Nothing left. One sistah' *heiau*, Paukini, was on a rock near where the end of the jetty is. Was connected to land then and the old *kahuna* of Kuhiau probably lived out there, walking up here to pray to his gods and talkin' to the *'amākua*, you know, the sharks of the ocean and the birds of the wiliwili tree, li' 'dat. The *heiau* had connections to the shark *'amākua*, you know. In those days people would throw *poi* to the sharks…'da kine', sacrifice."

Picking up a couple of seedpods from a *haole koa* tree, Joe absently ground them into pulp in his strong hands as he stared out to sea, looking beyond the jetty and the lighthouse, beyond the horizon even, to a place only he could see.

"The *wiliwili* trees is what Nawiliwili means, you know. In the old days, the blossoming *wiliwili* trees here was famous. Back then, the ocean came up much farther, all the jetty area you see now is just landfill. I still remembah' a grove of *wiliwili* trees from the days of my childhood. They had big blossoms in the spring—the shore was lined with them. The only boats then was canoes and maybe sometimes a sailing ship.

"Oh, was we ever rascals! Lucky we still alive, my friends and me. We'd climb to the top of Haupu, way up 'dere, to gather *mokihana* berries near the ruins of a small *heiau*–Keolewa–that was Laka's temple. She was the *hula* goddess. My old auntie, who pass away long time now, told me as a girl she was trained to sing Laka's song there, breaking off each leaf and flower of her *lei* to honor her.

"When we was *keiki* we'd dive off the point there at Ninini, where the lighthouse is, just like the *menehune* did. They wasn't only at the fishpond, you know. Their favorite sport was throwin' a big rock in the ocean and divin' in after it. One night they hauled one plenty big boulder all the way from Kipukai to Ninini. But when they crossed the river down where it gets shallow—they dropped 'da kine' and it split in two. You can still see one half down at Ninini, if you know where to look."

Joe turned and spit into the irrigation ditch while beckoning me to the taxi. We drove past the red-dirt playing fields of Kaua'i High and turned down the road to Puhi. At the lookout above Hulē'ia River and the Menehune Fishpond, we stopped. From our elevated vantage point we looked down upon the glassy, stadium-sized pond and the deep, lush valley carved by the curving river over millennia.

We gazed at the peaceful vista without speaking. The only sounds were the whistling of birds and the breeze rustling the branches of the *wiliwili* trees.

Suddenly the calm was shattered as a noisy, fuming tour bus pulled up next to us, stopped in front of the Hawaii Visitors Bureau sign and disgorged its cargo of picture-taking vacationers. Joe cleared his throat and stared downstream until the bus and its 30 pale passengers departed. Seeing the tourists actually heightened the experience. They, and their whirlwind perception of the wealth of things Hawaiian surrounding them, gave a deeper value to what Joe was showing me.

"The Alakoko Fishpond down there is the only project the *menehune* never *pau* with. Two *ali'i*, a bruddah' and a sistah', of Niumalu, down behind Nawiliwili, asked the *menehune* to build each of them a fishpond. To get enough rocks, the *menehune* lined up in one row for 20 miles, all the way from Makaweli Valley out by Waimea, and handed the rocks to here, one-by-one. But because the *menehune* nevah' worked more than one night at a time, they only finish the bruddah's one.

"The people of old would say you could hear the hum of the *menehune* at dawn…still working to try to finish the fishpond, I guess."

Jumping ahead in time, Joe drew me into his conversation, asking about my ancestors and where they had come from. Hearing of my New England Pilgrim roots, he laughed, crinkling his bloodshot, deep-brown eyes. He told me of the missionary descendants and their spouses and children who moved into Nāwiliwili beginning in the mid-1850's.

"Lihue was just a little *manini* town in those days. Governor Kaikioewa—back when Kauai had its own governor—built a house back of here on land called Papalinahoa. Later the Hawaiian church on the back road to Lihue was built and then a courthouse. Everyone lived down in Nawiliwili in those days, too.

"You know, what changed Nawiliwili, like 'da whole Kingdom, was sugar. The New England Yankee growers down at Koloa started everything in about 1835. They was not missionaries, but Yankee businessmen. Money was tight in those days. To make an honest dollar, people would try everything—no matter how hard the work. After the whalers stop coming, just about everybody work in the sugar field. The money even stopped comin' from New England for the missionaries. Lihue Plantation was started in the 1850's. Soon the forest—the *hau*, *koa*, the *wiliwili*, almost every old tree down hea' disappeared as the sugar cane spread. Many of the wealthy old Kauai families you see today made their first money on sugar.

"Old G.N. Wilcox began with just a few acres of sugar when he was young, bought Grove Farm from a German fellah'. Fifty years later, he had enough *kala* to buy the government bonds to build the harbor where the ships stay at Nawiliwili. He owned ships, even helped start the inter-island airplane.

"The Rice family, too. They stayed on after the mainland folks stopped sending money. They has a place down this side." We walked a ways along the road, then down an overgrown trail to the banks of the Hulē'ia River. Joe pulled back a thick stalk of wild cane which covered the rotting hulk of an outrigger canoe apparently carved from a single log.

I expected a diatribe about how the *haole*, especially the missionaries, had stolen his family's land, destroyed his culture and despoiled his world. I felt defensive. Surprisingly, though, Joe began, instead, the story of the visit of Hawai'i's Queen Lili'uokalani to Nāwiliwili.

"My grandfather took me here as a young boy and showed me this canoe. You see 'da big *puka* in the bow? The old man so shocked when he hear 'da Royal Hawaiian Band playing that he sail this canoe, blam, right into the *kahuna*'s rock. Had nevah' heard nothin' like 'dat before, you know! Later, he worked serving the *luau* to his beloved queen.

"She stayed with William Hyde Rice, you know. Rice was one *kama'aina*. Could speak Hawaiian fluently and, even though his parents were missionaries, straight from the mainland, he was like one of us. Local *haole* boy all 'da way. The queen rewarded him. Made him first *haole* to be governor of Kauai."

Joe dug into the canoe and fished out a woven net encircling a half dozen amber and deep green bottles, obviously hand-blown and very old.

"These bottles come over from Honolulu on the steamer that brought the queen. My grandfather took them from the luau grounds at Kalapaki, up on the Rice property where the old Kauai Inn used to be and where they built the Kauai Surf. Many years later the house they had there was smashed when a tsunami rolled across Nawiliwili."

Handing me a rare bottle embossed with the name of a Honolulu brewery long since shut down, Joe turned and headed back up to his taxi. We drove silently to the jetty, where I saw my friends parked, waiting for me.

As I picked up my small pack from the back seat of the cab, I accidentally tipped open one of the calabash lids. A sudden glimmer of bright light burst from the opening, momentarily blinding me. I thought of the lights of the old *heiau*, and wondered what ancient magic my guide possessed. Joe just grinned, exposing his mouthful of tobacco-stained teeth, and leaned over to tap the lid back on.

A bit dazed by the startling light and my sojourn with Joe, I slouched back in the rear seat of my new friend's station wagon, gently cradling my prized old bottle, and we departed.

I've never seen Joe or his taxi again, though I'm always looking for him. And whenever I mention him to the Hawaiians of Kaua'i who have since befriended me, I'm always met by an odd look, a pregnant pause and a quick change of subject.

Today, almost 15 years after my encounter with the cabby, times have changed again at Nāwiliwili, as they always will. However, the growing wealth of stories and events at the picturesque port town complement this change and ease the sometimes rapid transition from old to new. And the past still remains at Nāwiliwili. The ocean-going ships of Matson continue to bring in the world's goods and depart, for now, with tons of raw Kaua'i sugar as they have for decades, and the Hawaiian spirit of the place still underlies its day-to-day existence.

XXXII.   HURRICANE 'INIKI STRIKES KAUA'I

Hurricane Iniki devastated Kaua'i the late morning and afternoon of September 11, 1992. Packing winds of over 150 mph, the storm tore up the island. Entire towns crumbled and verdant mountainsides turned entirely brown in a few hours as if a huge weed whacker had been turned on them. Amazingly, the death toll was low.

As the weeks, months and years following Iniki roll on changes wrought by the hurricane continue to surface. Kaua'i has seen a mass emigration of long-time local residents and economic boom then bust. But perhaps the longest lasting impact is still playing out in the lives and souls of the survivors who spent a day at the center of nature's fury and lived to tell about it.

Here's my account, written for Garden Island *editor Rita DeSilva on a battery-powered laptop computer in the bombed-*

out shell of my home hours after the hurricane struck. My
family—and the computer holding the manuscript for this
book—came within 20 feet of being taken out by a flying
open beam ceiling that crashed through my master bedroom,
smashing everything in the room.

In the aftermath of Iniki I served as the tourism
spokesperson for the County of Kaua'i under Mayor JoAnn
Yukimura. Working inside her office during the critical early
weeks of recovery providing sound bites for national and local
media, and going around the island to see the devastation
first hand, gave me a close look at the massive effort she faced
in reviving the island, a daunting task that put Kaua'i on
the road to rebirth.

"HANALEI AND PRINCEVILLE look like a nuclear
bomb hit," more than one north shore resident said the
day after Hurricane Iniki hit.

A handful of homes at Princeville and Hanalei got
away with a few broken windows and missing shingles.
Most received serious damage, dozens were apparently
totaled—left with only one or two walls standing.
Hundreds of visitors were stranded. However, on Sunday
afternoon Aloha Island Air flights were taking people out
to Honolulu. Fred Matti, General Manager of Princeville
Hotel, led a valiant effort of his employees and volunteers
in housing hotel guests, other visitors and suddenly
homeless local residents.

The ordeal began Thursday afternoon when the
hurricane began to turn north. However, even late
Thursday night panic buying didn't set in like it would if
the community had fully realized what was to come.

Friday morning reality hit home. Foodland closed its
doors at 8:30 a.m., helping some of the community stock

up quickly, but also leaving some visitors weeping in front of the locked door. Big Save closed at 9:30 a.m. in Hanalei.

The air went very still at about noon. Still most residents and visitors weren't comprehending the threat of a major hurricane. One man pulled out a Hurricane Iwa souvenir book to show unbelievers what could happen.

By 3 p.m. the winds picked up from a southerly direction. The rapidly approaching low pressure made the air temperature and humidity almost unbearable.

While many people headed for shelter at the Princeville Hotel and Kilauea Neighborhood Center, many also chose to ride it out at home.

Then it hit. First palm frond leaves and birds flew by. The winds were maybe up to 70 m.p.h. By 4:30 or so the hurricane shifted gears and roof shingles began to fly by. Then roof sheeting began to appear.

Briefly, the winds subsided when the edge of the eye of the storm crossed. Two crazies on bicycles drove by, headed for who knows where.

"Is that it?" could be heard between homes. It wasn't. The sky darkened and the winds picked up quickly and immensely, coming from the west and across Hanalei Valley. Windows began to break, smashed by debris and pressure. The air was very hot and humid, like the exhaust of an air conditioner shot from the back of a jet plane.

Glancing out occasionally from secure shelter, the degree of damage became apparent. With Hurricane Iwa in mind, I determined this one would be worse. That was confirmed when the torrential winds and rain whipped up into a froth. It looked like a blizzard outside.

Palm trees were snapping, roofs were coming off. My wife and I and our two young sons barricaded ourselves in an interior bathroom, mattresses stacked outside the door. We had been hiding in a bedroom in the lee of the storm winds. A louver broke, driving us to the bathroom. About fifteen minutes later a window shattered in the bedroom, followed by a loud thud. We waited about 45 minutes for the wind to let down before I peeked in the bedroom, which looked like a lumberyard had been delivered into it. Two gaping holes, the entire length of the bedroom walls, were letting in the wind and rain. If we had stayed there we would have been smashed into the wall by a stack of wood four to five feet high.

Too shocked to realize how close we came to serious injury, if not death, I wandered out into the dark, ruined remains of Princeville. All our neighbors had made it too. The devastation, what I could see, was mind boggling. It was a miracle no one in the area was hurt.

Glass, fallen vegetation, roofs, palm tree heads and even a kitchen sink blocked sidewalks. Rental cars were smashed in the parking lot, but our trusty Subaru station wagon made it.

By 9 p.m. we had our candles out and on, the kids tucked in a makeshift bed. "Here we go again," I thought, recalling the lengthy aftermath following Hurricane Iwa.

At 3:30 a.m. I awoke. The air was dead still. The sky was crystal clear, the moon full and Orion hung in the midnight sky. Somehow the conditions were as amazing as the hurricane.

At first light the sun rose blood red and everyone climbed out of the wreckage and wandered around. It was unbelievable. Definitely much worse than Iwa. Every Norfolk Pine was stripped, the Princeville Visitor Center entrance flattened. Rows of houses devastated.

Word went around that a man had been killed in Kīlauea, and that the situation at the Kīlauea Neighborhood Center shelter had turned dangerous when the roof went off the nearby gym, striping the neighborhood center roof and exposing those huddled below to the hurricane.

A New Zealand man reported that a drunk man repeatedly screamed "This is the end!" over and over until a hefty local man slugged him.

The Princeville Hotel didn't appear too damaged. However, reportedly a man was sucked out a window and injured. Definitely many residents and visitors were thankful for the sturdy hotel to hide in.

Mike Arnold of Hale Moi condominiums was huddled in his upstairs bathroom when his roof blew off, almost taking him with it. His story was similar to dozens of others. Susan Glass, her husband Bill and their three children returned home that morning to find their Princeville home literally gone with the wind. Only the kitchen and a front wall remained. They weren't the only ones. In Hanalei many homes were striped of their roofs and gutted. The Haraguchi Rice Mill and Rodney Haraguchi's farm house were damaged.

A photographer spent the storm in the former Hawaiian Tel bunker on Kūhiʻo Highway in Hanalei. He leaned out occasionally to snap a photo. He spotted two men with T-shirts over their heads wheeling a safe on a dolly down the road.

The damage to cars also pointed out the force of the hurricane. Some looked like they were riddled with bullets, struck by roofing tiles. hurled through the air.

Island Hardware at Princeville opened at 7:30 Saturday morning to help out with what supplies were remaining. One of the store owners flew over on a chartered helicopter to Honolulu on Saturday to order emergency supplies.

Visitors wandered around stunned, but generally not

panicking, many offering sympathy for the locals who couldn't just fly away from the disaster.

Communication to the hurricane victims from state and local authorities was nil as of Sunday afternoon. Radio broadcasts and rumors were the only sources of news. Scanning the dial for word from the Honolulu stations usually brought in only music or normal programs. "It was a little like the *Twilight Zone,* there we were standing around what looked like a nuclear strike while Aretha Franklin was the only thing on the radio," someone said.

Princeville Hotel continued to serve meals, but limited them to only those registered to stay at their temporary Red Cross shelter. Alan Zingale of the hotel staff broadcast regular bulletins on "Radio Princeville Hotel," for both guests and local residents.

Foodland at Princeville reopened at noon on Saturday and a long line quickly formed. Milk was given out, plus ice in small containers.

Most roads were passable by Sunday. South of Kīlauea tall power poles lay across the road for several miles. Access to Līhu'e required driving along shoulders.

By Sunday reality set in that this was going to be a long-term project to return to normal. The magnitude of the disaster would not be truly known for probably six months.

Fears of looting also set in. Reportedly looters were spotted at Pali Ke Kua the night of the hurricane. The residents at the heavily damaged Paniolo Condominiums erected a sign which read, "Is this worth dying for?" As of Sunday afternoon no National Guard were visible at Princeville, though troops were at Kīlauea, some set in for the duration napping under a shade tree on the lawn of Kīlauea School.

Hanalei School also received severe damage with two kindergarten rooms demolished, and the roof torn or blown off the school library and cafeteria.

Sunday also brought a degree of calm and celebration as many groups of friends and relatives gathered. One group of Hawaiians near the Hanalei Police Station were entertained Saturday to an original epic song about the Hurricane, strummed by a local singer-guitarist.

Hurricane Iniki, although newsworthy, apparently will become a legend, probably the strongest hurricane to hit the north shore in known history.

■ ■ ■

XXXIII. CONQUERING KING'S REEF

Terry Chung & Titus Kinimaka

For surfers, King's Reef is the Mount Everest of Kaua'i's waves. The break only begins to show when winter swells 20 feet and higher hit the north shore. King's holds its round, tubular shape even when huge, breaking about a mile and a half outside of the Hanalei Pier. Riding the fast-breaking, pitching monstrous waves had only been a surfer's fantasy until a day in mid-November, 1996 when Titus Kinimaka and Terry Chung, two Native Hawaiians from Kaua'i, dared to risk their lives to conquer King's Reef.

They used a highly-tuned jet ski to tow each other into waves that had faces 40 feet and higher. Being whipped into a wall of water moving at about 40 miles per hour while taking a drop comparable to jumping off a five-story building became the newest trend in the 1000-year history of surfing on Kaua'i.

The 1990s saw the arrival of the jet ski tow-in as an addition to surfing technology which enabled riders to take off on giant waves they probably couldn't catch unaided. Hanalei-raised surfer Laird Hamilton and others pioneered tow-in surfing at Jaws, a huge wave that breaks near Pā'ia, Maui. Now many are riding formerly unridden "outer reef" breaks across Hawai'i.

The Kaua'i duo's feat rivals the deeds of mythological Hawaiian heroes, but unlike the champions of the island's past, Titus and Terry are here to tell all the details.

To describe their momentous ride Chung wrote down an account of the day, a first-hand tale of bravery and taking surfing literally to new heights, and Kinimaka added his tale of riding King's and events leading up to the ride.

TERRY

King's had never been surfed before, and I never thought I would surf it in my surfing career. The place only breaks when crests reach 18-20 feet or higher. The rock shelf under the break is 50 to 70 feet deep, dropping off to 120 feet. The wave actually breaks in 50 feet of water.

I probably wouldn't have been out at King's if it wasn't for Titus, and his will and determination to surf the never-ridden break. He wanted it and I was there to help him pull it off, and we did.

We're both 42 years old and not getting any younger. Experience gives us a few more years of big wave surfing, but probably neither of us would put ourselves in this situation again.

We didn't have any type of media or any sort of coverage photos or movies. It was all a spur of the moment thing. We were on our own out there. The energy level of our rides was over the red line on the Richter Scale for your average surfer. We're both stoked to have done it.

TITUS

We'd been training to ride King's for about eight months when my daughter Maluhia was born on September 2. I wanted to dedicate the reef to my daughter, because nobody had ever ridden King's Reef. It was destiny that particular day. I took my daughter's *piko* out to Hanalei and my paddleboard. Hōkūle'a was at the pier; it was an omen, a heavy visual thing to me. The last time, in 1977, Hōkūle'a was going around Kaua'i and Eddie Aikau was on board and we had a gathering at the pier, singing, playing music. I asked Nainoa Thompson if I could get a ride out there to leave the *piko*. I said it would mean a lot for me. He remembered me and said 'You were suppose to be on the first trip (of the Hōkūle'a).' They rigged the sail up and I put my paddleboard on board. A *kahuna* was on the boat. He gave a blessing to the *piko*. I took the helm and steered over to King's. We had a little ceremony and I threw my baby's *piko* off the canoe, from the side that belongs to Eddie Aikau. Everyone was crying. I jumped off the boat with my paddleboard to head back in. It was a flat day. There was a bump outside of Flat Rock, and I rode it all the way into the river mouth.

A month later, I was on O'ahu at the service for the one-year anniversary of Mark Foo's death (Foo, a top big wave rider at Waimea Bay on O'ahu, died in 1995 riding Maverick's, a big wave spot south of San Francisco). We were at Duke's restaurant at Waikīkī with Joey Cabell, talking about big waves. I asked him, 'You know where the biggest wave is?' We agreed King's is one of the biggest in the world. Cabell told me in 1969 (the year that what may be the largest swell of the century hit the north shore) he saw it breaking close to 50-60 feet. He said he tried to paddle out and it was beyond the capacity of his board, but he always wanted to try it. I said the next time it breaks we're going to be the first. We talked to 1 a.m. and I went back to my hotel. I woke up early in the morning in Waikīkī and was ready to go back to Kaua'i. The plane made a turn toward Mākaha and I saw giant lines marching to Kaua'i. I looked down and said it's got to be about 30 to 40 feet. The corduroy lines were going right across the channel.

I tore out to Kalihi Wai and found Terry who said it was 20 feet, and the outer reef was 40 feet. We went out past Lumaha'i Beach and saw King's Reef had a 60-foot face.

When got out to King's, I said, 'Okay here we go.' I was the first one to attempt it. It was my first time on waves that big. I tried to get in a couple times from the back side of the wave, whipping in. I got three false pitches, and got caught inside by a 60-foot high wave, by two closeouts. We had no sled. Terry came in and I used the handle of the rope to get out of the impact zone. I was totally out of breath. 'If I get caught again I don't know if I'll make,' I told Terry. I said we have to come from the frontside and I used the 50-foot rope and whipped myself down the face. Terry went up behind the wave.

When we turned around and faced toward Nā Pali Coast we saw one giant wave coming across the whole ocean. I thought, 'Oh my God, this thing is not normal.' Looking down this beast, I saw it was breaking from across the bay, connecting down past Hā'ena to Nā Pali in one big line. When I whipped down the face it was the first time I was going that fast. I was trying to handle the speed of the swell. As it jacked up my last view looking over at the bay was that I was in line with the lower clouds on Nāmolokama and Hi'imanu. I don't think anybody's seen this sight before. It was a horrifying experience.

The first few seconds were turmoil, big bumps and boils. You have to immediately get used to getting air, that's not normal for big wave riding. I was making 15-foot jumps.

The board was the first prototype of the design and the fins were cavitating. I thought I was going to die. I got it up on a rail and I made the wave all the way across. I was screaming at Terry. We were totally excited and overwhelmed—an incredible feeling. 'That's got to be the biggest wave I've ever seen in my life,' I said.

Then I whipped Terry into a couple of real big beasts. They were huge and scary. Terry made both the waves, and I said, 'Okay I'm done.' We gave each other a big hug and said we did it.

TERRY

Titus had just came back from Mark Foo's memorial on Oʻahu and checked out the surf here at home. King's was breaking consistent in one spot—the perfect condition for tow-in surfing.

King's was breaking about one and a quarter miles offshore and the spot stood out clearly. Watching it from a vantage point at Lumahaʻi, Titus called me on a cell phone. I was home eating lunch, waiting for his call.

'The surf at King's is doing it, let's go!" Titus said.

The green light was on, we're going out to King's to catch a few mackers. I was leery, but felt: this is it, our only chance. I'd thought about surfing King's, but never dreamt about really going out there. It's just too fricken big.

I threw the board I had made for Titus in my truck and drove from my home in Kīlauea to Titus' place near the beach at Hāʻena as fast as I could. I didn't even stop to look at the surf. I pulled up to Titus' place and the ski was on the beach. We suited up and were off in a matter of minutes. It felt like one of the practice runs we did all summer, but now we were heading out for the real thing, checking out the line up at King's from the water.

As we got closer to the spot you could see huge waves coming in. We pulled up to the west side of the break and watched a few waves break in what seemed like slow motion. After the first big set went by we drove around and checked the surface where the waves had broken. We had to sight landmarks to get a good sense of bearings on where to be at the right time when the next big sets came in. This took about 20 or 25 minutes.

Finding landmarks for the take-off zone was critical. North to south we chose the spot where the peak of Nāmolokama Mountain in the valley behind Hanalei Bay and Makahoa Point at Waikoko on the bay's west side. For the east to west line we picked Kīlauea Lighthouse as it lines up with Pu'upōā Point near the Princeville Hotel overlooking Hanalei Bay. Now we had a 90-degree reference point to start on.

Once all that was squared away it was time. Titus was the first to go—the first Hawaiian, and the first surfer, to ride King's. As I drove him into the first wave it all felt pretty shaky to me, but this is what we had practiced six months for. The waves were hard to judge at first; they're just so damn massive.

Titus jumped into the water with the red 7 foot 4 inch board I had shaped for him. It's a narrow spear that was made for this stuff, and just 15 and three-quarter inches wide.

I threw the tow rope to him and took up the slack. Titus was up on his feet within seconds. I could see something coming from outside and it looked like the sets were marching in toward us. Before we started Titus had told me he wanted the second or third wave of the set.

O.K. I got that. Heading out to set him up for the first ride I looked back at his face to see what the call was. He nodded 'No,' with the expression on his face telling me there was another wave coming that he wanted. I drove the ski over the second wave. Behind it was another swell. I turned slowly to catch it. The wave was moving at a surging speed almost impossible to catch up to. I gassed the throttle and the ski started to get major air, hitting chops. I could barely hang on and drive at the same time.

Titus was experiencing the same action back there too. We couldn't make contact with the right part of the wave. We pulled out and headed back outside to try again. This went on for a little while. I was having a hard time getting him into the face. We were dealing with a big and massive wave peak.

Then we had a few false take offs, one when Titus let go of the tow rope and couldn't keep up with the wave. On the next try he missed the wave and as I drove around to pick him up a solid 20 to 25 foot wave broke. I couldn't save him. Titus was on his own in the pit. He had to dunk under two bomber waves.

I was sitting on the ski to the west side of the sets, just watching. This isn't suppose to happen, I thought. It's too big and dangerous for any type of mistakes. But it was happening—the nightmare of all nightmares, to be caught in front of a couple of 20-25 footers and have to dive under them.

Titus faced it and dove under those set waves. He survived the situation in a normal manner. I was sorry, but glad everything was O.K. We regrouped and got ready to try again. He told me to get deeper into the other side of the peak and come back across from the east side, then go south for a better approach.

We waited for another set. The horizon started to rise up. Here it comes, I said to myself, get up and get one. This time I did what Titus suggested. I headed out to the wave he wanted and got the signal to go for it. I went toward the east end of the swell, got in front of it then turned south.

I looked over my shoulder to the west and saw this macking huge wall moving in and under us. Titus was now in prime position for the launch. I gave the ski a little more throttle to give him the speed to take off. Bam! He let go and was gone. I tried to get to the shoulder of the wave and watch, but couldn't keep up.

Titus was flying down and away from me. All I could do was follow his swell from behind and hope everything was going good. He covered a lot of distance fast on the ride. I saw the wave breaking and the whitewater churning up, but still couldn't see him.

Finally he popped out way inside of me. I throttled over to him. His arms were up in the air, fists clenched. He was screaming, 'Yeah, I did it! The first to ride King's!'

I drove over to Titus and he yelled that the fins on the board were too small. The board was coming out of the water and cavitating, the nose bouncing up and down. But he was stoked to have done it all without crashing. We shook hands and I congratulated him for his achievement.

Titus had done it, and that was enough for him that day. I could tell he was kind of worn out from all the false tries. He'd used a lot of his energy to get us more acquainted with the wave and the movement of the place.

Now it was my turn, a chance for me to try out the board I had made for King's. I worried about all the stuff Titus was telling me: keep the board down to prevent cavitation, get the speed you need to move.

I got to my feet and we were off to snag one of those beasts. The horizon looked like it was filling up again, a set was coming in. We let the first couple go by. Then I saw an opening and gave him the go signal.

Titus towed me out, turning east to west just as I did for him. This wave was a little mellower and probably smaller than the one he just rode. He pulled to the side and launched me in. I could see Titus up on the shoulder as I started to descend down the wave. He was keeping up with me and the wave, watching me ride. As I made it to the bottom I could hear the whitewater coming. It tried to gobble me up a little, but didn't knock me off. I made it to the safer part of the shoulder and glided off the side. I had just rode King's.

Titus was stoked. I could see it in his eyes. We shook hands again and congratulated each other.

That wasn't too bad, I thought, so decided to get one more then go in. Titus said O.K., one more for R&D.

I got to my feet again. This time the sets were looking more chunky. We went over the first couple of waves. Then I saw the one I wanted and gave him the signal. It was the same set up as Titus' wave. We started out on the east side of the swell, then made a turn to the south, then to the west. It was a huge swell to the right of us.

Titus throttled the ski into position and I got to where I had to let go of the tow rope. One more bump to clear and I was off. This time I leaned on my left rail to fade toward the peak, then leaned on the right rail to start my decent down the face. From the top it looked pretty smooth as I started down the wave. I started to pick up speed, super speed. I was flying down this mountain of water with the salty white grain coming up the wave face. I had a ways to go to the bottom when I saw a ripple of some sort part ways down. I raced toward it and all of a sudden was launched three or four feet in the air, still dropping, going God knows how fast, maybe 35 miles per hour. I made contact again and kept going, still having more down hill to go. After a few more feet and all of a sudden I was hopping another one of those upward surges. Airborne again, I hoped I wouldn't fall on the landing. I landed a little bit off and the board started cavitating. I corrected and angled for the shoulder. Right then I knew what Titus had been telling me about, the same thing that happened to him was happening to me. Scary stuff! You just can't and don't want to fall off at that speed—you could get really hurt.

I finally made it to the safety of the shoulder and glided to the side. Titus was coming from behind to get me. That was it. I didn't feel like doing that again. It was one of the biggest waves I'd ridden in my 31 years of surfing.

Titus came up to me and was glad to see I was in one piece. We again shook hands and congratulated each other. We'd done it, we had surfed King's. I wrapped up the tow rope, climbed on the ski and we headed for shore. Sometimes it's good to quit while you're ahead, and that's what we were doing.

SOURCES

W. D. Alexander *Proceedings of Russians on Kauai* 1814-16. Honolulu: Hawaiian Historical Papers No. 6, 1894, pp. 1-17.

W. D. Alexander, Hawaiian Historical Papers No. 13, pp. 24-31. Read before Hawaiian Historical Society, June 9, 1906.

George Washington Bates *Sandwich Island Notes By A Haole*. New York: Harper & Row, 1854.

Hiram Bingham *A Residence of Twenty-one Years in the Sandwich Islands*. Hartford: Hezekiah Huntington, 1847.

Hiram Bingham *Extracts from the Journal of Mr. Bingham, While at Atooi*, selection from The Missionary Herald, Boston, for August, 1822.

Isabella Lucy Bird *The Hawaiian Archipelago: Six Months Among the Palm Groves, Coral Reefs, and Volcanoes of the Sandwich Islands.* London, Murray, 1875.

H. Carrington Bolton *Some Hawaiian Pastimes.* Journal of American Folklore, Jan.-March, 1891.

James Cook and James King *A Voyage to the Pacific Ocean...* London: G. Nichol and T. Cadell, 1784.

Rev. Sheldon Dibble *A History of the Sandwich Islands.* Honolulu: T.G. Thrum, 1909.

Nathaniel Bright Emerson *Unwritten Literature of Hawaii.* Washington, D.C.: Bureau of American Ethnology, 1909.

Abraham Fornander *An Account of the Polynesian Race...3 vol.* London: Trubner, 1878-85.

Clifford Gessler *Hawaii, Isles of Enchantment.* New York: D. Appleton-Century Company, 1938.

Gorham D. Gilman *Journal of a Canoe Voyage along the Kauai Palis, made in 1845.* Honolulu: Papers of the Hawaiian Historical Society No. 14, Presented to the Society, August 27, 1908.

David Kalakaua *The Legends and Myths of Hawaii.* New York: C. L. Webster, 1888.

Eric Alfred Knudsen *Teller Of Hawaiian Tales.* Honolulu, Coca-Cola Bottling Co., 1945.

Jack London *Koolau The Leper.* From The House of Pride and Other Tales of Hawaii. New York: MacMillian 1912.

Rev. J.M. Lydgate *Na Pali Recollections.* Lihue: The Garden Island newspaper, Tuesday, Oct. 16, 1917.

George H. Read *The Last Cruise of the Saginaw.* Boston and New York: Houghton Mifflin Company, 1912.

Rerioterai Tava and Moses Keale *Niihau: The Traditions of a Hawaiian Island.* Honolulu: Mutual Publishing Co., 1989. Used by permission of Mutual Publishing, Co.

Thomas H. Thrum *Tales From the Temples–Kauai.* Honolulu: Hawaiian Annual for 1907.

Henry Martyn Whitney *Hawaiian Guide Book.* Honolulu, H. M. Whitney, 1875.

Charles Wilkes *Narrative of the United States' Exploring Expedition, During the Years 1838, 1839, 1840, 1841, 1842.* Philadelphia: Lea & Blanchard, 1845.

All other selections are by Chris Cook, from *North Shore* and *Sandwich Islands* magazines, 1987-92, except where noted.

◈ _____

SUGGESTED READINGS

NON-FICTION

Aikin, Ross. **Kilauea Point Lighthouse**. Illus. Kilauea Point Natural History Association, 1988. A history of Kaua'i's Kīlauea Point Lighthouse and the lives of its lighthouse keepers.

Alexander, Arthur C. **Koloa Plantation, 1835-1935: A History of the Oldest Hawaiian Sugar Plantation**. Illus. Honolulu: Star-Bulletin, 1937. A centennial history of Hawai'i's first commercial sugar plantation from the Kauai Historical Society.

Alexander, W. D. **Proceedings of Russians on Kauai 1814-16**. Honolulu: Hawaiian Historical Papers No. 6, 1894, pp. 1-17. A thorough, scholarly look at the historical record of the Russians on Kauai in the 1810's, and of the aftermath of their intrigues.

Anderson, Rufus. **The Hawaiian Islands: Their Progress and Condition Under Missionary Labors.** Illus. Boston: Gould & Lincoln, 1864. A look at Kauai in the 1860's with an emphasis on the ongoing work of the mission stations at Waioli, Waimea and Koloa. B.

Bates, George Washington. **Sandwich Island Notes By A Haole.** New York: Harper & Row, 1854. Early nonmissionary tour of Kaua'i by outspoken "cultured" visitor. Except for the too-frequent illusions to classical Greek poetry, this firsthand account offers an intimate look at major Kaua'i towns and districts in the 1850's. B

Beaglehole, J.C. **The Life of Captain James Cook.** Stanford: Stanford University Press, 1974. Perhaps the most authoritative life of Cook. Australian sailor and author Alan Villars' biography of Cook is also recommended.

Bennett, Wendall C. **Archaeology of Kauai.** Illus. Honolulu: Star-Bulletin, 1937. A comprehensive survey of archaeological sites of Kaua'i made in the 1930's.

Bingham, Hiram. **A Residence of Twenty-one Years in the Sandwich Islands.** Hartford: Hezekiah Huntington, 1847. New England missionary Bingham's account of his life in Hawai'i offers a detailed look at Kaua'i in the 1820's-30's. His description of the attempted salvaging of Cleopatra's Barge at Hanalei offers a look at the conflict between Bingham the adventurer and Bingham the straight-laced Yankee.

Bird, Isabella Lucy. **The Hawaiian Archipelago Six Months Among the Palm Groves, Coral Reefs, and Volcanoes of the Sandwich Islands.** Murray, 1875. Pioneer female travel writer visits Kaua'i and enjoys a stay at Kōloa.

Bolton, H. Carrington. **Some Hawaiian Pastimes**. Journal of American Folklore, Jan.-March, 1891. Observations of Hawaiian fireworks, surfing and other activites by Columbia University professor during visit to Ni'ihau and Kaua'i. Bolton refers to photographic plates of surfers on Ni'ihau, which, if found, could be earliest known photographs of Hawaiian ʻsurfers, pre-dating early Waikīkī photos. B

Clark, John C. **The Beaches of Kauai and Niihau**. University of Hawaii Press, 1991. Interesting and informative descriptions of every beach. Glimpses of Hawaiian legends and history, plus excellent water safety advice abound in this excellent work.

Cook, Chris. **The Kaua'i Movie Book**. Honolulu: Mutual Publishing 1996. The definitive story of feature filmmaking on Kaua'i.

Cook, James and James King. **A Voyage to the Pacific Ocean. . .** London: G. Nichol and T. Cadell, 1784. The journal of Captain Cook's third and final circumnavigation of the world.

Damon, Ethel Moseley. **Koamalu, A Story Of Pioneers on Kauai, and of What They Built in That Island Garden**. Honolulu: Honolulu Star-Bulletin Press, 1931. A rare, two-volume history of post-contact Kauai through the point of view of the Rice Family. Well written, excellent source for historical material.

Dibble, Rev. Sheldon. **A History of the Sandwich Islands**. Honolulu: T.G. Thrum, 1909. This update of missionary Dibbles' 1830's work includes Thrum's additions.

Emerson, Nathaniel Bright. **Unwritten Literature of Hawaii**. New Era Printing Co., 1906. Missionary son records ancient art of hula for Smithsonian. This anthropological work has become a classic on the subject.

Feher, Joseph. **Hawaii: A Pictorial History**. Honolulu: Bishop Museum Press 1969. A factual, coffee-table picture book with hundreds of illustrations and photos of Hawai'i from ancient days to the mid-1960's. Considered a comprehensive book on Hawai'i's past.

Finney, Ben R. and Houston, James D. **Surfing: The Sport of Hawaiian Kings**. Rutland, Vt.: Tuttle, 1966. Includes a list of ancient Kauai surfing sites at Wailua and other beaches. Kauai surfers were considered among the best in Hawai'i.

Fornander, Abraham. **An Account of the Polynesian Race.** . . . . . 3 vol. London: Trubner, 1878-85; Rutland, Vt.: Tuttle, 1969. Fornander, a Hawaiian-speaking circuit court judge in the mid- to late-1800's collected the oral traditions of Hawaiians and compiled an extensive English collection of the myths and legends.

Gessler, Clifford. **Hawaii, Isles of Enchantment**. New York: D. Appleton-Century Company, 1938. A very readable account of Hawai'i's history plus a travelogue of visits to all major islands by a Honolulu journalist.

Gilman, Gorham D. **Journal of a Canoe Voyage along the Kauai Palis, made in 1845**. Honolulu: Papers of the Hawaiian Historical Society No. 14, Presented to the Society, August 27, 1908. A Hawai'i judge's adventurous trip down Nā Pali.

Halford, Francis John. **9 Doctors & God**. Honolulu: University of Hawaii Press, 1954. Hawai'i's missionary doctors from the viewpoint of a Hawai'i physician in the early 1950's.

Hind, Norman E.A. **The Geology of Kauai and Niihau**. Honolulu: Bernice P. Bishop Museum Bulletin 71, 1930. A classic look at the islands' geology.

Joesting, Edward. **Kauai–The Separate Kingdom**. Honolulu: University of Hawaii Press, 1984. Engrossing historical account of Kaua'i from ancient days to end of nineteenth century. The late Hawai'i author knew how to compress a treasure trove of information into each paragraph. Highly recommended as an overall book on Kaua'i's history.

Kamea, Lori. **The Empty Throne**. Honolulu: Topgallant, 1980. The life of Prince Jonah Kūhiō Kalaniana'ole. Born on Kaua'i, "Prince Cupid" led Hawai'i into the twentieth century as an elected official. A probable King of Hawai'i, had not the Hawaiian kingdom been overthrown.

Kauai Historical Society. **The Kauai Papers**. Illus. Līhu'e, Kaua'i: Kauai Historical Society, 1991. Kaua'i's villages and their stories described in 13 pieces from the archives of the Kauai Historical Society, plus three trips around Kaua'i in 1849, 1865 and 1895, respectively.

Knudsen, E.A. and Noble, Gurre P. **Kanuka of Kauai**. Honolulu: Tongg Publishing Co., 1944. A slim volume on a west side and Poipu *haole* pioneer from Norway who went broke in the gold fields of California before starting a successful sugar plantation on Kaua'i.

Knudsen, Eric Alfred. **Teller Of Hawaiian Tales**. Honolulu, Coca-Cola Bottling Co., 1945. Tales from Knudsen's "Sunday Kauai" radio show, offered by sponsor. Tales also recorded on rare 78 rpm record set.

Krauss, Bob with W.P. Alexander. **Grove Farm Plantation**. Palo Alto, Calif.: Pacific Books, 1965. The story of George N. Wilcox, missionary son, creative engineer, and founder of Grove Farm Plantation. Wilcox served in Hawai'i's legislature, was a key figure in development of the port at Nāwiliwili, and a generous donor to many philanthropic works on Kaua'i.

London, Jack. **Koolau The Leper**. From The House of Pride and Other Tales of Hawaii. New York: MacMillan 1912. B

Ludwig, Myles. **Kauai - In the Eye of Iniki**. 1992. A firsthand account in words and photographs of Hurricane 'Iniki both during the devesating storm and its aftermath.

Lydgate, Rev. J.M. **Na Pali Recollections**. Lihue: The Garden Island Newspaper, Tuesday, Oct. 16, 1917. Interview with a Hawaiian born and raised along Nā Pali coast who was one of the last generation to inhabit the isolated valleys.

Moriarty, Linda (with photographs by Leland A. Cook and Chris Cook). **Niihau Shell Leis**. Illus. Honolulu: University of Hawaii Press, 1986. The definitive book on the only Native Hawaiian craft to be practiced continuously since Western contact.

Nordhoff, Charles. **Northern California, Oregon, and the Sandwich Islands**. New York: Harper, 1874. By the grandfather of Charles Nordhoff of Nordhoff-Hall writing fame, who toured Kaua'i in 1873.

Peebles, Douglas with Chris Cook. **From the Skies of Paradise - Kauai**. Illus. Honolulu: Mutual Publishing. A unique, comprehensive and colorful look at Kaua'i from a helicopter. The towns and villages of each district are pictured in color aerial photograhs and described district by district in the text.

Porteus, Stanley David. **And Blow Not The Trumpet**. Pacific Books, 1947. A firsthand detailed account of World War II in Hawai'i. Especially interesting chapter on Kaua'i. The maybe too-dramatic writing is offset by a wealth of factual information.

Read, George H. **The Last Cruise of the Saginaw**. Boston and New York: Houghton Mifflin Company, 1912. An engrossing firsthand account of a shipwreck at Kure Atoll and subsequent open-boat sail of 1,200 miles to Kaua'i to alert rescuers.

Riznick, Barnes. **Waioli Mission House**, Hanalei, Kaua'i. Illus. Līhu'e, Kaua'i: Grove Farm Homestead and Waioli Mission House, 1987. Well written, interesting and detailed history of the home of Congregational missionaries at spectacularly beautiful Hanalei.

Schleck, Robert J. **The Wilcox Quilts in Hawaii**. Photographs by Hugh deVries. Līhu'e: Grove Farm Homestead Museum & Waioli Mission House, 1987. The colorful and historic art of Hawaiian quiltmaking well described and illustrated with full color photographs.

Smith, Robert. **Hiking Kauai**. Berkeley: Wilderness Press. One of the first and best hiking books to describe the island's trails and scenic vistas.

Tava, Rerioterai and Moses Keale. **Niihau: The Traditions of a Hawaiian Island**. Honolulu: Mutual Publishing Co., 1989. A unique, in-depth look at Ni'ihau by a Tahitian woman and a Niihauan. Place name descriptions are especially valuable.

Thrum, Thomas H. **Tales From the Temples–Kauai**. Honolulu: Hawaiian Annual for 1907, Thomas Thrum. Thrum's careful record of the ruins of Kauai's heiaus from his popular Hawaiian annual. B

Valier, Kathy. **On the Na Pali Coast**. Illus. Honolulu: University of Hawaii Press, 1988. A wilderness exploration guide of Nā Pali by a veteran Nā Pali hiker. Excellent maps and natural history information of this isolated area.

Von Holt, Ida Elizabeth Knudsen. **Stories of Long Ago: Niihau, Kauai, Oahu.** Honolulu: Daughters of Hawaii (Rev. Ed.), 1985. Stories of Kauai's kamaaina west-side families.

Wenkam, Robert, **Kauai and the Park Country of Hawaii.** San Francisco: Sierra Club, 1967. A beautiful essay in words and color photos pleading for the preservation of Kaua'i's natural beauty.

Whitney, Henry Martyn. **Hawaiian Guide Book.** Honolulu, H. M. Whitney, 1875. Newspaper publisher from Honolulu writes first visitor-oriented guide to Hawai'i.

Wilkes, Charles. **Narrative of the United States Exploring Expedition, During the Years 1838, 1839, 1840, 1841, 1842.** Whittaker and Co., 1845. Wilkes, a Naval officer, and his men explore Kaua'i as part of the United States' first worldwide scientific research expedition.

Wilcox, Carol. **The Kauai Album.** Illus. Līhu'e: Kauai Historical Society, 1981. A survey in words and photographs of Kaua'i's existing historic buildings, late-1970's, early 1980's. Hurricane 'Iwa and Hurricane 'Iniki destroyed or seriously damaged a number of the structures.

Yzendoorn, Reginald. **History of the Catholic Mission in the Hawaiian Islands.** Honolulu: Star-Bulletin, 1927. A key source of information about the history of the Roman Catholic Church's work on Kaua'i.

FICTION ·
Kalakaua, David. **The Legends and Myths of Hawaii.** New York: C. L. Webster, 1888. The history, warfare and politics of pre-contact Hawai'i by Hawai'i's last king. Probably transcribed by R.M. Daggett, a United States Minister to Hawai'i.

London, Jack. **The House of Pride**. New York: MacMillan, 1912. A still very readable collection of Jack London's Hawaiian short stories.

Rice, William Hyde Rice. **Hawaiian Legends**. Illus. Honolulu: Bishop Museum Press. One of Kaua'i's favorite Hawaiian legends collection. Rice grew up speaking Hawaiian. His tales are from native informants of the 1800's.

Wichman, Frederick B. **Kauai Tales**. Honolulu: Bamboo Ridge Press, 1985. A collection of Kaua'i legends and myths by a *kama'aina* writer and place name researcher.

Note: All selections by Chris Cook are from The Sandwich Islands Journal, 1987-92 except where noted.

TALES OF THE PACIFIC

JACK LONDON

Stories of Hawai'i by Jack London
Thirteen yarns drawn from the famous author's love affair with Hawai'i Nei.
$8.95 mass market • 282 pp • ISBN 0-935180-08-7

The Mutiny of the Elsinore by Jack London
Based on a voyage around Cape Horn in a windjammer from New York to
Seattle in 1913, this romance between the lone passenger and the captain's
daughter reveals London at his most fertile and fluent best. The lovers are forced
to outrace a rioting band of seagoing gangsters in the South Pacific.
$5.95 mass market • 378 pp • ISBN 0-935180-40-0

South Sea Tales by Jack London
Fiction from the violent days of the early century, set among the atolls of
French Oceania and the high islands of Samoa, Fiji, Pitcairn, and "the terrible
Solomons."
$7.95 mass market • 288 pp • ISBN 0-935180-14-1

HAWAI'I

Ancient History of the Hawaiian People by Abraham Fornander
A reprint of this classic of precontact history tracing Hawai'i's saga from
legendary times to the arrival of Captain Cook, including an account of his
demise. Originally published as volume II in *An Account of the Polynesian
Race: Its Origins and Migration,* this historical work is an excellent reference
for students and general readers alike. Written over a hundred years ago, it still
represents one of the few compendiums of precontact history available in a single
source.
$9.95 mass market • 432 pp • ISBN 1-56647-147-8

A Hawaiian Reader edited by A. Grove Day
Thirty-seven selections from the literature of the past hundred years, including
such writers as Mark Twain, Robert Louis Stevenson and James Jones.
$7.95 mass market • 380 pp • ISBN 0-935180-07-9

Hawai'i and Its People by A. Grove Day
An informal, one-volume narrative of the exotic and fascinating history of
the peopling of the archipelago. The periods range from the first arrivals of
Polynesian canoe voyagers to attainment of American statehood. A "headline
history" brings the story from 1960 to 1990.
$10.95 trade • 360 pp • ISBN 1-56647-705-0

A Hawaiian Reader, Vol. II edited by A. Grove Day
A companion volume to *A Hawaiian Reader.* Twenty-four selections from the
exotic literary heritage of the Islands.
$7.95 mass market • 352 pp • ISBN 1-56647-207-5

Kona by Marjorie Sinclair
The best woman novelist of post-war Hawai'i dramatizes the conflict between a daughter of Old Hawai'i and her straitlaced Yankee husband.
$6.95 mass market • 256 pp • ISBN 0-935180-20-6

The Wild Wind, a novel by Marjorie Sinclair
On the Hana Coast of Maui, Lucia Gray, great-granddaughter of a New England missionary, seeks solitude but embarks on an interracial marriage with an Hawaiian cowboy. Then she faces some of the mysteries of the Polynesia of old.
$6.95 mass market • 256 pp • ISBN 0-935180-30-3

Rape in Paradise by Theon Wright (large mass market)
The sensational "Massie Case" of the 1930's shattered the tranquil image that mainland U.S.A. had of Hawai'i. One woman shouted "Rape!" and the island erupted with such turmoil that for 20 years it was deemed unprepared for statehood. A fascinating case study of race relations and military-civilian relations.
$11.95 trade • 336 pp • ISBN 1-56647-703-4

Mark Twain in Hawai'i: Roughing It in the Sandwich Islands
The noted humorist's account of his 1866 trip to Hawai'i at a time when the Islands were more for the native than the tourists. The writings first appeared in their present form in Twain's important book, *Roughing It*. Includes an introductory essay from *Mad About Islands* by A. Grove Day.
$5.95 mass market • 144 pp • ISBN 0-935180-93-1

The Trembling of a Leaf by W. Somerset Maugham
Stories of Hawai'i and the South Seas, including *Red,* the author's most successful story, and *Rain,* his most notorious one.
$4.95 mass market • 302 pp • ISBN 0-935180-21-4

Horror in Paradise: Grim and Uncanny Tales from Hawai'i and the South Seas edited by A. Grove Day and Bacil F. Kirtley
Thirty-four writers narrate "true" episodes of sorcery and the supernatural, as well as gory events on sea and atoll.
$8.95 mass market • 304 pp • ISBN 0-935180-23-0

HAWAIIAN SOVEREIGNTY

Kalākaua: Renaissance King by Helena G. Allen
The third in a trilogy that also features Queen Liliuokalani and Sanford Ballard Dole, this book brings King Kalākaua, Hawai'i's most controversial king, to the fore as a true renaissance man. The complex facts of Kalākaua's life and personality are presented clearly and accurately along with his contributions to Hawaiian history.
$6.95 mass market • 320 pp • ISBN 1-56647-059-5

Nahi'ena'ena: Sacred Daughter of Hawai'i by Marjorie Sinclair
A unique biography of Kamehameha's sacred daughter who in legend was descended from the gods. The growing feelings and actions of Hawaiians for their national identity now place this story of Nahi'ena'ena in a wider perspective of the Hawaiian quest for sovereignty.
$6.95 mass market • 224 pp • ISBN 1-56647-080-3

Around the World With a King by William N. Armstrong, Introduction by Glen Grant
An account of King Kalakaua's circling of the globe. From Singapore to Cairo, Vienna to the Spanish frontier, follow Kalakaua as he becomes the first monarch to travel around the world.
$5.95 mass market • 320 pp • ISBN 1-56647-017-X

Hawai'i's Story by Hawai'i's Queen by Lydia Lili'uokalani
The Hawaiian kingdom's last monarch wrote her biography in 1897, the year before the annexation of the Hawaiian Islands by the United States. Her story covers six decades of island history told from the viewpoint of a major historical figure.
$13.95 trade • 464 pp • ISBN 1-56647-684-4
$8.95 mass market • 464 pp • ISBN 0-935180-85-0

The Betrayal of Lili'uokalani: Last Queen of Hawai'i 1838-1917 by Helena G. Allen
A woman caught in the turbulent maelstrom of cultures in conflict. Treating Liliuokalani's life with authority, accuracy and details, *Betrayal* also is tremendously informative concerning the entire period of missionary activity and foreign encroachment in the Islands.
$8.95 mass market • 432 pp • ISBN 0-935180-89-3

HAWAIIAN LEGENDS

Myths and Legends of Hawai'i by Dr. W.D. Westervelt
A broadly inclusive, one-volume collection of folklore by a leading authority. Completely edited and reset format for today's readers of the great prehistoric tales of Maui, Hina, Pele and her fiery family, and a dozen other heroic beings, human or ghostly.
$10.95 trade • 288 pp • ISBN 1-56647-706-9
$7.95 mass market • 288 pp • ISBN 0-935180-43-5

The Legends and Myths of Hawai'i by David Kalākaua
Political and historical traditions and stories of the pre-Cook period capture the romance of old Polynesia. A rich collection of Hawaiian lore originally presented in 1888 by Hawai'i's "merrie monarch."
$9.95 mass market • 576 pp • ISBN 0-935180-86-9

Teller of Hawaiian Tales by Eric Knudsen
Son of a pioneer family of Kauai, the author spent most of his life on the Garden Island as a rancher, hunter of wild cattle, lawyer, and legislator. Here are 60 campfire yarns of gods and goddesses, ghosts and heroes, cowboy adventures and legendary feats among the valleys and peaks of the island.
$6.95 mass market • 272 pp • ISBN 0-935180-33-8

SOUTH SEAS

Best South Sea Stories **edited by A. Grove Day**
Fifteen writers capture all the romance and exotic adventure of the legendary
South Pacific, including James A. Michener, James Norman Hall, W. Somerset
Maugham, and Herman Melville.
$10.95 trade • 320 pp • ISBN 1-56647-771-9

The Lure of Tahiti **selected and edited by A. Grove Day**
Fifteen stories and other choice extracts from the rich literature of "the
most romantic island in the world." Authors include Jack London, James A.
Michener, James Norman Hall, W. Somerset Maugham, Paul Gauguin, Pierre
Loti, Herman Melville, William Bligh, and James Cook.
$5.95 mass market • 324 pp • ISBN 0-935180-31-1

Home from the Sea: Robert Louis Stevenson in Samoa **by Richard Bermann**
Impressions of the final years of R.L.S. in his mansion, Vailima, in Western
Samoa, still writing books, caring for family and friends, and advising
Polynesian chieftains in the local civil wars.
$10.95 trade • 280 pp • ISBN 1-56647-788-3

U.S. Orders
For U.S. orders, send credit card information,
check or money order to
Mutual Publishing
1215 Center Street, Ste 210
Honolulu, HI 96816

Priority Mail via USPS, U.S. orders only:

up to $15	add $7.00 for shipping
$15.01–$30	add $9.00
$30.01–$45	add $11.00
$45.01–$60	add $13.00
$60.01–$75	add $15.00
$75.01–$100	add $18.00
$100.01–$200	add $25.00
$200.01 and over	add 15% of total invoice

For express delivery, please add $10.00 to the shipping rates. For international
deliveries, please contact us.

International Orders
For orders outside of the U.S., please visit our website:
www.mutualpublishing.com
or email us at info@mutualpublishing.com